Moroni's America

-→≫ ≪←-

The North American setting for the
Book of Mormon

MORONI'S AMERICA

-->» «<--

The North American Setting
For the Book of Mormon

JONATHAN NEVILLE

Moroni's America: The North American Setting for the Book of
Mormon
Copyright © 2015 by Jonathan Neville
All rights reserved.

This is a work of nonfiction. The author has made every effort to be
accurate and complete and welcomes comments, suggestions, and
corrections, which can be emailed to lostzarahemla@gmail.com.

All opinions expressed in this work are those of the author alone.

Dedicated to open-minded people everywhere.

Special thanks to my wife, Beverly.

12-5-15
ISBN-13: 978-1512087987
ISBN-10: 151208798X

Cover:
Pounds Hollow, an ancient fortress along the Ohio River
American Flag 1840
The Hill Cumorah, New York
Photos by Jonathan Neville

Maps in this book are adapted from the sources indicated, including Google
Earth and a relief layer for Google Maps created by Hans Braxmeier at
http://maps-for-free.com/ under the Creative Commons CCO.

TABLE OF CONTENTS

—⇒≫ ≪⇐—

List of Figures

Preface

Right up front, I stipulate that the spiritual messages of the Book of Mormon are more important than its geography.

And yet the historicity—the historical accuracy—of the book is also important. The Book of Mormon could not accomplish its objective if it was not a true history of real people. As a *restored history*, it is a tangible symbol of the *restored gospel*. The book's very existence is a manifestation of the reality of divine revelation in our day.

President Ezra Taft Benson once said, "We do not have to prove the Book of Mormon is true. The book is its own proof."[1] I completely agree with that statement. However, in my view, over the last few decades an interpretive gloss has accumulated[2] that is inconsistent with the text and obscures much of its meaning and impact. I offer this book to help refocus on the book and its actual, real-world setting.

Every book I write is an answer to a question I had. Here, the question is simple and universal: *Where did the Book of Mormon take place?*

The answer has been a long time coming.

When I was a teenager, my family visited Italy and Greece. We were in Athens when my father took us to Mars Hill and explained that this was where the Apostle Paul had preached. I vaguely remembered some guy in the Bible named Paul, but drew a blank regarding Mars Hill. I went back and read in Acts 17. For the first time, the scriptures became real to me.

Since then, I've visited Biblical sites many times, always gaining a greater appreciation for the scriptures. It is striking how the Old Testament setting is also the setting for much of the New Testament. History repeats itself in surprising ways. I've also been to Church history sites many times, learning more about those wonderful events with each visit.

But what about the Book of Mormon?

In the 1970s, I took Book of Mormon classes at BYU. I read extensively about Central America (Mesoamerica) and all the discoveries that seemed to correlate with the Book of Mormon. I visited sites in Central America. Although I wanted to believe what I was being taught, there were too many inconsistencies and gaps to satisfy me.

It was only in the last few years that I realized what was wrong. I also discovered that when I was visiting Church history sites in New York, Ohio, Illinois, and Missouri, *I was also visiting Book of Mormon sites.*

For decades, the search for the real-world setting of the Book of Mormon has resembled the old joke in which a man is crouched next to a streetlight. A policeman approaches and asks what he is doing.

"Looking for a quarter I dropped."

"Where did it fall?"

"A block down the street."

"Then why are you looking here?"

"Because the light is better."

In a similar way, many LDS scholars have been searching in Mesoamerica for evidence of the Book of Mormon because they think there is more "light" there—more archaeological data—than in North America. I respect the academic work done and do not question anyone's motives, but I have to ask, is this the type of light by which we should be guided?

Joseph Smith and Oliver Cowdery shed more light on the question than all the scholars combined. But instead of searching the text with the aid of that light, some scholars have been *obscuring* the light Joseph and Oliver provided. These scholars insist that Joseph and Oliver were merely speculating about Book of Mormon locations; their statements should be considered an endorsement of a purely scholarly approach.

Consequently, anonymous articles in the 1842 *Times and Seasons* that linked the Book of Mormon to Central America became the light under which they searched.[3] Their scholarly conclusions have led to confusion and discord, even among themselves. Many faithful members have ignored the whole debate, but others who read about illusory Mayan connections have come to question the authenticity of the Book of Mormon.

When we read the Book of Mormon under the light Joseph and Oliver provided, we see it in a completely new way.

We come to realize that the Gospel was *restored* where it was *lost*.

The light of the Gospel was extinguished in the Old World when the Apostles were killed and the Church fell into apostasy, but that light endured in the New World until the Nephite civilization was finally destroyed in New York around 400 A.D. What better place for the restoration of the Gospel than the scene of its disappearance? And from the New World, the gospel is taken back to the Old World.

We come to realize that the early history of the Church paralleled Nephite history, in reverse.

The Nephites were destroyed in New York, so the Church was established there. The Nephites had been driven from Zarahemla and diminished on their way to Cumorah, so the Church grew on its way to Zarahemla from Cumorah. Joseph Smith was eventually buried in an ancient Nephite cemetery in Nauvoo—across the river from Zarahemla.

Finally, we come to realize that just as the Gospel was taken *from* the entire Earth, now it is spreading *to* the entire Earth.

And the Book of Mormon is the means for making that possible.

My objective in writing this book is not to persuade or convince anyone of anything. I have simply assembled and organized information that I think everyone interested in the Book of Mormon should be aware of. While I am convinced about the geography I present, I frame each element as a proposal or plausible interpretation. Feel free to agree or disagree. Each of us makes our own decisions about what to believe, and I recognize how complex that process is. And yet, well-informed decisions tend to be better than uninformed decisions.

I write to those interested in the Book of Mormon, but even more so to those who are *not* interested in the book. I'm familiar with many people who have dismissed the text—or turned away from it after having once accepted it—because they think it is fiction. If you're among that group, I empathize with you. There are good reasons to doubt what you've been told about its historicity if all you've heard is the Mesoamerican theory. And there are many alternatives to the Mesoamerican theory that are equally perplexing and difficult to reconcile with the text and modern revelation.

Bear with me a while and let me show you another perspective.

Let's consider the North American setting for the Book of Mormon.

Acknowledgements

Although I am solely responsible for the content of this book, I have been educated and influenced by many people who have written and spoken about Book of Mormon geography. I acknowledge a few of them here.

Joseph Smith and Oliver Cowdery wrote more about the real-world setting of the Book of Mormon than anyone else—not in terms of total word count, but in terms of their unique qualifications. They worked together to translate and record the text. They received revelations together. They shared interactions with John the Baptist, Peter, James and John, Moroni, modern Lamanites, Moses, Elias, Elijah, and the Lord Himself.

W.W. Phelps, Parley P. Pratt and Orson Pratt, Benjamin Winchester, and William Smith were early Church authors who focused on geography issues. They all agreed the Hill Cumorah was in New York, but they had various ideas about the location of other Book of Mormon lands. Their work gave me insights into the development of the Mesoamerican theory.

Hugh Nibley, the well-known prolific author who inspired so many LDS members to study more deeply, encouraged me to study Latin and Greek and many other aspects of antiquity and languages.

John L. Sorenson, author of *Mormon's Codex* and many other books and papers, brought to my attention the need to think of the people in the text as real people living in a real-world setting. While I think he made a fundamental mistake by emphasizing the one verse that refers to a "narrow neck of land," Brother Sorenson's attention to detail has contributed greatly to my understanding of the text, despite his Mesoamerican focus.

John W. Welch, Editor-in-Chief, *BYU Studies*, has written and edited numerous wonderful books and articles about the Book of Mormon. He discovered chiasmus in the text and has offered many valuable insights about historicity of the text, particularly related to the Old World setting.

Wayne May, publisher of *Ancient American Magazine*, has written and edited many books and articles about Book of Mormon geography. His focus on early American history, including the contemporary accounts given by Native American Indians,[4] has been especially helpful.

Rod Meldrum, Director of the FIRM Foundation, has written extensively on the topic of the Book of Mormon in North America. His book, titled *The Book of Mormon in America's Heartland*, brings together an assortment of evidences from Church history, archaeology, geology, and anthropology.

There are innumerable other books, articles, and web pages I've read, seminars I've attended, people I've met with, etc. This has been a long and a very enjoyable journey. But one thing I've learned is that initials at the end of one's name don't stand for "an open mind."

Figure 1 - Bibliography (partial)

[Note on sources: I have cited accessible sources as much as possible, including web links, to encourage additional research and comment.]

Jonathan Neville

NOTES

[1] Ezra Taft Benson, "A New Witness for Christ," *Ensign*, October 1984.

[2] By this, I mean the theory that the Book of Mormon took place in Central America, also called Mesoamerica. This has led scholars to interpret the text as a Mayan document, incorporating Mayan mythology and concepts.

[3] Some scholars have lately retreated from that reliance, but the record shows the Mesoamerican theory originated from those articles. As recently as 2005, the articles were an integral part of the "Worlds of Joseph Smith" symposium at the Library of Congress, celebrating the 200th anniversary of Joseph Smith's birth. They have been cited in innumerable papers, books and presentations developing and supporting the Mesoamerican setting. I addressed the historical background of these articles in my book, *The Lost City of Zarahemla*, and other articles and blog entries explaining how and why those articles were published. My conclusion: Joseph Smith had nothing to do with them. There is not a single document that can be directly linked to Joseph Smith that has anything to do with South America, Central America, or Mesoamerica. (The "narrow neck of land" argument relies on a single verse—Ether 10:20—that is a throwaway comment about the location of a Jaredite marketplace. See Chapter 20 for more discussion.)

[4] Throughout this book, I use the term Indian to refer generically to the Native American people and tribes. There is a variety of opinion and preferences for nomenclature, but historical documents—and the Constitution itself—use the term Indian to refer to the tribes that lived in North America when the Europeans arrived. The term is used in federal legislation. The Bureau of Indian Affairs in the U.S. Department of the Interior continues to use the term Indian.

Section 1 – Overview of Geography

Chapter 1 – Why *Moroni's* America?

-→→⟫ ⟪←←-

FOR DECADES, I BELIEVED THE BOOK OF MORMON TOOK PLACE in Central America (specifically, Mesoamerica). I read books and articles written by LDS scholars, visited sites in Mesoamerica, attended lectures, engaged online and in person—let's say I studied the issue in depth. I know the evidence and can recite the arguments backwards and forwards.

But now I'm convinced everything happened in North America.

The settings for major Book of Mormon events are not in Mexico and Guatemala but in Florida and Tennessee, Missouri and Iowa, Illinois and Ohio, and, ultimately, in New York.

If you're surprised to read this, join the club. Many Church members are surprised, as I was myself. We've been conditioned to associate the Book of Mormon with Central America. I know from my own experience that the change in paradigm can be startling and even difficult.

But I also know what a difference it makes to finally realize that everything Joseph Smith and Oliver Cowdery said about the Book of Mormon and North America is true.

For example, on June 4, 1834, after crossing Ohio, Indiana, and Illinois as part of Zion's Camp, Joseph Smith wrote a letter to his wife Emma saying he had been "wandering over *the plains of the Nephites*, recounting occasionally the history of the Book of Mormon, roving over *the mounds of that once beloved people of the Lord*, picking up their skulls and their bones, as a proof of its defined authenticity"[5] (emphasis added). Revelations in the Doctrine and Covenants identify the American Indians in New York, Ohio and Missouri as Lamanites (D&C 28:8-9; 32:2; 54:8). Oliver Cowdery wrote accounts of early Church history including a description of the final battles of the Jaredites and Nephites near the Hill Cumorah in New York. Joseph helped Oliver write this history and had his scribes copy it into his journal as part of his history.[6]

All of these and more are not only consistent with a North American setting, but they *require* such a setting. Once you think of the Book of Mormon taking place in New York, Ohio, Illinois, Missouri, and Tennessee, I think you'll feel, as did I, a greater appreciation for the scriptures and enjoy a more vibrant engagement with them.

At the outset, let me be clear that my purpose isn't to criticize the scholars who developed and promoted the Mesoamerican theory. While I think it was a mistake, I also think they have been sincere, hard-working and faithful, trying to vindicate what they believed were the teachings of Joseph Smith. The problem is, they started with a false premise[7] and ended up constructing an entire theory that has led to unnecessary confusion and controversy.[8]

Officially, the Church has no position on Book of Mormon geography. Individual members are free to believe whatever they want on the topic.

Nevertheless, the Mesoamerican theory has dominated LDS culture, including Church media, lesson manuals, and artwork in chapels and temples. We find it in the *Ensign*, in LDS books, and in scholarly publications published by FARMS, the Maxwell Institute, and others. More recently, it has made its way into the Joseph Smith Papers.[9]

As I said, I think this is all a mistake, however innocent and well intentioned.

To be sure, scholars have done tremendous work that helps us understand the Book of Mormon in terms of linguistics, influences from Hebrew culture, the setting in ancient Israel and the Arabian Peninsula. But the effort to find Mayan culture in the Book of Mormon has been futile and counterproductive because it has given millions of people an erroneous perception of what the text says and even what it means.[10]

There is abundant evidence of a sophisticated ancient civilization in North America that matches the descriptions in the Book of Mormon. The evidence includes extensive earthworks that involved mathematics and sophisticated celestial alignments over large distances. The population was extensive; one expert says there were over one million mounds in North America, although fewer than 100,000 still exist because of farming, construction, and other destructive activities.[11] Many of these date to

Jaredite and Nephite timeframes, in the locations we would expect from the scriptures and the statements of Joseph Smith and Oliver Cowdery.

The most astonishing thing for me as I've studied these issues is how well the Book of Mormon describes the United States as it existed in 1842. The geography in the text is not only internally consistent, but every verse fits in the real world.

There is no need to look anywhere other than where Joseph and Oliver said we should look, starting with Cumorah in New York.

Much of life consists of asking and answering questions, ranging from the mundane and repetitive ("What's for dinner?") to the profound and life-changing ("What's the purpose of my life?"). Questions are like hunger and thirst; answers are the food and drink that satisfy us.

A given question can be more important for one person than it is for another. For many people, the question "What's for dinner?" is easily answered by a quick stop at the store or choosing from a menu at a restaurant, but it could be the most important question of the day for an impoverished parent when asked by a hungry child.

The question addressed in this book—*where did the Book of Mormon take place?*—may fall anywhere along the spectrum of importance for you. If you're curious about Mormonism, this question might be a pre-requisite for reading the Book of Mormon. If you're a critic, you may consider the question a challenge to find fault. If you already believe the Book of Mormon is scripture equal to the Bible, you might think the question doesn't matter because you have a spiritual witness of the book; you might find the answers interesting and useful to enhance your understanding and appreciate of the book, but not essential. Or, you might find the answer critical to resolving doubts you are harboring.

Maybe you once believed in the Book of Mormon but have lost your faith because you think there is no physical evidence of the people and cultures it describes. In that case, I suggest you have been looking in the wrong place—as so many people have been for far too long.

Regardless of where the question falls on your spectrum, I think the very first readers of the Book of Mormon—Oliver Cowdery and Joseph Smith—

asked themselves that very question. They, maybe more than anyone since, wanted to know where the events took place. In Chapter 7, I'll look at what they had to say on the topic.

Since 1830, millions of people around the world have encountered the Book of Mormon one way or another. Most have wondered where the events occurred. Answers are plentiful and varied. Hundreds of books, articles, and web pages have proposed different settings, ranging from a single county in New York to the entirety of North and South America, and from locations in Asia and Africa to nowhere on Earth (for those who think it is fiction).

The last thing the world needs is yet another answer—unless this answer is different. And it is.

Until now, proposed settings for the Book of Mormon failed to reconcile all the available evidence from the text itself, additional latter-day scripture, teachings of Joseph Smith and the Three Witnesses, and the real-world geology, geography, anthropology and archaeology. The North American setting embraces all of these sources and harmonizes them in a way I didn't think possible. A table comparing geography theories in light of these elements is included in Chapter 29.

One reason this book is titled Moroni's America is because Moroni holds the keys to the Book of Mormon (D&C 27:5). What does that mean?

I suggest it means that Moroni was given stewardship over the record, both anciently and in modern times. It was he who completed his father's work, added his own writing to the record, sealed most of it, and buried it in the hill in New York. It was Moroni who gave the plates to Joseph Smith and took back possession of them. Presumably it will be Moroni who makes the sealed portion available sometime in the future.

Although he engraved only 9.8% of the Book of Mormon,[12] Moroni's contributions were exceptional in several ways.

1. He finished the record by writing things that his father, Mormon, commanded him to write. (Mormon 8:1)
2. He had two unique qualifications. First, he knew the history his father had written. Second, he saw our day. "Behold, I speak unto you as if ye were

present, and yet ye are not. But behold, Jesus Christ hath shown you unto me, and I know your doing." (Mormon 8:35)

3. Hundreds of years after Christ's ministry, Moroni personally met the disciples of Jesus who had been promised to tarry (Mormon 8:10-11).

4. He knew more than he could write. He explained that "were it possible, I would make all things known unto you." (Mormon 8:12) Because that wasn't possible, he selected choice teachings and knowledge specifically for our benefit.

5. He abridged the record of the Jaredites and provided important warnings about secret combinations in our day.

6. He wrote, "And then shall ye know that I have seen Jesus, and that he hath talked with me face to face, and that he told me in plain humility, even as a man telleth another in mine own language, concerning these things."

7. He gave instructions on Church operations and Priesthood ordinances, spiritual gifts, and sanctification.

8. He explained the manner by which anyone who reads the Book of Mormon can find out, directly from God, whether it is true.

Another reason for the title is that Moroni lived in what is now western New York. It was in America—Moroni's America—where he saw his father die, where he observed the destruction of his people, where he finished the record, where he buried the plates, where he died, and where he, as a resurrected being, returned to give the plates to Joseph Smith.

By his own words, he was in the area where the Jaredites and Nephites were destroyed—which was the same place where he buried the plates. He called it "this north country" (Ether 1:1).

Oliver Cowdery explained that the plates were *written and deposited* in New York.

He [Moroni] then proceeded and gave a general account of the promises made to the fathers, and also gave a history of **the aborigines of this country**, and said they were literal descendants of Abraham. He represented them as once being an enlightened and intelligent people, possessing a correct knowledge of the gospel, and the plan of restoration and redemption. He said **this history was written and deposited not far from that place** [i.e., Joseph's home].[13]

Moroni referred to the Hill Cumorah, where the plates were written and deposited. It is "not far from" Joseph's home—about two miles south.

Although their message is universally applicable to every child of God on Earth, Moroni and his father (as well as Nephi, Jacob, and the other contributors) were writing *in* America, *about* America, *to* Americans.

The Book of Mormon took place in Moroni's America.

There is another Moroni who deserves mention here. When he raised the title of liberty, Captain Moroni

> prayed mightily unto his God for the blessings of liberty to rest upon his brethren, so long as there should a band of Christians remain to possess the land—
> And it came to pass that when he had poured out his soul to God, he named all the land which was south of the land Desolation, yea, and in fine, all the land, both on the north and on the south—A chosen land, and the land of liberty. And he said: Surely God shall not suffer that we, who are despised because we take upon us the name of Christ, shall be trodden down and destroyed, until we bring it upon us by our own transgressions. (Alma 46:13, 17, 18).

This relevance of this message is apparent to those who live in Moroni's America today.

I titled this book *Moroni's America*, but maybe I should have titled it *Lehi's America*. For Lehi, the place where he landed was a promised land, a land of inheritance for his descendants.

Where are those descendants today?

Soon after the Book of Mormon was published in 1830, the Lord called Oliver Cowdery, Parley P. Pratt, Ziba Peterson, and Peter Whitmer, Jr., to go on a mission to the Lamanites. These were the living descendants of Lehi. Where were they sent?

New York, Ohio, and Missouri.

Sometimes we forget who originally possessed the land now called the United States of America. Before the Europeans arrived, millions of Indians inhabited North America. By the year 1900, their numbers had declined to 237,000.[14] Even where the former inhabitants have been killed or removed from their land, their presence endures through Indian place names. More than half of the States, as well as dozens of counties, cities, towns, villages, rivers, and landmarks throughout the country, are known by Indian names. All of the states in the Heartland of America have Indian names—except for Indiana, which is a Latin-derived name that means "Land of the Indians."

American States with Indian names
Alabama - Thicket Clearers (Choctaw)
Alaska - Great Land/Peninsula (Aleut)
Arizona - Silver Slabs/Small Springs (O'odham)
Arkansas - Downstream People (Kansa)
Connecticut - Upon the Long River (Algonquian)
Dakota (North/South) - Related People/Allies (Sioux) (Dakota tribe)
Illinois - Men/Great Men or Speaks Normally (Algonquian)
Indiana - Land of the Indians
Iowa - Drowsy People (Dakota) (Iowa tribe)
Kansas - People of the South Wind (Kansa) (Kaw tribe)
Kentucky - Hunting Ground, the Meadow (Iroquoian)
Massachusetts - Great Hill (Algonquian)
Michigan - Great Water (Ojibwe)
Minnesota - Sky Tinted Water (Dakota)
Mississippi - Father of Water, Great River (Ojibwe)
Missouri - Long Canoe People (Illinois) (Missouri tribe)
Nebraska - Flat Water (Chiwere)
Ohio – Good River (Seneca/Iroquoian) (for both Ohio and Allegheny)
Oklahoma - Land of the Red People (Choctaw)
Oregon - Beautiful Water (unknown Native American)
Tennessee – Winding River, meeting place, river of the great bend
Texas - Tejas or Allies (Caddo)
Utah - Those Who Dwell High Up (Apache)
Wisconsin – It Lies Red (Miami) or Red Stone Place (Ojibwe)
Wyoming – Big River Flat (Munsee Delaware)

Canadian Provinces
Manitoba – Strait of the Spirit (Cree or Ojibwa)

Jonathan Neville

Ontario – Beautiful Lake (Wyandot)
Quebec – Strait, Narrows (Mikmaq)
Saskatchewan – Swift Flowing River (Cree)

Another important reason for the title *Moroni's America* is that Moroni specifically addressed the future inhabitants of his homeland. One of the purposes of the Book of Mormon, the thread that runs throughout from Nephi through Moroni, is connecting the past (Jaredites), present (Nephites), and future (Americans).

When he abridged the writings of Ether, the Jaredite prophet, Moroni included his own editorial comments about the land of promise that had been occupied by the Jaredite nation and the Nephite nation, and would in the future be occupied by another nation.

- And now, we can behold the decrees of God concerning **this land**, that it is a land of promise; and **whatsoever nation** shall possess it shall serve God, or they shall be swept off when the fulness of his wrath shall come upon them (Ether 2:9)
- Behold, **this is a choice land**, and **whatsoever nation** shall possess it shall be free from bondage, and from captivity, and from all other nations under heaven, if they will but serve the God of the land, who is Jesus Christ, who hath been manifested by the things which we have written (Ether 2:12).
- And **whatsoever nation** shall uphold such secret combinations, to get power and gain, until they shall spread over the nation, behold, they shall be destroyed; (Ether 8:22).

These writings of Moroni deserve serious attention. In one sense, they may have universal application, but Moroni specifically refers to the land of promise that is "this land," meaning the land where he lived. Hence, it is important to know where that land was.

There is another reference to "this land" in modern revelation that ties in with what Moroni wrote. "And for this purpose [to protect moral agency and freedom] have I established the Constitution of this land, by the hands of wise men whom I raised up unto this very purpose" (D&C 101:80).

Often we think of the Founding Fathers as the "wise men" referred to, but they were influenced by the Iroquois League of Nations. The wise men referred to in section 101 included American Indians. "Benjamin Franklin, Thomas Jefferson, George Washington, and Thomas Paine were well aware of the inner workings of many tribal governments such as the Iroquois Confederacy, the Cherokee, and the Shawnee. In fact, an Iroquois chief suggested to Franklin in 1744 that the 13 colonies should form a union such as the six tribes had formed in the Iroquois Confederacy."[15] "The Iroquois League was, and still is, the oldest participatory democracy on Earth."[16]

It is fitting that the government established in Moroni's America was established on principles and practices developed by the ancient inhabitants of this land. Those ideas were embodied in the "laws and constitution of the people, which I have suffered to be established, and should be maintained for the rights and protection of all flesh, according to just and holy principles."

In a sense, then, Moroni's America is everyone's America. The promised land sought by Lehi was sought by the Jaredites. Today it is called America. True, it is an actual, physical location on Earth. But ultimately, it is a symbol for the promised land of salvation, available to "all flesh."

Yea, thus we see that the gate of heaven is open unto all, even to those who will believe on the name of Jesus Christ, who is the Son of God.
Yea, we see that whosoever will may lay hold upon the word of God, which is quick and powerful, which shall divide asunder all the cunning and the snares and the wiles of the devil, and lead the man of Christ in a strait and narrow course across that everlasting gulf of misery which is prepared to engulf the wicked—
And land their souls, yea, their immortal souls, at the right hand of God in the kingdom of heaven, to sit down with Abraham, and with Isaac, and with Jacob, and with all our holy fathers, to go no more out. (Helaman 3:28-30).

Jonathan Neville

NOTES

⁵ Joseph Smith, Letter to Emma Smith, 4 June 1834, in JS Letterbook 2, pp. 56-59, online at http://bit.ly/Moroni4.

⁶ Oliver Cowdery, *Letter VII*, Joseph Smith 1834-1836 Journal, online at http://bit.ly/Moroni5.

⁷ The Mesoamerican theory originated in three articles in the 1842 *Times and Seasons*. As I noted in the Preface, my book, *The Lost City of Zarahemla*, explains how and why those articles were published. My conclusion: Joseph Smith had nothing to do with them. Without these articles, there was no reason to look in Mesoamerica in the first place.

⁸ There are dozens of variations of the Mesoamerican theory, each supported by web pages, books, videos, etc. The Mesoamerican theory requires that the Hill Cumorah—the scene of the last battles of the Nephites and Jaredites—be located in Mexico. This contradicts what Joseph Smith and Oliver Cowdery said on the topic, as well as other statements Joseph made about the Book of Mormon in North America. This is just one element of controversy.

⁹ "In fall 1830, four missionaries were commanded by revelation to preach to various tribes of American Indians west of the Missouri border who were considered by Joseph Smith and many church members to be descendants of Lamanites." *Revelations and Translations*, Volume 3, part 1, Printer's Manuscript of the Book of Mormon (The Church Historian's Press, 2015), p. xxvii. A similar explanation appears in the Church History Museum's display titled "The Indian Mission." In my view, if Joseph Smith "considered" them to be Lamanites it was because the Lord himself designated them as such in the revelation. A comment not influenced by the Mesoamerican theory would read "In fall 1830, four missionaries were commanded by revelation to preach to the Lamanites west of the Missouri border."

¹⁰ Efforts to impose a Mayan interpretation on the text have led some scholars to conclude the text is mistranslated and merely metaphorical in some respects.

¹¹ Gregory L. Little, Ed.D., *The Illustrated Encyclopedia of Native American Mounds & Earthworks*, (Eagle Wing Books, Inc., Memphis, TN, 2009), p. 2.

¹² Wayne A. Larsen and Alvin C. Rencher, "Who Wrote the Book of Mormon? An Analysis of Wordprints," in *Book of Mormon Authorship: New Light on Ancient Origins*, ed. Noel B. Reynolds (Provo, UT: Religious Studies Center, Brigham Young University, Provo, Utah, 1982), pp. 157-88, Appendix A

¹³ Oliver Cowdery, Letter IV. Oliver wrote a series of letters to W.W. Phelps, describing events in early Church history. They were published in the *Messenger and Advocate*, the *Times and Seasons*, and the *Gospel Reflector*. Joseph Smith had them copied into his personal journal (History, 1834-1836, p. 69), online here: http://bit.ly/Moroni6. The letters are discussed in my book, *Letter VII: Oliver Cowdery's Message to the World about the Hill Cumorah*.

¹⁴ Estimates of pre-Columbian population numbers vary widely. See Guenter Lewy, "Were American Indians the Victims of Genocide," History News Network, online at http://bit.ly/Moroni136 and Charles C. Mann, *1491* (Knopf 2005), pp. 97-101.

¹⁵ Robert J. Miller, "American Indian Influence on the United States Constitution and its Framers," *American Indian Law Review*, 18:1 (1993), at http://bit.ly/Moroni137.

¹⁶ "American History Myths Debunked," *Indian Country Today*, at http://bit.ly/Moroni138.

Chapter 2 – Pins in the Map

THE BOOK OF MORMON PRESENTS A UNIQUE CHALLENGE when it comes to geography. The text contains many named locations, but the names are ancient. There is nothing comparable to Jerusalem, for example. We know where Jerusalem is because it never moved and it has been continuously inhabited. By contrast, there are no named sites in the Book of Mormon that have maintained their location and name through the present.

The text describes a comprehensive, consistent geography, but it is quite flexible. Locations and directions are given in vague terms. Distances are measured by travel time, not by miles or kilometers. There are lands *northward* and *southward*, relative terms whose meaning depends on the frame of reference. There is a narrow neck, a small neck, a narrow pass, and a narrow passage. There are seas and rivers and mountains and hills, some named but most not.

With such ambiguity, no two people can independently develop an identical map merely from reading the text. Matching such maps to real-world locations is just as problematic.

What we need is a solid starting point—a reliable pin in the map.

That's why we need modern revelation.

Because the Book of Mormon does not refer to places we recognize, we look to modern revelation, where there are scriptural references to two Book of Mormon sites: Cumorah and Zarahemla.

Regarding Cumorah, D&C 128:20 says, in part:

And again, what do we hear? Glad tidings from Cumorah! Moroni, an angel from heaven, declaring the fulfilment of the prophets—the book to be revealed. A voice of the Lord in the wilderness of Fayette, Seneca county, declaring the three witnesses to bear record of the book!

Oliver Cowdery explicitly and unequivocally located the hill Cumorah is in New York, outside of Palmyra. Joseph Smith repeatedly endorsed Oliver's statements about Cumorah.[17] Every one of Joseph's contemporaries accepted the New York setting.

I stick a Cumorah pin in the map in western New York.

⟶≫ ≪⟵

Regarding Zarahemla, D&C 125:3 says, in part, "Let them build up a city unto my name upon the land opposite the city of Nauvoo, and let the name of Zarahemla be named upon it."[18]

This verse is not conclusive about geography, but it doesn't need to be. The Lord named the site Zarahemla. I want to see if it fits, so I stick a pin in eastern Iowa, along the Mississippi River across from Nauvoo.

Here is how the two pins fit on a map.[19]

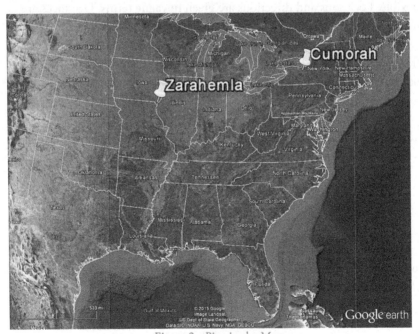

Figure 2 - Pins in the Map

There it is. Book of Mormon geography in a nutshell.

⟶≫ ≪⟵

I expect you have some questions. Most people ask, what about the narrow neck of land? What about the sea west? What about...

I'll get to all those questions, but for now I want to focus on *this* question: If figuring out Book of Mormon geography based on modern revelation is so easy, why has it been so complicated and confusing?

A detailed answer would take an entire book to answer,[20] so I'll summarize some of the factors.

Fundamentally, we have more resources than people had in the past. Some of these factors may fit within Article of Faith 9: "We believe all that God has revealed, all that He does now reveal, and we believe that He will yet reveal many great and important things pertaining to the Kingdom of God."

1. The Book of Mormon was translated into English from an ancient text that contained unusual terminology that has been difficult to understand. It contains ancient literary structures (such as chiasmus, discussed in Chapter 27) that were unknown to Joseph Smith and his contemporaries. I think Joseph knew where the Book of Mormon took place but couldn't figure out how the text described the geography. That's why he identified Book of Mormon places and people but didn't link them to the text.

With modern understanding of these ancient literary structures and terminology, we can see how the text describes a comprehensive, consistent geography in a way previous generations could not.

2. Ancient languages lacked punctuation. Joseph Smith dictated the text without punctuation (another evidence of its antiquity, by the way). The original printer and subsequent editors have used punctuation to make sense of the text, but in doing so have unintentionally obscured some of the meaning. The text has also been divided into chapters and verses that also affect the meaning.

Thanks to the Joseph Smith Papers project and the work of Dr. Royal Skousen, we have access to portions of the original manuscript dictated by Joseph and the entire printer's manuscript (the copy Oliver Cowdery made for the printer).[21] We can see where changes have been made in the text, whether by innocent mistake or in an effort to clarify the meaning. The closer we get to the original, the better—even on the geography issues.

3. In the 1830s and 1840s, overzealous missionaries sought to prove the truthfulness of the Book of Mormon by citing impressive ruins in Central America. The public was fascinated by the accounts of explorers in that area and some Mormons thought linking the Book of Mormon to these exotic locales would motivate more people to read the book. Some of these ideas were published in the Church newspaper, the *Times and Seasons*, in 1842. Different ideas about Book of Mormon settings in Central and South America were published in footnotes to the official text starting in 1879. The footnotes were deleted in 1920, but artwork by Arnold Friberg depicting Central America was included in official editions of the Book of Mormon and reinforced the Mesoamerican theory. Over the years, Mormon scholars persisted in seeking links between the Mayans and the Book of Mormon, and these ideas have remained dominant in Church culture, despite the official position of neutrality.

Thanks to the Joseph Smith Papers and other electronic resources, we now know much more about Church history and can see that the early links to Mesoamerica and South America originated not with Joseph Smith but with others. It is also becoming more apparent that the purported cultural links between Mayans and Book of Mormon peoples are illusory.

4. Everyone reads the Book of Mormon in the light of their own culture and knowledge. In the 19th century, people knew relatively little about archaeology, geology, geography, anthropology, etc.[22] This led to misunderstandings about what the text actually said, leading to unwarranted assumptions about geography and Nephite culture that have persisted.

With far greater knowledge and understanding of the scientific context of ancient America—North, Central, and South—we can re-evaluate previous beliefs and match the text to what we discover.

We simply know more now than those who preceded us. And the more we learn, the more we realize Joseph Smith was right all along.

An open-minded evaluation of the text is essential for anyone approaching this topic in the pursuit of truth. As Brother John L. Sorenson points out, "If we are to progress in this task, we must chop away and burn the conceptual underbrush that has afflicted the effort in the past."[23]

Ironically, some of that conceptual underbrush has been the basis for the Mesoamerican theory itself. Brother Sorenson declined to even consider North America:

> The prospect that any other part of America than Mesoamerica was the scene of Book of Mormon events is so slight that only this obvious candidate area will be considered here.[24]

Answering the question *before* examining the evidence leads to confirmation bias, a common error that superficially resembles testing a hypothesis. I am sensitive to the risk of confirmation bias. When I started this process, I was fully prepared to take the pins out of the map if they didn't fit. Unlike Brother Sorenson, I didn't view any setting as unworthy of consideration. But after considering the Mesoamerican geography for decades, I realized is just didn't work. So I came up with a different hypothesis.

The search for Book of Mormon geography is akin to application of the scientific method. I asked a question (where did the Book of Mormon take place?), did background research (reading, talking, traveling), constructed a hypothesis (put two pins in the map), tested the hypothesis (read the text carefully), analyzed my data, and drew a conclusion. The final step, communicating my results, consists of this book.

The rest of Section 1 of this book discusses *how* the text describes Moroni's America and what Joseph Smith and others said about it. Section 2 goes through the text, verse by verse, to put the geographical references in context. Section 3 discusses frequently asked questions about geography issues and examines how the chiastic structure of Alma 22 describes North America.

NOTES

[17] I recognize that some scholars dispute the validity of Oliver's account. They even claim Joseph merely adopted a "tradition" about the New York Cumorah that was started by unknown Church members at an unknown time. I address this in my short book, *Letter VII, Oliver Cowdery's Message to the World about the Hill Cumorah*, so I don't address it in detail in this book.

[18] William Clayton recorded a slightly different version in his journal on 8 April 1841. "A short revelation was also read concerning the saints in Iowa. The question had been asked what is the will of the Lord concerning the saints in Iowa. It read to the following effect-- Verily thus saith the Lord let all those my saints who are assaying to do my will gather themselves together upon the land opposite to Nauvoo and build a city unto my name and let the name of Zarahemla be named upon it. And all who come from the east and West and North and South who have desires let them settle in Zarahemla that they may be prepared for that which is in store for a time to come &c. Brother Joseph when speaking to one of the brethren on this subject says you have hauns Mill for a sample. Many of the brethren immediately made preparations for moving in here but on account of its being so late in the season President John Smith advised to get through with planting and then proceed to move in." Clayton, *Manchester*, p. 208. I discuss the issues related to the designation of Zarahemla in Iowa in *The Lost City of Zarahemla*.

[19] I used Google Earth in this book because it is easily accessible to anyone who has access to the Internet. Those interested can experiment with the text on their own, using my maps as a start. I haven't put my maps on the Internet because I'm constantly adjusting them, but if you'd like my .kml file for your personal use, just email me at the address listed on the copyright page.

[20] The complications arose from what people read into the text. For example, where Joseph and Oliver stated clearly and simply that the Hill Cumorah was in New York, some scholars in the 20th century claimed that was wrong; they think Cumorah has to be in southern Mexico. They reached this conclusion by 1) establishing their own criteria for the scene of the last battles of the Jaredites and the Nephites and 2) deciding New York didn't meet their criteria. For example, see David A. Palmer, *In Search of Cumorah*, Horizon Publishers, 1982, also cited in Sorenson, *Mormon's Codex*, p. 142. Brother Sorenson discusses Cumorah in more detail on pages 688-695, where he ridicules those who believe the final battles took place in New York. See also Brant A. Gardner, *Traditions of the Fathers*, pp. 375-379, in which Brother Gardner refers to the "sacralization of the New York hill."

[21] In this book, I reference the printed books (Joseph Smith Papers, *Revelations and Translations*, Volume 3) as well as Brother Skousen's work available online. Information about the books is available here: http://bit.ly/Moroni7.

[22] People were aware that many ancient sites were being destroyed, so they made efforts to document what they found. Squier and Davis conducted an extensive survey and published it in *Ancient Monuments of the Mississippi Valley*, which I reference later in this book.

[23] Sorenson, *Geography*, p. 210.

[24] Ibid, p. 407.

Chapter 3 – The North American Map

MANY YEARS AGO I SERVED A MISSION IN FRANCE. EVEN BACK THEN, people we contacted said they were not interested because there was no evidence of the Book of Mormon. The same objection was faced by missionaries in the 1830s such as Parley P. Pratt. It has become even more pervasive in modern times through the Internet. The claim of no evidence is a persistent narrative.

But it's a false narrative.

There *is* evidence of the historicity—the historical authenticity—of the Book of Mormon. We just have to look in the right place.

I'm sympathetic with those who have questioned the Book of Mormon because, as they have concluded, there is no physical or external evidence of the people and history described in the text. For decades, the dominant ("consensus") view of Book of Mormon geography has focused on Central America, particularly southern Mexico and Guatemala (Mesoamerica). I actually agree with critics who say there is no direct evidence to support the Book of Mormon narrative in Mesoamerica.[25]

However, anyone who rejects—or has lost faith in—the Book of Mormon because of concerns about physical evidence ought to reconsider. What could be worse than making an important decision based on incorrect information (i.e., the Mesoamerican theory of geography), when there is actually abundant evidence of the Book of Mormon in North America?

Evidence comes in many forms, direct and circumstantial, documentary and physical, scientific and literary, anecdotal and statistical, etc. When integrated and harmonized, a combination of these forms of evidence can become persuasive, even convincing.

That said, many people may want a map to help *prove* to someone else the reality, or historical authenticity—the historicity—of the Book of Mormon. This is not realistic. *Proof* is a subjective concept; evidence that convinces one person may seem irrelevant to another. (This is how the Mesoamerican theory became so prevalent in the first place. People who wanted to believe it accepted maps that defied common sense, such as a "narrow neck" over 100 miles wide).[26]

However, a map that matches up with the text, with real-world geography and geology, and with the teachings of Joseph Smith and Oliver Cowdery and other sources, would undoubtedly be of great worth to those who believe—or who want to know if—the Book of Mormon recounts a true history, apart from its spiritual teachings.

The Book of Mormon contains hundreds of verses that describe, or at least refer to, its geographical setting. They can be confusing without a visual reference. This chapter sets out the basic map—a replacement for the hourglass so many people have been accustomed to.[27]

In Chapter 1, I mentioned that the Church of Jesus Christ of Latter-day Saints has no formal position on Book of Mormon geography, which leaves the question open to individual interpretation.[28] Some may conclude this official position means geography doesn't matter, but for many people it does matter. It matters a lot.

For readers, a map helps clarify the narrative. When we know where Cumorah and Zarahemla are, for example, we can understand where other things happened, why certain places were strategic, why people would get lost in the wilderness, etc. A map may help us identify the promised land so often mentioned in the text. Using such a map, we might even be able to identify known (or unknown) archaeological sites that will give us greater insight into the narrative.

Once I concluded that the Mesoamerican model has too many problems to be viable—among other things it contradicts the text and relies on illusory "correspondences" that amount to wishful thinking—I took another look at the text and the external evidence, including what Joseph Smith and his contemporaries said and wrote, and what the real-world geography, geology, and archaeology tell us.

In my opinion, they tell us to look in North America.

The bulk of the Nephite record (Omni through 3 Nephi) describes events that took place from around 200 B.C. to the visit of Christ after his resurrection. The capital city of the Nephites was Zarahemla, which is by far the most often mentioned city and land in the text. The scene of the destruction of the Nephites was Cumorah.

In Chapter 2, I placed the two pins in the map. Now I'm going to show the overall picture of Nephite vs Lamanite territory.

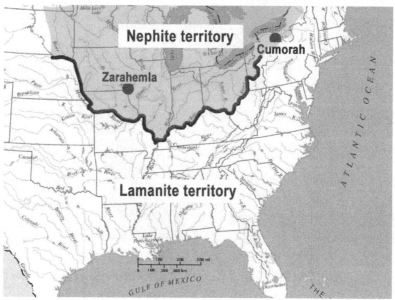

Figure 3 – Nephite and Lamanite territory

The thick black line is the "narrow strip of wilderness" mentioned in Alma 22. It consists mainly of the Ohio and Missouri Rivers.

My proposed border—the narrow strip of wilderness—is a natural border that has been recognized even in modern times.

Historians may notice something familiar about these borders. At the conclusion of the French and Indian War, British King George III issued the Proclamation of 1763. The British had defeated France and taken over territory west of the British colonies. To reward the American Indians and separate them from the British colonists, the proclamation created an "Indian Reserve" along the Appalachian mountains, with the Mississippi River as the western border and the Ohio River, Lake Ontario, Lake Erie, and St. Lawrence River as the northern border. The line from the Ohio River to Lake Ontario later became the western border of Pennsylvania.

The white line in the map below[29] shows my proposed border between the Nephites and Lamanites at one point of Nephite history. It is just 100 miles west of the border established in 1763.

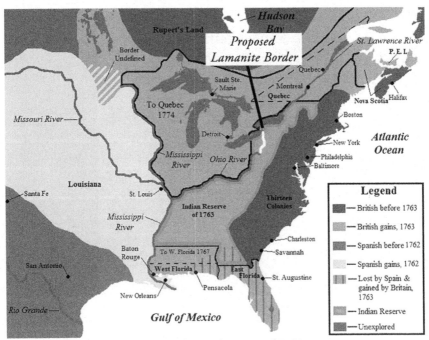

Figure 4 - Proclamation of 1763

This historical comparison demonstrates the practical, real-world reality of Mormon's description of the borders in Alma 22, which we will explore in more detail throughout this book.

Obviously, the British were not enforcing the Nephite border; the Book of Mormon hadn't been published in 1763. However, this and other historical analogies can help inform our understanding of the text and help show that the distances and time frames mentioned in the text fit in the real world.

One of the most common questions asked about the North American setting is, "what about the narrow neck of land?" People have been taught to think the Book of Mormon describes two large land masses connected by the "narrow neck of land." The hourglass shape has been depicted in many LDS publications. When we look on a globe, we immediately think of Panama as a narrow neck of land connecting North and South America. However, scholars have pointed out that a hemispheric interpretation of Book of Mormon geography contradicts the text; the distances are simply too great.

Instead, scholars have proposed a more limited territory. Two articles in the 1984 *Ensign*[30] introduced the limited model of Book of Mormon geography in Mesoamerica to a wide LDS audience. The author of those articles, John Sorenson, has also written that "A key feature of any geographical correlation must include a narrow neck of land connecting two sizable land masses... Only one geographical correlation avoids fatal flaws: The narrow neck of land was the Isthmus of Tehuantepec."[31]

Figure 5 - Hourglass shape

Figure 5 is an application of this interpretation of the text.[32]

It may be surprising to realize that the term "narrow neck of land" is used *only once* in the entire Book of Mormon. The passage is in Ether 10:20: "And they built a great city by the **narrow neck of land**, by the place where the sea divides the land."

That's it.

A single passage.

Despite its solitary appearance in Ether, many commentators have considered the "narrow neck of land" to be a defining feature. They think the verse in Ether refers to the same feature as a verse in Alma 22:32, which says "thus the land of Nephi and the land of Zarahemla were nearly surrounded by water, there being **a small neck of land** between the land northward and the land southward." That interpretation is a mistake. Besides the difference in terminology (*narrow* does not mean *small*), the context and frame of reference of the two passages are entirely different, and they were written by different authors.

I'll explain this in more detail in the next chapters, but notice that the *small* neck of land is an exception to the two lands being "nearly surrounded by water." No location in Central America is nearly surrounded by water because at both ends there are enormous continents. In North America, both the land of Zarahemla and the land of Nephi *are* nearly surrounded by water, with a small neck of land between them, as I'll explain.

Furthermore, the narrow neck of land in Mesoamerica is over 100 miles wide. Many people have observed the incongruity of describing such a wide stretch of difficult terrain as "narrow." A feature this wide might appear "narrow" from a satellite, but to someone on the ground, this Isthmus is as wide as the adjacent land.

When we read the text, we need to put ourselves in the place of the authors, in their time and place. They didn't have satellites. They described their territory as they saw it, from the surface. Perspective is key.

In this book, I refer to scholarly resources to help define terms in the geography passages, but I don't spend a lot of space debating the semantics of previous interpretations. Instead, I take a fresh look at the text to see whether, and how, it describes North America in a manner that harmonizes the other evidence.

One reason why the overall shape of the setting has been erroneously portrayed for so long is punctuation. There was no punctuation in the original manuscript; Oliver wrote down the words Joseph spoke without sentence breaks or any form of punctuation. The punctuation we have today was added later, by the typesetter.[33] Punctuation is used to imitate speech and show the reader how the sentence should be read. It imposes a particular meaning. For that reason, throughout this book I disregard punctuation in the text.

Another point: the current chapters and verses were created by Orson Pratt and first published in 1879. They were intended to facilitate citations to specific passages, but unfortunately they also impose a particular interpretation that may or not be valid. We aren't bound by them.

For those who have thought of the Book of Mormon geography in terms of an hourglass shape, here is the paradigm shift.

Alma 22:27 says the border between the Nephites and Lamanites was a narrow strip of wilderness. Conceptually, think of it as a fence. (As I'll show, it was a water barrier that acted as a border—effectively, a fence.)

Now, picture the small neck of land between the land of Nephi and the land of Zarahemla as a gate in the fence.

Figure 6 - A Gate in the Fence

Like many gates, the small neck of land required attention. It had to be defended. But it wasn't the defining feature of the landscape, and it was not the narrow neck of the Jaredites.

Jonathan Neville

NOTES

[25] Although I don't believe the events described in the Book of Mormon took place in Central America, there is a caveat. The text leaves plenty of room for "hinterland" people and events outside the narrative of the book itself. In other words, descendants of Book of Mormon people could have—and likely did—migrate southward from North America and were absorbed into Mesoamerican civilizations. I address this point in Chapter 31.

[26] In Chapter 22 I address the problems of evidence, proof, and persuasion in more detail.

[27] The most common question people ask me is, where is the narrow neck of land? Many people don't realize there is only a single verse in the Book of Mormon that refers to a "narrow neck of land." That verse, Ether 10:20, has little to do with the overall geography. See chapter 22 for a discussion of the hourglass concept.

[28] Anyone who peruses the Church's web page, manuals, magazines, and officially approved art might conclude that the policy, in practical terms, is actually to not take an official position on *where in Mesoamerica* the Book of Mormon events took place. For example, when the Church published the manual titled *Teachings of the Presidents of the Church: Joseph Smith*, Chapter 38 was titled "The Wentworth Letter." The Wentworth letter was published in the 1 March 1842 *Times and Seasons* and is the source of the Articles of Faith, among other things. The chapter deleted only one portion of the letter—the section about the "history of ancient America" including these sentences Joseph wrote "The principal nation of the second race [i.e., Lehi's descendants] fell in battle towards the close of the fourth century. The remnant are the Indians that now inhabit this country." Why would that section be deleted if the official Church position accommodated a North American setting? A significant exception to the Mesoamerican dominance is the video presentation titled "Scriptures Legacy" which appears to portray Christ visiting the Nephites in a North American setting. But other parts of the film depict Book of Mormon events in Mayan-looking buildings and cities.

[29] Map adapted from http://bit.ly/Moroni8 under the creative commons license. For more background, see http://bit.ly/Moroni9.

[30] John L. Sorenson, "Digging into the Book of Mormon: Our Changing Understanding of Ancient America and Its Scripture," parts 1 and 2, Ensign, September and October 1984. Available online at http://bit.ly/Moroni119 and http://bit.ly/Moroni120. Brother Sorenson wrote several other pieces for Church magazines on this topic.

[31] Sorenson, *Mormon's Codex*, pp. 21-22.

[32] John L. Sorenson, *An Ancient American Setting for the Book of Mormon* (FARMS 1985), 11. Online at fairmormon.org, http://bit.ly/Moroni139.

[33] In some cases, the punctuation in the original text was later edited by Joseph Smith. The current chapter and verse structure was created by Orson Pratt and first published in 1879. See the narrative and notes at "Book of Mormon Translation" on lds.org, available here: http://bit.ly/Moroni121.

Chapter 4 – The Map in Alma 22

THE FRAMEWORK FOR BOOK OF MORMON GEOGRAPHY is set forth in Alma 22, in which Mormon describes the way the land was divided between the Nephites and the Lamanites. He is writing several hundred years in the future, looking back on the events as a historian providing an overall perspective.

Alma 22 can be confusing because we are not used to the method Mormon used to describe the various lands. Plus, the current chapter and verse divisions make the text a little more confusing than it could be. (In the next chapter I suggest two changes that would help, although I realize we can't change the chapters and verse at this point.)

One point to keep in mind is that Mormon describes the overall picture of Nephite and Lamanite lands in the first section, then he focuses on a particular region of Nephite territory (Bountiful and Desolation) before coming back to summarize the overall picture.

He begins in verse 27, where he gives a general outline of the Lamanite King's territory. Here is how verse 27 appeared as originally translated by Joseph Smith and recorded by Oliver Cowdery, without punctuation:[34]

And it came to pass that the king sent a proclamation throughout all the land amongst all his people who were in all his land who were in all the regions round about which was bordering even to the sea on the east and on the west and which was divided from the land of Zarahemla by a narrow strip of wilderness which ran from the sea east even to the sea west and round about on the borders of the seashore and the borders of the wilderness which was on the north by the land of Zarahemla through the borders of Manti by the head of the river Sidon running from the east towards the west and thus were the Lamanites and the Nephites divided.

As you can imagine, this long sentence has been interpreted in many different ways. For example, the meaning of the passage changes completely depending on what each clause beginning with the word *which* modifies.

When I analyzed this passage, I considered what others had written.[35] But then I wondered *why* Mormon wrote it this way, and how he thought it would be intelligible to his future readers.

(Actually, I wondered why Mormon didn't just include a map on the plates. Presumably, as a military leader, Mormon used maps. If a picture is worth a thousand words, it seems like a map would be worth a thousand words of description. Of course, it is possible that Mormon did draw a map on the plates, and that Joseph saw it, but neither he nor any of the Three or Eight Witnesses mentioned it. If there was a map engraved on the plates, we don't have a copy of it. The only things traced from the plates were the characters that Martin Harris took to Charles Anthon and the other scholars.[36])

Although we don't have a map from the plates, the text works well enough when we combine the other elements we've been given.

A key point to understanding Alma 22:27 is the ancient poetic form of *chiasmus* that is also found in the Hebrew Bible.

Chiasmus is an inverted parallel structure in which a series of thoughts are repeated in reverse order. The structure helps convey meaning, serving a function similar to modern punctuation. (Chapters 27 and 28 explain chiasmus and its application to the geography passages in more detail.)

It should not be surprising that Mormon and other Book of Mormon authors would use chiasmus, since they lived in a Hebrew culture and knew the language. In fact, it would be more surprising if they didn't use chiasmus.

It is helpful to re-format chiastic passages so the parallel structure is more apparent. When formatting parallel structures in a text, scholars commonly put a capital letter at the beginning of each line to clarify the correspondence between the two branches of the chiasm.

A simple chiasmus would look something like this:

A
  B
    C
    C¹
  B¹
A¹

There are several passages in the text that use this structure. Here is an example Don Parry offers from Mosiah 2:56.

A And it came to pass that when they came up to the <u>temple</u>,
  B they pitched their tents round about,
    C every man according to his <u>family</u>,
      D consisting of his wife, and his <u>sons</u>, and his <u>daughters</u>,
      D and their <u>sons</u>, and their <u>daughters</u>, from the eldest down to the youngest,
    C every <u>family</u> being separate one from another.
  B And they pitched their tents round about
A the <u>temple</u> (chiasmus)[37]

Mormon constructed Alma 22:27 and subsequent verses in discreet lines of text and phrases that make sense when viewed in this chiastic—or parallel—format. Chapter 28 includes a step-by-step analysis of the chiastic format. Here I am merely summarizing it.

Parallel terms are underlined for convenience. In my proposed structure below, I've also bolded the word **which** because of its importance to the structure and meaning of the passage. In this format, each of the *which* clauses modifies the original focus of the passage—the extent of the king's land. Together, they describe an oval or a rectangle. This clarifies the meaning of the text and produces a general overview of the geography in The Book of Mormon.

Jonathan Neville

Alma 22:27—Chiastic format

And it came to pass that the king sent a proclamation throughout all the land

A   amongst all his <u>people</u> who were in all his land who were in all the regions round about
  B   **which** was <u>bordering</u> even to the sea on the <u>east</u> and on the <u>west</u> and
    C   **which** was divided from the <u>land of Zarahemla</u> by a narrow strip of wilderness
      D a   **which** ran from the <u>sea east</u>
         b   even to the <u>sea west</u>
      D¹ a   and round about on the <u>borders</u> of the seashore
         b   and the <u>borders</u> of the wilderness
    C¹ **which** was on the north by the <u>land of Zarahemla</u>
  B¹ through the <u>borders</u> of Manti by the head of the river Sidon running from the <u>east</u> towards the <u>west</u>
A¹ —and thus were the <u>Lamanites</u> and the <u>Nephites</u> divided.

Here's how this verse looks in graphic form:

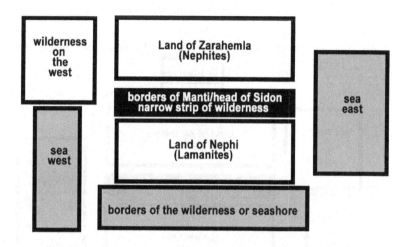

Now this abstract map, based on the text, can be overlaid on the map to see if it fits the pins in Cumorah and Zarahemla.

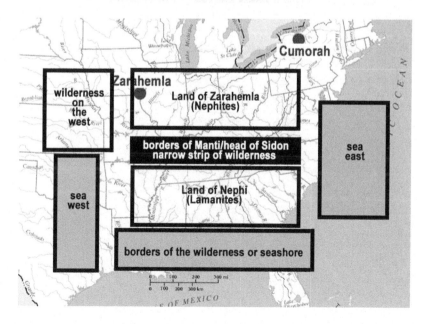

This is not bad for an approximation, but there are details to work out, such as the sea west. Setting those details aside for a moment—I'll come back to them soon—we can put the remaining verses of Alma 22 into parallel format and add them to verse 27.

This leads to a general abstract overview of Book of Mormon geography.

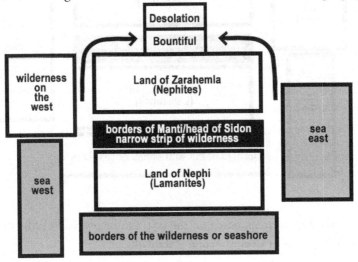

When overlaid on the map, it looks like this:

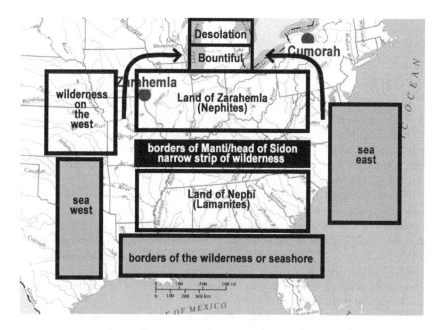

(A step-by-step analysis is contained in Chapter 25.)

Given the general and abstract nature of the description in Alma 22, this is a promising fit. With this overview, we can examine the text in more detail, including every geography-related verse in the Book of Mormon, and see if we can fine tune the map. The goal is to see if, using the scriptural pins, the real-world geography matches up with the text. Then we can examine other factors, including geology, archaeology, and anthropology, to clarify the setting.

There are some obvious questions, such as the location of the sea west and the narrow strip of wilderness, that I will address in the next chapters.

Brother Sorenson identifies over 130 sites in The Book of Mormon text.[38] Forty-five of these are named cities. Other sites described in the text include named "lands," various wilderness areas, hills, unnamed seas, the "narrow neck of land" and the "narrow pass," and the plains. Most of these I'll discuss in Section 2, Verse by Verse.

Jonathan Neville

NOTES

---

[34] The earliest manuscript we have for this section of the text is the printer's manuscript, which shows punctuation added by the printer. Placement of punctuation makes a difference in the meaning; because punctuation was added after Joseph dictated the words, punctuation reflects someone's interpretation of the text. Disregarding the punctuation offers a chance for an unimpeded interpretation.

[35] In the year 2000, John Sorenson published *Mormon's Map*, an overview of what The Book of Mormon text says about geography. He writes, "The nearest thing to a systematic explanation of Mormon's geographical picture is given in Alma 22:27-34... He [Mormon] must have considered that treatment full and clear enough for his purposes, because he never returned to the topic."[35] Sorenson takes the approach of creating an abstract map based on The Book of Mormon text, and then seeing if it fits in a real-world location. I agree with Sorenson about the importance of Alma 22, as well as the utility of creating an abstract map and finding a fit in the real world.

However, Sorenson's analysis of Alma 22 seems to be influenced by the *Times and Seasons* article published on 1 October 1842, which declares that the Nephite city of Zarahemla "stood upon" "Central America or Guatimala [sic]." Sorenson cites this passage from the *Times and Seasons*, although he recognizes the "fact that the geography question had not been settled authoritatively."[35] In *Mormon's Codex*, Sorenson relegates the *Times and Seasons* articles to a footnote in support of his unequivocal conclusion: "Joseph Smith became convinced in the last years of his life that the lands of the Nephites were in Mesoamerica."[35]

Sorenson's assumptions about Central America lead him to a preconceived concept of Book of Mormon geography; i.e., a narrow neck of land between two larger land masses. Perhaps he felt somewhat bound by the *Times and Seasons* articles and his inference that Joseph Smith agreed with them. As such, Sorenson's work could be viewed as an effort to vindicate the Prophet's words.

[36] Joseph Smith copied characters from the plates for Martin Harris to take to scholars, but the whereabouts of that document is unknown. There are three existing documents that contain characters from the plates that may have been copied from the paper Joseph prepared. See http://bit.ly/Moroni10.

[37] Donald W. Parry, *Poetic Parallelisms in* The Book of Mormon (Neal A. Maxwell Institute for Religious Scholarship, BYU, Provo, Utah, 2007), p. 160. The book, cited herein as Parry, is available here: http://bit.ly/Moroni11.

[38] Sorenson, *Geography*, pp. 319-326.

Chapter 5 – The Sea West

THE FIRST QUESTION I HAD WHEN I OVERLAID THE CHIASTIC MAP over the real-world map was, what about the sea west?

It was apparent that the Pacific Ocean was much too far away. I agree with Brother Sorenson and other scholars that a hemispheric model that includes North and South America is excluded by the text. Even a model that covers the whole of the North American continent would be too vast to match the descriptions of the wars and other travels.

Because the Nephites referred to their seas with only general directional designations and not proper nouns or names, it is possible there were multiple seas; i.e., the "sea west" could refer to one body of water in one passage, and a different body of water in another passage. Some Book of Mormon scholars resolve geographical conflicts between the text and their theories by claiming the sea north and the sea south in the text are only metaphors,[39] while the sea west is actually south and the sea east is actually north.[40]

I don't think either of those are viable explanations.

Before we can find any feature, of course, we need to know what the text means by the terms used. In this case, what is a *sea*?

Because the Nephites were Hebrew and knew the Hebrew language even after a thousand years in the New World, Hebrew terms may be useful references when we seek to understand and define the English terms Joseph dictated to Oliver Cowdery. Moroni noted that Hebrew had advantages over the characters he used on the plates. He implied that Hebrew would be more precise and leave less room for ambiguity.

And now, behold, we have written this record according to our knowledge, in the characters which are called among us the reformed Egyptian, being handed down and altered by us, according to our manner of speech. And if our plates had been sufficiently large we should have written in Hebrew; but the Hebrew hath been altered by us also; and if we could have written in Hebrew, behold, ye would have had no imperfection in our record. (Mormon 9:32-3)

I looked up the word *sea* in Biblical Hebrew concordances.[41] *Strong's Concordance* transliterates the Hebrew as *yam*, with the number 3220. The NAS Exhaustive Concordance defines *yam* as *sea* and notes variations, including seacoast, west, west side, and westward. Brown-Driver-Briggs offer usages in context, including the Mediterranean Sea, Red Sea, Dead Sea, Sea of Galilee—and "a mighty river."

The example given for "a mighty river" is the Nile River. The Hebrew term *yam* is used in Isaiah 19:5 and Nahum 3:8 (twice in one verse), both in connection with Thebes, or the modern Luxor.

Alternate translations show the term is translated as either sea or river.

KJV Isaiah 19:5 – And the waters shall fail from the **sea**, and the river shall be wasted and dried up.

NIV Isaiah 19:5 – The waters of the **river** will dry up, and the riverbed will be parched and dry.

If Biblical translators used the English word *sea* for the Hebrew term *yam*, even when it clearly referred to the Nile River, then Joseph Smith could have done the same when referring to a mighty river.

The next step was to find a mighty river that would fit both the chiastic map and the real-world geography.

That was the easy part.

The *sea west* in Alma 22:27 had to be the lower Mississippi.

The lower Mississippi is considered a separate river from the upper Mississippi. On Google Earth, the outline of the ancient boundaries of the lower Mississippi (the Mississippi Alluvial Valley or MAV) is plainly visible. In some places it is over 100 miles wide.

The lower Mississippi was originally part of the Gulf of Mexico. Over time, silt from the upper Mississippi and Ohio Rivers filled in the gulf, transforming it into a river. Now the river is controlled by reservoirs, levees and dikes, but it remains an impressive sight, particularly in times of flood.

The similarity between the Nile and the Mississippi was so apparent that European settlers gave names such as Memphis, Cairo, Themes, and Metropolis to cities along the Mississippi and its tributaries. Lower Illinois is still known as "Little Egypt."

The U.S. Geological Survey has quantified the water discharge of the rivers in the Mississippi system.[42] The Ohio River is the biggest contributor to the lower Mississippi, followed by upper Mississippi, the Tennessee, and the Missouri Rivers. This is portrayed on the USGS map below.

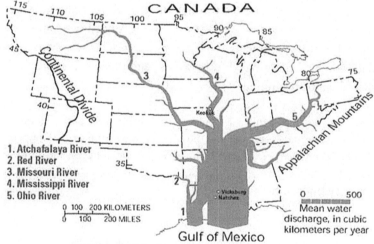

Figure 7 - Mississippi River Water Discharge

Figure 7 depicts the discharge rate, not the physical dimensions of the rivers, but it shows that the lower Mississippi River is significantly larger than any of its tributaries.

It is not clear from the text where the river ended and the sea began. It could have been at the confluence of the Missouri, Mississippi and Illinois Rivers, or at the confluence of the Mississippi and Ohio Rivers.

Either way, it is easy to understand why early settlers compared this *mighty river* to the Nile and why Mormon could have described it as a *sea* the same way Isaiah and Nahum described the Nile.

But that doesn't solve all the issues with seas in the Book of Mormon. It doesn't even solve all of Alma 22.

Alma 22:27 says the land of the Lamanites runs from the sea east (the Atlantic) even to the sea west (the Lower Mississippi). But when verses 32 and 33 describe the land Bountiful and the land Desolation, they use the phrase "from the east to the west sea." Does this mean the same sea west?

I think not.

Verses 27-29 distinguish between the lands of the Nephites and the lands of the Lamanites. Then, at the end of verse 29, Mormon switches to a parenthetical discussion about Bountiful and Desolation that continues through the first part of verse 33, through the phrase "unto the west sea."

The way Orson Pratt divided the verses here is confusing because he combines Mormon's comments about Bountiful with his summation of the overall geography, beginning when he writes "and thus the Nephites…" This should be the beginning of its own verse.[43]

Current:

33. And it came to pass that the Nephites had inhabited the land Bountiful, even from the east unto the west sea, and thus the Nephites in their wisdom, with their guards and their armies, had hemmed in the Lamanites on the south, that thereby they should have no more possession on the north, that they might not overrun the land northward.

Proposed:

33. And it came to pass that the Nephites had inhabited the land Bountiful, even from the east unto the west sea.

34. And thus the Nephites in their wisdom, with their guards and their armies, had hemmed in the Lamanites on the south, that thereby they should have no more possession on the north, that they might not overrun the land northward.

This restructuring would make it clearer that Mormon was talking about two different areas when he mentioned these seas; i.e., he referred to the *sea west* when he was describing the narrow strip of wilderness that separated the lands of the Nephites from the lands of the Lamanites, and he referred to the *west sea* when he was describing the land Bountiful, a subset of the larger lands of the Nephites.

People commonly refer to natural features using their own frame of reference. For example, if a person in Boston refers to "the ocean," everyone will understand the Atlantic Ocean. If a person in Los Angeles refers to "the ocean," everyone will understand the Pacific Ocean.

In the same manner, when Mormon was describing the boundary between the Nephites and Lamanites, he referred to the *sea west* because everyone knew the sea west—the Lower Mississippi—was related to that border. When describing the land Bountiful, he referred to the *west sea* because everyone knew Bountiful extended all the way to the west sea—Lake Michigan.

There were times when Mormon made a distinction between the west seas, however. In Alma 53, verses 1-6 discuss Moroni's activities in Bountiful. Verse 7 relates that Moroni spent the rest of the year making fortification and providing food for his armies and their women and children. Then verse 8 relates what happened in a different part of the land.

> And now it came to pass that the armies of the Lamanites on the **west sea south** while in the absence of Moroni on account of some intrigue amongst the Nephites which caused dissensions amongst them had gained some ground over the Nephites yea insomuch that they had obtained possession of a number of their cities in that part of the land (emphasis added and punctuation omitted).

I think Mormon clarified he was referring to the west sea south (Lower Mississippi) as opposed to the west sea north (Lake Michigan) because he had to explain that verse 8 starts a discussion of a different area than the previous verses. (This is another case where the text would be clearer if chapter 53 started with verse 8. Verses 1-7 are really a continuation of chapter 52.) Mormon reiterates that the action took place on the southern west sea in verse 22:

> And now it came to pass that Helaman did march at the head of his two thousand stripling soldiers, to the support of the people in the borders of the land **on the south by the west sea** (emphasis added).

Although it may seem confusing to us that the Nephites used the same designation for these two separate seas, we have a similar situation today with the Upper and Lower Mississippi. Although both sections are called

"Mississippi," they are really two different rivers geologically. The upper section is rocky and steeper—like a river. The lower section is sandy and flatter—more like a sea. Because of all the silt and sand brought by the Upper Mississippi, the bedrock beneath the Lower Mississippi is thousands of feet below the surface.

The two sections of the Mississippi are treated as two rivers on river charts. Navigation mileage markers for the Lower Mississippi begin at the mouth of the river, south of New Orleans, and end at the confluence of the Ohio River at Cairo, Illinois. Mile zero for the Upper Mississippi begins at Cairo and continues northward to Minneapolis, Minnesota.

All of this is another example of how geographical references in the Book of Mormon tend to be relative. Once we know the overall geography, and we understand the frame of reference for a particular passage, the terminology makes sense. But if we don't keep these specifics in mind, we run the risk of thinking two entirely different features are the same thing because they are called by the same or similar names, even though they are described in different parts of the book within different frameworks.

NOTES

[39] Brant A. Gardner, *Traditions of the Fathers: The Book of Mormon as History* (Greg Kofford Books, Salt Lake City, Utah 2015), p 143. Brother Gardner quotes John E. Clark as writing, "I am convinced that the reference to a north sea and a south sea is devoid of any concrete geographical context... Any geography that tries to accommodate a north and south sea, I think, is doomed to fail... The main point is that the reference to north and south seas fits nicely into the Mesoamerican scene as part of a metaphor for the whole earth and was probably used in a metaphorical sense in the Book of Mormon."

[40] John L. Sorenson, *An Ancient American Setting for the Book of Mormon*, p. 37, Map 5 "Plausible Locations in Mesoamerica for Book of Mormon Places." Also see Sorenson, *Mormon's Codex*, Map 9, "Plausible Sites of the Nephite Wars."

[41] A useful online source is here: http://bit.ly/Moroni12.

[42] See http://bit.ly/Moroni13.

[43] In the printer's manuscript, the compositor placed a semicolon after "sea" but the original has no punctuation. The ampersand (&) is at the beginning of what is now verses 29, 30, 31, 32, and 33. It should also be at the beginning of what I propose as a new verse 34.

Chapter 6 – Interpretive Keys

→≫ ≪←

ALTHOUGH ALMA 22 PROVIDES THE GENERAL OVERVIEW of the respective territories of the Lamanites and the Nephites, numerous other passages in The Book of Mormon also refer to their geography and must be integrated into the map. The information provided by the text is too vague to locate every Book of Mormon site on a map of the real world, but it does give us some useful clues. Until further discoveries are made, we can only make educated guesses about where some of these might be.

Brother Sorenson outlined an effective conceptual approach to the problem. "We need instead to use *the entire scripture, without exception . . .* We must understand, interpret and deal successfully with *every statement in the text*, not just what is convenient or interesting to us"[44] (emphasis added). This "requires writing out our work in detail; only written communication permits the careful examination by others that such work demands . . . By this repetitive process all should move toward consensus."[45]

As you read the Book of Mormon, here are some interpretive keys to keep in mind.

Up, Down and Over

Although we might think of *up* and *down* in connection with a map (up = north and down = south), as used in the Book of Mormon the terms in a geographical context probably refer to elevation.[46] Brother Sorenson often infers that "up" and "down" mean an ascent or descent of mountainous terrain. While that is a plausible interpretation, my assumptions on this regard differ slightly.[47] I think those terms more likely mean simply moving with or against a river current. Ancient peoples navigated by waterways whenever possible, and these directional clues make sense in such a context. One could paddle (or walk) "up" or "down" a river even when the terrain is not mountainous at all.

Jonathan Neville

When I read the text, I usually think of *upstream* when I read *up*, and *downstream* when I read *down*.

When Mosiah left the land of Nephi, he went "down" into the land of Zarahemla. (Omni 1:13) This means he went downriver. Zeniff came "up" out of the land of Zarahemla; i.e., he went upstream. (Mosiah 7:9)

In some cases, the term "over" means crossing a river. For example, Alma "took his journey over into the land of Melek, on the west of the river Sidon." (Alma 8:3) "Zoram and his sons crossed over the river Sidon." (Alma 16:7) This helps interpret verses that don't explicitly mention a river, such as Alma 30:21 in which Alma "came over into the land of Gideon."

Distances

The length of a journey or the distance between cities is never described in terms of miles or kilometers. Instead, the text describes distance in terms the time traveled, such as "a day and a half" or "eight days." But how far can a person walk? On average, people walk about 3.1 miles per hour. An adult male in good health will walk 4.5 to 5 miles in an hour. How long is a day? It could be 12 hours, 24 hours, or anything the society agreed upon. A day's journey could be 48 miles (4 mph x 12 hours), or twice or half that, all depending on assumptions about how fast a person—or "a Nephite" as the text says—could travel in a given time frame.

It is a fallacy to think "a day's journey for a Nephite" would be equivalent to a particular measurement in miles or kilometers that would always be the same. The distance one can travel in a day depends on the particular route. Travel through dense brush would take longer than travel over grasslands or plains; ascending hills or mountains takes longer than descending them.

As an example, let's say the Nephites walk across a flat grassland from point A to point B in one day. We measure that distance as 48 miles (4 mph x 12 hours). They also walk from point A to point C in one day, but this route is over a mountain. It's one day's journey to them, but they only travel 3 mph. We would measure 36 miles.

Nephites: A to B = one day's journey for a Nephite
Us: A to B = 45 miles
Nephites: A to C = one day's journey for a Nephite
Us: A to C = 36 miles.

40

In other words, distance and travel times, for the Nephites, are route-specific.

Assumptions about the means of transportation also make a big difference. People can travel faster by boat than by land; by boat, they can travel faster downstream than upstream, and the river's speed makes a big difference in relative speed.

Although the text only mentions a few travels by water (Ether, Lehi, Hagoth, and shipping timber), that doesn't preclude the possibility that Book of Mormon people used boats more extensively. Mormon specifically mentioned he didn't take the time to give an account of "their shipping and their building of ships" (Helaman 3:14). When the text refers to "crossing" Sidon, as when Zoram and his sons crossed over the river Sidon with their armies in Alma 16:7, they could have waded, swam, or used boats. They could have even constructed a bridge.

All of this makes estimating distance traveled by time of travel highly speculative. At most, we can establish broad parameters and infer relative distances. Once we can tie an abstract geography to a real-world setting, more specificity may be possible.

Lines

Related to the issue of distances is the question of what the text means by the term "line." There are five geographic references to *lines* in the text:

- Alma 22:32 "it was only the distance of a day and a half's journey for a Nephite, on the line Bountiful and the land Desolation."
- Alma 50:11 "fortifying the line between the Nephites and the Lamanites,"
- Alma 50:13 "it was on the south by the line of the possessions of the Lamanites."
- Helaman 4:7 "it being a day's journey for a Nephite, on the line which they had fortified and stationed their armies to defend their north country."
- 3 Nephi 3:23 "to the line which was between the land Bountiful and the land Desolation."

The context of the term *line* in these verses suggests that *line* probably refers to a border, or a river that serves as a border. A possible corroboration of this interpretation arises from a surprising source.

In the fall of 1827 or winter of 1828, Joseph Smith created a document with characters copied from the plates.[48] Martin Harris took the document to scholars in Albany, NY, Philadelphia, and New York City. The Joseph Smith papers feature three documents that "were all purported to include characters copied from the gold plates, and they likely are representative of characters Joseph Smith copied from the plates."

The most familiar of these is the document containing characters copied by John Whitmer.[49]

Figure 8 - Caractors

One analysis of these characters finds similarities between them and Egyptian characters. The author concludes that

> the mention of a "line" in the Book of Mormon is a reference to a river. The River Sidon is not mentioned as a "line", and it is fairly obvious what the difference is. There is no indication that the River Sidon ever served as a boundary line between nations or lands, while the other two rivers did.[50]

Egyptian hieroglyphs that depict boats show the river as a line. This interpretation corroborates the idea that the "narrow strip of wilderness" from Alma 22 is a river because a *narrow strip* is a synonym for a *line*.

If the term *line* in the passages quoted above refers to a river, the Nephites and Lamanites may have traveled by water more than has been commonly assumed.

At the same time, not every instance of line needs to be a river. It can also be a fortified defensive position.

Directions

Directions to and from various sites are given in general terms, referring to cardinal directions. I accept these as literal; i.e., north in the text is what we refer to as north today.[51]

When Nephi was in the Old World, the directional information he gave about the Arabian Desert correlate to modern cardinal directions. There is no reason why he would change those directions once he arrived in the New World. The sun still rises in the east.

In fact, after arriving in the new world, Nephi records that the Lord spoke in terms of cardinal directions: "I command all men, both in the east and in the west, and in the north, and in the south." (2 Nephi 29:11) Maybe Nephi would have understood this in some Mayan cultural sense, but that seems implausible.

Related to this is the question of *southward* and *northward*. Together, they appear 60 times in the text (19 and 41 times, respectively). The terms mean simply "the southern regions or countries" and "being towards the north, or nearer to the north than to the east and west points,"[52] respectively. These are context-specific terms; i.e., a land could be both *northward* and *southward* from different perspectives. The United States is the land *northward* for someone in Mexico; it is the land *southward* for someone in Canada.

A similar issue involves the seas. They are unnamed; instead, they are described in generic directional terms that imply relative position. A particular sea could be east or west depending on which side is the frame of reference.

The Hill Cumorah

The Cumorah pin on the map is in western New York. That location excludes a Mesoamerican setting because the text does not support the idea of a 2,500 chase from southern Mexico to western New York. Some people have developed lists of criteria for the Hill Cumorah that exclude the New

York hill from consideration. One of these, David A. Palmer, wrote the entry on the Hill Cumorah for the *Encyclopedia of Mormonism*, which includes this statement:

> This annual [Hill Cumorah] pageant has reinforced the common assumption that Moroni buried the plates of Mormon in the same hill where his father had buried the other plates, thus equating this New York hill with the Book of Mormon Cumorah. Because the New York site does not readily fit the Book of Mormon description of Book of Mormon geography, some Latter-day Saints have looked for other possible explanations and locations, including Mesoamerica. Although some have identified possible sites that may seem to fit better (Palmer), there are no conclusive connections between the Book of Mormon text and any specific site that has been suggested.[53]

In my view, the criteria Brother Palmer set forth are not stated or implied by the text. For example, he says the hill in New York couldn't be the Book of Mormon Cumorah because it is not distinctive or strategic. But if you look on the map, you see it is in a strategic location in western New York. It is the highest hill in the area, with a mile-wide valley to the west that makes a good battlefield—just as Oliver Cowdery described it.

So when you read about Cumorah, think western New York.

Escaping into the south countries

In Mormon 6:15, Mormon describes the fate of his people this way:

> 15 And it came to pass that there were ten more who did fall by the sword, with their ten thousand each; yea, even all my people, save it were those twenty and four who were with me, and **also a few who had escaped into the south countries**, and a few who had deserted over unto the Lamanites, had fallen; and their flesh, and bones, and blood lay upon the face of the earth, being left by the hands of those who slew them to molder upon the land, and to crumble and to return to their mother earth.

The scene of the last battle would have to be a place where people could escape south, but not north, east or west. When you look at the topography of the area around Cumorah, you have Lake Ontario to the north—no escape there. To the west, you have the forces of the Lamanites—no escape there. To the east, you have large north/south finger lakes, which extended farther north than they do today (as is easily viewed on Google Earth), almost to Lake Ontario—no escape there. But to the south, there are ridges and north/south finger lakes that would provide numerous escape routes and places to hide. Mormon's description fits the geography.

The River Sidon

One of the major geographic features in the text is the river Sidon. It is mentioned twenty-eight times in the Book of Mormon. I think the Sidon River is the upper Mississippi River. The text explains that it flows past the city of Zarahemla, which is on the west bank.

A fundamental question is whether the river flows north or south. I address this issue in detail in Chapter 24, but I'll summarize it here.

Nephites and Lamanites are always traveling *up* from the land of Zarahemla to the land of Nephi, and *down* from the land of Nephi to the land of Zarahemla. Nephi is south of Zarahemla; therefore, the thinking goes, south is a higher elevation and the river must flow north. As corroboration, the "head of Sidon" is south of Zarahemla. Some people think the "head of Sidon" means the *headwaters* of Sidon; i.e., the source of the river.

The first answer to this is that it is the *riverbed*, not the surrounding terrain, that determines the flow of a river. There are many examples of rivers flowing downstream through countryside that rises in elevation. This is characteristic of the Nile, the Rhine, and the Mississippi Rivers, all of which have cut channels through elevated areas after flowing through flat areas.

The second answer is that nowhere does the text say Sidon flows past the city of Nephi. Yet people do travel up to the land of Nephi to get to the city. Because I think this means they are following (or traveling upon) a river, it is a river different from Sidon, and one that is not part of the narrow strip of wilderness; i.e., it's the Tennessee River, which does actually flow north. So from the land of Zarahemla, you would have to go upstream on the Tennessee River to get to the land and city of Nephi.

The third answer is that, for the reasons set forth in Chapter 24, the *least likely* meaning of the term "head of Sidon" is the *source* of the river. In my view, the term refers to a confluence of rivers (in this case, the Illinois and Missouri). (It may also refer to the confluence with the Ohio River, but I think that's less likely.) The head of the river is also where the river Sidon flows into the sea west (discussed in the next chapter).

Consequently, when you read the text, think of the geography from Alma 22; i.e., the Sidon is the upper Mississippi River, and it flows south.

Names

Names play an important role in Nephite society. For example, when they were converted, Ammon's converts "called their names Anti-Nephi-Lehies; and they were called by this name and were no more called Lamanites" (Alma 23:17). In addition, "it was the custom of the people of Nephi to call their lands, and their cities, and their villages, yea, even all their small villages, after the name of him who first possessed them" (Alma 8:7). However, the text never states there was only one city per name.

There is considerable duplication of names, such as multiple men named Nephi, Lehi, Alma, Mosiah, Moroni and Helaman. Could there be multiple cities named after the different individuals? For example, there is a city Moroni, and General Moroni was a great military leader, but the text does not say the city Moroni was founded by or named after him. That would mean there was another Moroni who founded that city.

At one point, General Moroni chased the Lamanites so they "fled into the land of Moroni which was in the borders by the seashore" (Alma 62:25). Does Mormon use this designation to tell us where the land was, or does he use it to distinguish this land of Moroni from another land of Moroni?

In the modern day, if we are writing about Paris, we would avoid confusion with the city in France, by referring to Paris, Idaho. Mormon would make that clarification by writing "Paris which was in the land of Idaho." That designation doesn't mean there is only one Paris; to the contrary, the identification is necessary because there is more than one Paris.

In like manner, we can't assume that every named location in the Book of Mormon is unique.

NOTES

---

[44] Sorenson, *Geography*, p. 210.

[45] Ibid, p. 211.

[46] Ibid, 215; Lawrence Poulsen, "Book of Mormon Geography," 2008 FAIR Conference, http://bit.ly/Moroni14.

[47] The text doesn't mention mountains until the Book of Helaman, a point I discuss in Chapter 16. Brother Sorenson sometimes infers that an elevation is a mountain when the text does not require—or even suggest—that.

[48] Appendix 2: Copies of Book of Mormon Characters, Introduction, Documents, *The Joseph Smith Papers*, available online here: http://bit.ly/Moroni15.

[49] This document was used as the source for a special edition of the Book of Mormon, published in 1976, in which the front and back covers were made to look like gold plates. The characters were embossed in black onto the shiny gold-colored covers.

[50] Jerry D. Grover, Jr., "Translation of the 'Caractors' Document," p. 182. Brother Grover's interpretation of the characters is insightful, especially regarding the use of rivers, but because he tries to fit the passage into Mesoamerica, it doesn't work very well. Online here: http://bit.ly/Moroni16.

[51] This approach to cardinal directions may seem straightforward, but some scholars disagree. For example, because Brother Sorenson believes the predominant orientation in the text is north/south, while Mesoamerica has a predominantly east/west orientation, he assumes that the cardinal directions in the Book of Mormon text do not correspond to the directions modern cultures use. To Brother Sorenson, Nephite *north* is not modern-day *north*. He explains it this way:

> I conclude this appendix by drawing attention to two scenarios that have been proposed as possibilities to help explain Nephite direction references as they seem to have been developed to fit a physical land (Mesoamerica, in general the only reasonable correlation evident at this time) which is basically not oriented to the cardinal points. Sorenson, *Geography*, p. 413

One Mesoamerican supporter, Brandt A. Gardner—whom I consider one of the finest LDS scholars in this field—has reached a startling conclusion on this point. He writes, "We have evidence that Joseph dictated 'north.' What we do not have evidence of is what the text on the plates said." Brant A. Gardner, "An Exploration in Critical Methodology: Critiquing a Critique, *FARMS Review* 16/2 (2004): 173-223, at 218. The article is available online at: http://bit.ly/Moroni17.

If Joseph's translation is not evidence of what the plates said, what good is the translation at all? And what better evidence *could* there be than Joseph's translation? Brother Gardner's candor regarding the implications of the Mesoamerican theory leaves these questions unanswered.

At any rate, Brother Sorenson supports his assumption that *north* is not *north* by noting that "Directions and how they are referred to are cultural products, not givens in nature . . . labeling of directions is not obvious nor intuitive but really highly cultural." *Geography*, p.

---

401. He cites numerous examples to demonstrate that "the lexical coding of cardinal directions is a relatively recent development." Anyone interested in pursuing the Egyptian and Hebrew usage referenced in the quotation above should review Brother Sorenson's book.

[52] "southward" and "northward" in Webster's Dictionary 1828. Online at http://bit.ly/Moroni18.

[53] David A. Palmer, "Cumorah," *Encyclopedia of Mormonism*, http://bit.ly/Moroni19. The article cites Palmer's own book, *In Search of Cumorah*.

Chapter 7 – Narrow Places

THE TEXT REFERS TO SEVERAL NARROW PLACES: A NARROW STRIP of wilderness, a narrow neck, a narrow neck of land, a narrow pass, and a narrow passage. There is also a small neck. Each of these will be addressed in the verse-by-verse section, but here I'd like to give an overview of all of them together.

With a plausible candidate for the sea west, another question that arises from Alma 22 is the narrow strip of wilderness in verse 27: "The king sent a proclamation throughout all the land... which was divided from the land of Zarahemla by a narrow strip of wilderness."

The phrase is used nowhere else in the scriptures, and yet this narrow strip of wilderness was the main border between the two nations.

Some scholars interpret this phrase to refer to a mountain range. Nothing in the text supports that view; mountains in the new world are not even mentioned until the Book of Helaman, and then only in connection with hills. (See Chapter 16 on Helaman.) The mountain interpretation is purely an inference designed to fit a theory of Mesoamerican geography.

Put yourself in the position of a Mormon looking at a mountain range from the ground. You will likely think of descriptive terms such as high, or tall, or steep. Perhaps you will think of inaccessible, barrier, or impassable. Maybe *wilderness* will come to mind, since some mountain ranges are not inhabited. But *narrow*? Or *strip*? Not likely.

Ultimately, the only thing that matters is what Mormon meant when he wrote this unique phrase.

Jonathan Neville

As explained by the chiastic structure of Alma 22:27, the narrow strip of wilderness divides the Lamanite king's land from the land of Zarahemla. However, it is the *territory* of the Lamanites, *not* the narrow strip of wilderness, that extends from the sea east to the sea west. This suggests that the border—the *narrow strip of wilderness*—may not be extend all the way to either sea.

The phrase is a peculiar combination of terms; by definition a *strip* is *narrow*. He could have written simply *a strip of wilderness* and conveyed the idea that this border was narrow. So why did Mormon add *narrow* as an adjective?

Mormon lived in a Hebrew culture and knew that language, so it may be useful to consider how he may have derived this unique phrase.

Strong's Concordance offers several Hebrew terms translated into English as *narrow*, including *tsar* (narrow or tight), *emeq* (vale) *gay* (valley) and other terms with similar connotations. Of particular interest is *nachal*. As a noun, *nachal* refers to *rushing water in a narrow channel, brook, flood, river, stream or valley.*[54] As a verb, *nachal* means *to get or take as a possession,* and also has connotations of *divide, have inheritance, take as a heritage,*[55] all of which make sense because Mormon is describing a boundary between the Nephites and the Lamanites. No Hebrew terms for *narrow* relate to mountains or mountain ranges.

For *strip*, Strong's offers no relevant nouns, but it proposes verbs that connote 1) removing vegetation and 2) plunder or raid. These have obvious connections to the concept of a border.

The term *wilderness* is associated with several Hebrew words having a connotation of *desert, waste.* The English conveys this idea as well: a wilderness is *wild* and uninhabited by humans.

The Hebrew is helpful, but I wanted more data so I consulted the Oxford English Dictionary and found these relevant definitions:

Narrow:
1.a. Small in breadth or width in proportion to length; lacking breadth; constricted.
2. a. Lacking space or area; of limited size or extent; confined.
3. a. Limited in range or scope; precise; restricted.

Strip:
1. a. A narrow piece (primarily of textile material, paper, or the like; hence gen.) of approximately uniform breadth.
b. A long narrow tract of territory, of land, wood, etc.
1816 J. K. Tuckey Narr. Exped. River Zaire (1818) vi. 206   The banks [of the river here] have in some places low strips of soil and sand.
1841 W. Spalding Italy & Ital. Islands I. 27   The county of Nice and duchy of Genoa, which form a long narrow strip between the southern side of the mountains and the sea.

Wilderness
1. a. (without article) Wild or uncultivated land.
Distinguished from desert, in that the latter denotes an uninhabitable and uncultivable region, and implies entire lack of vegetation.
1. b. (with article or other defining word) A wild or uncultivated region or tract of land, uninhabited, or inhabited only by wild animals; 'a tract of solitude and savageness' (Johnson).
2. transf. or gen. A waste or desolate region of any kind, e.g. of open sea, of air.

Border
1. A side, edge, brink, or margin; a limit, or boundary; the part of anything lying along its boundary or outline.
2. a. The district lying along the edge of a country or territory, a frontier; pl. the marches, the border districts.
b. The boundary line which separates one country from another, the frontier line. on the border: on or close to this line, on either side; hence, in the border district. on the borders of (Wales): close to, the frontier of (Wales). over the border: across the frontier line.
c. With various prepositions, e.g. within, in, out of, and in other connections, borders is equivalent to 'territories, dominions, limits'. (Latin fines.)
3. a. (Eng. Hist. and Sc. Hist.) the Border, the Borders: the boundary between England and Scotland; the district adjoining this boundary on both sides; the English and Scottish border-land. (The term appears to have been first

established in Scotland, where the English border, being the only one it has, was emphatically the border.)

No man's land
1. (A piece of) waste or unowned land; an uninhabited or desolate area. Esp. in early use as a place name, often referring to a place on a boundary or between boundaries; spec. †a piece of ground outside the north wall of London, formerly used as a place of execution (obs.).

With these definitions in mind, Mormon's explanation that the strip is a border makes perfect sense. A *narrow strip of wilderness* is visible from the ground and confined in scope. It could be a valley, vale, channel, or even a river, and it is uninhabited by humans. It runs mainly east to west and separates the Nephites from the Lamanites.

I propose that the narrow strip of wilderness is a major river—or system of rivers—that serves as an effective border.

Here is my rationale.

First, Moroni tells us it is a border. The "narrow strip" element suggests a feature that is visible and obvious to people on the ground; i.e., narrow enough that observers can see how wide it is, and long and thin enough that it is not mistakable. It is a definite border, not a vague region.

Second, the definitions of the terms offer similar connotations. *Narrow* suggests a vale, valley, or river bed. *Strip* suggests something that is long and thin—like a river.

Third, *wilderness* indicates the feature is uninhabited. A river cannot be inhabited. People could live near, or even along, a river, but not in the river itself. The concept of a *narrow strip of wilderness* that also serves as a border requires a feature that can be watched and defended. This would exclude a feature such as a long thin stand of trees.

Assuming the narrow strip of wilderness is a river, why didn't Mormon simply use the term *river*? He could have written that the lands were divided by a river and saved all the trouble.

There is a good reason why he didn't, which becomes evident only after we identify the likely candidate.

Given the chiastic map and the touchstones of Cumorah and Zarahemla, I propose that the narrow strip of wilderness consists of the Ohio and Missouri Rivers, as shown on this map (together with the sea west or Lower Mississippi River). This narrow strip makes a well-defined border from western New York all the way through the wilderness in the west in what is now Nebraska and the Dakotas.

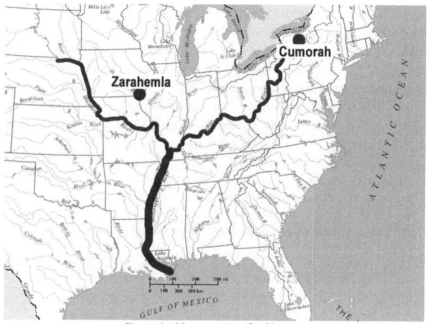

Figure 9 - Narrow strip of wilderness

With the Ohio River as part of the *narrow strip of wilderness*, the term makes good sense. In modern times, a series of dams and channels controls the Ohio River. Flooding is now rare, and droughts have less impact than they used to.

In the past, however, the Ohio River often dried up in late summer (unless there were heavy summer rains). This left the riverbed as an expanse of silt and mud. In that state, it could not be called a river. But it could still be a border, and it could still be called a *narrow strip of wilderness*.

It turns out, Mormon picked (and Joseph translated) an *ideal term* for the feature.

Jonathan Neville

The Narrow Neck

The mistaken "hourglass" shape for Book of Mormon geography was based on the "narrow neck of land" that is actually mentioned only once in the text. The phrase is often conflated with three verses that mention a "narrow pass" and one verse that mentions a "narrow passage." To correctly understand the text, it is important to stick with what the text actually says.

Different terms refer to different features.

Ether refers to a *narrow neck of land*, while Alma refers only to a *narrow neck*. These verses each qualify the term "narrow neck" differently, indicating that they are referring to two different locations.

> Alma 63:5 – "And it came to pass that Hagoth, he being an exceedingly curious man, therefore he went forth and built him an exceedingly large ship, on the borders of the land Bountiful, by the land Desolation, and launched it forth into the west sea, by **the narrow neck** which led into the land northward."

> Ether 10:20 – "And they built a great city by **the narrow neck of land**, by the place where the sea divides the land."

The narrow neck in Alma.

Although many people have assumed this narrow neck is a land feature, the text doesn't require that. A careful reading shows that Hagoth built a ship on the borders of the land Bountiful "by" the land Desolation. The text doesn't say he built it in the west sea; instead it says he launched it into the west sea by the narrow neck. "By" here could mean "at the side or edge of, in the vicinity of, near, close to, or beside." But it could also mean "by means of" or "through."

It is also strange that the verse uses the preposition "by" twice; i.e., Hagoth built the ship "by the land Desolation" and launched it "by the narrow neck." Does this mean he built it in one place and launched it in another? Is Mormon giving us parallel structure? What relationship is there between Desolation, the narrow neck, and the land northward?

From wherever he built the ship, Hagoth launched it into the west sea by the narrow neck which led into the land northward.

Neck also has a variety of possible meanings. The Oxford English Dictionary[56] includes these definitions of "neck" that should each be considered:

5.c. Fortification. The narrow part of a bastion or embrasure.
5.d. A pass between hills or mountains; the narrow part of a mountain pass.
5.e. A narrow channel or inlet of water; the narrow part of a sound, etc.
7.a. A narrow piece of land with water on each side; an isthmus or narrow promontory.
7.b. orig. U.S. A narrow stretch of wood, pasture, ice, etc.

As with the term *narrow strip of wilderness*, the text uses an adjective to modify a noun that already means a narrow place; by definition, a "neck" is narrow. Furthermore, a "neck" can be land or sea, which may explain why Ether specifies a neck *of land*. Here in Alma, we don't have that limitation.

Punctuation here, as in many places of the text, is critical. Here are some alternate readings:

Text	Interpretation
Into the west sea, by the narrow neck which led into the land northward	Hagoth launched it near the narrow neck, a land bridge or pass people recognized because it led into the land northward.
Into the west sea, by the narrow neck which led into the land northward	Hagoth launched it through the narrow neck, a narrow channel or inlet of water, or the narrow part of a sound that led into the land northward.
Into the west sea, by the narrow neck, which led into the land northward	The place of entrance was near the narrow neck, but it was the west sea that led into the land northward.
Into the west sea by the narrow neck, which led into the land northward	The place of entrance was through the narrow neck, from which the ship entered the west sea that led into the land northward.

Jonathan Neville

Some readers may prefer one interpretation over another, but they are all plausible.

There are other clues. Alma 63 and Helaman 3 are the only chapters from the new world that mention ships being used. Alma 63:4 indicates that 5,400 Nephite men and their families left Zarahemla for the land northward, but it doesn't say how they traveled. They could have gone by boat or over land. Alma 63:10 says "Corianton had gone forth to the land northward in a ship, to carry forth provisions unto the people who had gone forth into that land." Because he went in a ship, he traveled by water. If it was possible to travel from Zarahemla to the land northward in a ship, maybe the people in verse 4 did the same.

Helaman 3:10 confirms that the Nephites used ships to reach the land northward: "And it came to pass as timber was exceedingly scarce in the land northward, they did send forth much by the way of shipping." We wish we had more details, but Mormon tells us in verse 10 that the account of "their shipping and their building of ships" "cannot be contained in this work," presumably because of space constraints.

We're left with the question, why did Hagoth go to the west sea to build his ship when others traveled north by river? Could it be that the ship he built was too big for the river? If so, that may mean transporting 5,400 men and their families would have required many river-worthy ships.

Alma 63:5 gives us several possibilities to consider as we seek to place this account on a map.

The narrow neck in Ether.

The "narrow neck" in Ether was by the place where the sea divides the land. Moroni specifies that this neck was "of land," an important clarification.

The term "divide" means "to separate an entire thing, to part a thing into two or more pieces, to cleave,"[57] etc. Therefore the phrase "sea divides the land" suggests that the sea was smaller than the land; it cut through or split up the land.

Lake Erie is the most obvious choice. It divides the land both on the east and on the west. On the east, it looks like a knife blade with the tip at Buffalo, dividing the land north and south

The other requirement is a "great city" by this place. There should be evidence of a significant ancient civilization here. There is evidence of ancient civilization in the area around both Buffalo on the east and Detroit on the west, although most sites have been long since destroyed by subsequent civilizations.

The Small Neck

Alma 22 includes several clauses that begin with thus. This term usually signifies a summary or conclusion. Verse 23 includes the small neck.

And thus the land of Nephi and the land of Zarahemla were nearly surrounded by water, **there being a small neck of land between the land northward and the land southward.**

Many have concluded that this neck of land is the same as Alma's narrow neck and Ether's narrow neck of land. Nothing in the text requires that. "Small" is clearly a different adjective than "narrow" and the words were chosen for a reason. A "small" neck of land is therefore not necessarily a "narrow" neck of land. A neck can be narrow, wide or anything in between. It can also be short, long, or anything in between.

The description in Alma 22 conveys the point that this small neck was an exception to both lands being nearly surrounded by water. By implication, it must be a small neck of land.

Notice the text does not say the lands were surrounded by seas. *Water* can include rivers or lakes as well as sea or ocean. It can mean a swampy area. The text also does not say the small neck was the only exception to being nearly surrounded by water; it was merely the only exception that separated the lands of the Nephites and the Lamanites.

From the perspective of people who used water as boundaries and highways for travel, it would be significant that these lands were nearly surrounded by water.

Here is my proposal for how the two lands were each nearly surrounded by water.

The land of Nephi is defined by water borders, starting at the northeast with the narrow strip of wilderness. This is the Allegheny down to the Ohio, then south on the lower Mississippi (Sea West) to the Gulf Coast, east to the

57

Atlantic Ocean, and north to one of the river systems flowing out of western New York, such as the Susquehanna River or the Mohawk and Hudson Rivers. This leaves a gap—a small neck—in western New York by the Pennsylvania border in the area of the triple divide, where two continental divides meet. This area is about 80 miles south of the Hill Cumorah and is the location of the headwaters of three rivers that can take a traveler to the Chesapeake Bay, the Gulf of Mexico, or the Gulf of St. Lawrence.

The land of Zarahemla, which encompassed the land of Bountiful and the other Nephite territories, was also nearly surrounded by water. Starting at the gap, or small neck, in western New York and moving southwest, the land is bordered by the Allegheny River, the Ohio River, the upper Mississippi River, and the Missouri River to the wilderness in the northwest. The rivers and lakes of Minnesota and Wisconsin border the north. Moving east are the Great Lakes, all the way back to the gap or small neck.

This is depicted on the following map.

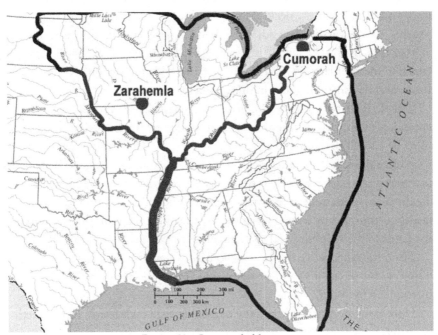

Figure 10 - Surrounded by water

The triple divide is shown on the map below, with the three rivers:
- The Genesee River flows north into the Gulf of St. Lawrence

- The Allegheny River flows southwest to the Gulf of Mexico.
- The west branch of the Susquehanna River flows southeast to Chesapeake Bay.

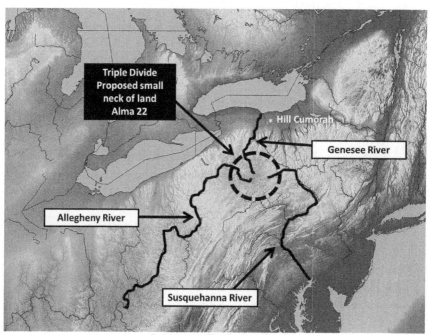

Figure 11 - Triple Divide map

The Other Narrow Places

The other verses in the text that mention narrow places are these:

Alma 50:34 – And it came to pass that they did not head them until they had come to the borders of the land Desolation; and there they did head them, **by the narrow pass which led by the sea into the land northward**, yea, by the sea, on the west and on the east.

Alma 52:9 – And he also sent orders unto him that he should fortify the land Bountiful, and **secure the narrow pass which led into the land northward,** lest the Lamanites should obtain that point and should have power to harass them on every side.

Mormon 2:29 – And the Lamanites did give unto us the land northward, yea, even to **the narrow passage which led into the land southward**. And we did give unto the Lamanites all the land southward.
Mormon 3:5 – And it came to pass that I did cause my people that they should gather themselves together at the land Desolation, to a city which was in the borders, **by the narrow pass which led into the land southward**.

In Alma, both verses refer to the narrow pass which led into the land northward; in Mormon the *passage* and the *pass* led into the land southward. The terms *northward* and *southward* are relative to where the speaker is.

In Alma 22, the land controlled by the King of the Lamanites was the land southward, meaning south of the narrow strip of wilderness. In that frame of reference, the land of Zarahemla (including the land of Bountiful) was northward. Alma 50 and 52 are written from the perspective of Bountiful, which is northward compared to the land of Nephi but southward of the land of Desolation.

In Mormon 2 and 3, Mormon and his people have been chased to the land of Desolation, which is northward of Bountiful. From the perspective of Desolation, the land of Bountiful is southward.

Alma 50:34 is the only verse that says the pass led by the sea. This raises the possibility that verse 34 refers to a different narrow pass; i.e., Mormon specified it as the one that led by the sea, as opposed to other passes that didn't lead by the sea.

None of these verses are from Ether. While it is not impossible that Ether's *narrow neck of land* is the same as one of the other narrow places, the word choice suggests they are different features.

NOTES

[54] See http://bit.ly/Moroni20.
[55] See http://bit.ly/Moroni21.
[56] http://bit.ly/Moroni22.
[57] "divide," 1828 Webster's Dictionary, http://bit.ly/Moroni23.

Chapter 8 – Joseph Smith's Teachings

-->>> <<<--

ON 12 AUGUST 1841, JOSEPH SMITH MET IN NAUVOO with a group of about one hundred chiefs and braves of the Sac and Fox nation, with their families, who were then temporarily encamped across the Mississippi River near Montrose, Iowa.

The ferryman this morning brought over a great number on the Ferry boat and two Flat boats for the purpose of visiting me. The Military band, and a detachment of Invincibles were on shore ready to receive & escort them to the grove, but they refused to come on shore until I went down. I accordingly went down, and met "Keokuk," "Kish-ku-Kosh," "Appenoose," and about 100 Chiefs and Braves of those tribes with their families at the landing, introduced my brother Hyrum to them, and after the usual salutations, conducted them to the meeting grounds in the grove, and **instructed them in many things which the Lord had revealed unto me concerning their Fathers, and the promises that were made concerning them in The Book of Mormon**; and advised them to cease killing each other and warring with other tribes, and keep peace with the whites; which was interpreted to them. Keokuk replied **he had a Book of Mormon at his Wickaup which I had given him some years before**. "I believe," said he, "you are a great and good man; I look rough, but I also am a Son of the Great Spirit. I've heard your advice— we intend to quit fighting and follow the good talk you have given us." After the conversation they were feasted on the green with good food, dainties, and melons by the brethren; and they entertained the spectators with a specimen of their dancing.[58]

I highlighted two particularly interesting things in this account. First, Joseph mentioned things the Lord had revealed to him *apart* from the promises made in the Book of Mormon. This is consistent with other statements Joseph made about things he knew about the Indians beyond what was in the Book of Mormon. In this instance, the Lord had revealed to Joseph "many things" about the ancestors of these specific tribes.

Jonathan Neville

The second item of interest is that Joseph had given Keokuk a Book of Mormon "some years before." There is no record of this event, but it demonstrates Joseph's ongoing concern for these people. That they refused to come ashore until Joseph greeted them is another indication of his special relationship with the Sac and Fox nation.

When the Europeans arrived, the Sac (or Sauk) were living near Saginaw Bay of Lake Huron and on the shores of Lake Michigan.[59] Forced from their homeland, the Sac and Fox lived in Illinois from 1764 to 1830 (Chicago got its name from the Sauk word for "land of onions"). In 1832, they joined with other tribes to fight against the United States in the Black Hawk War, which took place in northern Illinois and what is now southern Wisconsin. Abraham Lincoln, at age 23, volunteered to serve in the militia. It would be his only military service. Although he did not participate in combat, he did see scalped corpses. This was the final armed resistance to the Federal Government east of the Mississippi River.

By 1841, the Sac and Fox nation lived in Iowa. They encamped across from Nauvoo for "several days" before crossing to meet Joseph, suggesting that they may have come to the area specifically to meet with him. Later, in May 1844, just a month before he was murdered, Joseph met these Indians again and reiterated his teaching that The Book of Mormon tells about their fathers.

Hill Cumorah

For about 100 years, it was universally accepted in the Church that the Book of Mormon Cumorah—the scene of the final battles of the Jaredites and the Nephites—was located in New York. It was the same hill where Joseph obtained the plates. Oliver Cowdery wrote a detailed account of the final battles, explaining that they took place in the valley west of the hill. Oliver called this a fact.[60] In 1835, Oliver's account was published in the *Messenger and Advocate* (the official Church newspaper in Kirtland). Joseph had his scribes copy the account into his own journal as part of his history. In 1840, Orson Pratt published Oliver's account in his pamphlet, *A[n] Interesting Account of Several Remarkable Visions.*[61] The account was republished in 1841 in the *Times and Seasons* (the official Church newspaper in Nauvoo, edited by Joseph's brother Don Carlos). Joseph also gave permission to Benjamin Winchester to republish the account in his Philadelphia newspaper, the *Gospel Reflector*, in 1841.

In my view, Joseph Smith fully endorsed Oliver Cowdery's history, including the New York setting for the Hill Cumorah. Who more than Joseph and Oliver would be in a position to know? It was just a few months after Oliver published Letter VII and Joseph had it copied into his journal that the Lord appeared to them in the Kirtland temple, along with Moses, Elias, and Elijah (D&C 110). In the years following this visitation, Joseph had Letter VII republished at least two more times. He even referenced it in D&C 127.

It is difficult to imagine what more Joseph could have done to communicate the point.

Needless to say, the New York setting for the Hill Cumorah is incompatible with a limited geography setting in Mesoamerica. [62]

I encourage all students of the Book of Mormon to read Letter VII and the related history and commentary.

Mission to the Lamanites

As early as 1830, Joseph received revelations to send missionaries to the Lamanites. The first one called was Oliver Cowdery, in September 1830, just five months after the Church was organized (D&C 28:8-10). Later that month, Peter Whitmer, Jr., was called to accompany Oliver (his future brother-in-law) on the mission (D&C 30:5-6). In early October, Parley P. Pratt and Ziba Peterson were called to go with Oliver and Peter (D&C 32:1-3). Parley later wrote that they "distributed the record of their forefathers among three tribes, viz.: The Cattaraugus Indians, near Buffalo N.Y., the Wyandots, of Ohio, and the Delawares, West of Missouri."[63]

Zion's Camp

On 4 June 1834, during the Zion's Camp march, Joseph sat on the banks of the Mississippi River and dictated a letter to his wife Emma. He and the other members of the camp, including Benjamin Winchester, had just traversed Ohio, Indiana, and Illinois, and were about to cross into Missouri. He wrote:

The whole of our journey, in the midst of so large a company of social honest and sincere men, wandering over the plains of the Nephites, recounting occasionally the history of The Book of Mormon, roving over the mounds of that once beloved people of the Lord, picking up their skulls & their bones, as proof of its divine authenticity, and gazing upon a country the fertility, the splendor and the goodness so indescribable, all serves to pass away time unnoticed.[64]

In this letter, Joseph seems to allude to Alma 52:20 (meet them upon the *plains* between the two cities) and Alma 62:18 (they did pitch their tents in the *plains* of Nephihah). In addition to those plains of the Nephites, the Jaredites referred to specific plains in Ether 13: 28-9 (until he came to the *plains* of Heshlon, gave him battle again upon the *plains*) and Ether 14:15-6 (Lib did pursue him until he came to the *plains* of Agosh, he had come to the *plains* of Agosh).

Zelph's Mound

Two days before writing the letter, Joseph and other brethren ascended a mound along the Illinois River where they dug up a large skeleton. Several accounts were written. Here is what Wilford Woodruff wrote:

While on our travels we visited many of the mounds which were flung up by the ancient inhabitants of this continent probably by the Nephites & Lamanites. We visited one of those Mounds and several of the brethren dug into it and took from it the bones of a man.
We visited one of those Mounds: considerd to be 300 feet above the level of the Illinois river. Three persons dug into the mound & found a body. Elder Milton Holmes took the arrow out of the back bones that killed Zelph & brought it with some of the bones in to the camp. I visited the same mound with Jesse J. Smith. Who the other persons were that dug in to the mound & found the body I am undecided.
Brother Joseph had a vission respecting the person. He said he was a white Lamanite. The curs was taken from him or at least in part. He was killed in battle with an arrow. The arrow was found among his ribs. One of his thigh bones was broken. This was done by a stone flung from a sling in battle years before his death. His name was Zelph. Some of his bones were brought into the

Camp and the thigh bone which was broken was put into my waggon and I carried it to Missouri. Zelph was a large thick set man and a man of God. He was a warrior under the great prophet /Onandagus/ that was known from the hill Camorah /or east sea/ to the Rocky mountains. The above knowledge Joseph receieved in a vision.[65] (spelling original)

Because there are variations among the accounts, some LDS scholars have claimed this account has no bearing on Book of Mormon geography. Yet Woodruff's journal is considered highly reliable and is the sole source for many teachings attributed to Joseph Smith. The other journal accounts corroborate what Woodruff recorded.

Note that Woodruff uses the Book of Mormon term "east sea" in proximity to the Hill Camorah,[66] which is also what I propose in this book.

Despite the consistency of Joseph Smith's statements about the Book of Mormon in North America, some LDS authors claim Joseph changed his views later in life. One wrote that "Joseph Smith became convinced in the last years of his life that the lands of the Nephites were in Mesoamerica."[67] The basis for that conclusion is the publication of the articles in the 1842 *Times and Seasons*, which I've shown have nothing to do with Joseph.

Others say Joseph was merely speculating because he never specifically claimed revelation about the setting. However, his mother wrote about Joseph's familiarity with Book of Mormon people:

In the course of our evening conversations, Joseph gave us some of the most amusing recitals which could be imagined. He would describe the ancient inhabitants of this continent, their dress, their manner of traveling, the animals which they rode, the cities that they built, and the structure of their buildings with every particular, their mode of warfare, and their religious worship as specifically as though he had spent his life with them.[68]

Critics say Joseph had an active imagination, but Joseph himself explained the source of his knowledge in the Wentworth letter published March 1, 1842.

Jonathan Neville

"I was also informed concerning the aboriginal inhabitants of this country [The United States of America] and **shown** who they were, and from whence they came; a brief sketch of their origin, progress, civilization, laws, governments, of their righteousness and iniquity, and the blessings of God being finally withdrawn from them as a people, was [also] made known unto me."[69]

During Moroni's initial visits, Joseph was shown some things, while others were "made known" unto him. He had this knowledge before he had the plates. Moroni may have shared this knowledge with Joseph to help with the translation. So far as we know, he did not elaborate beyond the records we have, but his recognition of the "plains of the Nephites" makes sense when we understood he had been shown these things in vision.

Joseph used the Wentworth letter to provide insights on Book of Mormon geography. The letter had its origins in a pamphlet written by Orson Pratt titled *An Interesting Account of Several Remarkable Visions, and of the Late Discovery of Ancient American Records.* Joseph used Pratt's pamphlet as a source, adopting some of it word for word. However, he made some detailed and significant doctrinal changes to Pratt's material.

One of the most significant changes involved Book of Mormon geography. Pratt described in some detail a hemispheric model for Book of Mormon setting.

Joseph Smith edited it out.

He replaced it with a simple statement that the remnant of the Book of Mormon people are the Indians that live in this country.[70]

Here is a side-by-side comparison between the two documents.

AN INTERESTING ACCOUNT OF SEVERAL REMARKABLE VISIONS, AND OF THE LATE DISCOVERY OF ANCIENT AMERICAN RECORDS Orson Pratt 1840	"CHURCH HISTORY" *Times & Seasons* 3:9, 1 Mar. 1842, pp. 706-710 (known as the Wentworth Letter) Joseph Smith
By these Records we are informed that America, in ancient times, has been inhabited by two distinct races of people. The first or more ancient race	We are informed by these records that America in ancient times has been inhabited by two distinct races of people. The first were called Jaredites and came directly from the

came directly from the great tower of Babel, being called Jaredites.	tower of Babel.
The second race came directly from the city of Jerusalem, about six-hundred years before Christ, being Israelites, principally the descendants of Joseph.	The second race came directly from the city of Jerusalem, about six hundred years before Christ. They were principally Israelites, of the descendants of Joseph.
Comment: In this passage Joseph makes an important doctrinal clarification. Instead of Lehi's group "being Israelites, principally the descendants of Joseph," they "were principally Israelites, of the descendants of Joseph." The correction specifies that not everyone in Lehi's party was an Israelite.	
The first nation, or Jaredites, were destroyed about the time that the Israelites came from Jerusalem, who succeeded them in the inheritance of the country.	The Jaredites were destroyed about the time that the Israelites came from Jerusalem, who succeeded them in the inheritance of the country.
The principal nation of the second race, fell in battle towards the close of the fourth century.	The principal nation of the second race fell in battle towards the close of the fourth century.
The remaining remnant, having dwindled into an uncivilized state, still continue to inhabit the land, although divided into a "multitude of nations," and are called by Europeans the "American Indians."	The remnant are the Indians that now inhabit this country.
Comment: Here and in Pratt's ensuing paragraphs, Joseph deletes 2,700 words of Pratt's speculation about Lehi's descendants inhabiting all of North and South America and simply declares that the "remnant are the Indians that now inhabit this country."	

David Whitmer, too, had an experience with Cumorah in New York. He related the account to Orson Pratt and Joseph F. Smith, who interviewed David in Richmond, Missouri, on September 7, 1878. They sent their report to President John Taylor and the Council of the Twelve, and it was published in the *Millennial Star*, No. 49, Vol XL, December 9, 1878.

David said that in 1829 he went to Harmony to get Joseph and Oliver and bring them to David's father's house.

When I was returning to Fayette, with Joseph and Oliver, all of us riding in the wagon, Oliver and I on an oldfashioned wooden spring seat and

Joseph behind us; while travelling along in a clear open space, a very pleasant, nice-looking old man suddenly appeared by the side of our wagon and saluted us with, "good morning, it is very warm," at the same time wiping his face or forehead with his hand. We returned the salutation, and, by a sign from Joseph, I invited him to ride if he was going our way. But he said very pleasantly, "No, I am going to Cumorah." This name was something new to me, I did not know what Cumorah meant. We all gazed at him and at each other, and as I looked around enquiringly of Joseph, the old man instantly disappeared, so that I did not see him again… It was the messenger who had the plates, who had taken them from Joseph just prior to our starting from Harmony."

David's statement is significant because at the time, he had never read the Book of Mormon. The messenger who carried the plates mentioned Cumorah before David had heard the term anywhere else. The New York setting for the Book of Mormon was not a tradition started by unnamed people at an unknown time; it was directly established by a divine messenger. It was part of David Whitmer's testimony, just as Letter VII was part of Oliver Cowdery's. Rejecting either David's experience or Oliver's Letter VII, in my view, is rejecting their testimony of the Book of Mormon.

Joseph Smith was consistent his entire life when he taught about the Book of Mormon in North America. Although some of his associates speculated about Central and South America, there is not a single document that can be directly linked to Joseph Smith that puts the Book of Mormon events outside "this country" as he referred to the United States in the Wentworth letter.

NOTES

---

[58] History, 1838-1856, volume C-1 Addenda, 12 August 1841, Joseph Smith Papers. Available online at http://bit.ly/Moroni24. Also, see History of the Church 4:401-2.

[59] Timothy James McCollum, Sac and Fox, Oklahoma Historical Society, available online at http://bit.ly/Moroni25.

[60] Oliver wrote this account as a letter to W.W. Phelps. It is available from many sources. My short book, *Letter VII: Oliver Cowdery's Message to the World about the Hill Cumorah*, provides the text and commentary. Here is the link to Joseph's journal: http://bit.ly/Moroni26.

[61] Pratt's influential pamphlet was a source Joseph apparently used when writing the Wentworth letter that contains the Articles of Faith. The Historical Introduction in the Joseph Smith Papers explains that the letter echoes some wording from Pratt's pamphlet. The letter is available online at http://bit.ly/Moroni27 http://bit.ly/Moroni27. (Don't refer to the chapter on the Wentworth letter in *Teachings of the Presidents of the Church: Joseph Smith*. Recall that this version inexplicably edits out some key points of the letter.) Pratt had speculated about Book of Mormon geography encompassing both North and South America, but Joseph omitted that material and simply said the remnant of the Book of Mormon people are the Indians who live in this country. I explain all of this in detail in *The Lost City of Zarahemla*. Pratt's pamphlet is available in the Joseph Smith Papers here: http://bit.ly/Moroni28.

[62] Consequently, proponents of the Mesoamerican setting have claimed Joseph and Oliver were merely speculating about the New York setting. Not only were they speculating, the theory goes, but they were *wrong*. Rather than address the implications of Letter VII, in his book *Mormon's Codex*, published by Deseret Book, John Sorenson *ridicules* the idea of the Hill Cumorah being in New York:

> There remain Latter-day Saints who insist that the final destruction of the Nephites took place in New York, but any such idea is manifestly absurd. Hundreds of thousands of Nephites traipsing across the Mississippi Valley to New York, pursued (why?) by hundreds of thousands of Lamanites, is a scenario worthy only of a witless sci-fi movie, not of history. *Mormon's Codex*, p. 688.

Despite Letter VII, the theory of a Mesoamerican Cumorah seems to have prevailed. Sorenson's Mesoamerican geography has been published in the *Ensign* September 1984, available online at http://bit.ly/Moroni29, and and has been widely published by scholars affiliated with BYU. Each year, a replica Mayan temple is built on the New York Hill Cumorah as part of the pageant. Artwork in the Visitor's Center in New York depicts a Mesoamerican setting for the Book of Mormon.

[63] *Autobiography of Parley P. Pratt*, (Deseret Book Co., Salt Lake City, Utah 1938): 56-61.

[64] Joseph Smith, letter, Pike County, IL, to Emma Smith, Kirtland, OH, 4 June 1834; in JS Letterbook 2, pp. 56-59. Available online at http://bit.ly/Moroni30.

---

[65] Donald Q. Cannon, "Zelph Revisited," in *Church History Regional Studies-Illinois*, BYU Department of Church History and Doctrine, 97-109, available online here: http://bit.ly/Moroni31 Cannon's paper includes the other accounts of the event.

[66] This is how it was spelled in the first edition of the Book of Mormon. Oliver Cowdery noted in Letter VII that this was an error, and it should have been spelled Cumorah. Presumably it was Joseph Smith who made that correction. Joseph spelled out many of the proper nouns in the text, while Oliver recorded others phonetically.

[67] Sorenson, Mormon's Codex, p. 694.

[68] Proctor, ed., *The Revised and Enhanced History of Joseph Smith by his Mother*, (Bookcraft, SLC, 1996) p. 112.

[69] Joseph Smith, Wentworth Letter, also known as "Church History," 1 March 1842, *Times and Seasons*. The letter is available at the Joseph Smith papers here: http://josephsmithpapers.org/paperSummary/church-history-1-march-1842.

[70] That statement was part of the passage omitted from the 2011 Church manual.

Chapter 9 – Reaching Consensus

IT HAS BEEN SAID THAT THERE ARE TWO THINGS most people don't like:

1) the way things are, and

2) change.

It is safe to say that few people are satisfied with the current status of Book of Mormon geography. The uncertainty and competing ideas about where the events took place are unsettling for believers. We want to know where Lehi landed, where the city of Zarahemla was, and where the Savior appeared to the Nephites. More importantly, we seek unity and resolution on this question. And yet, those who hold opinions about Book of Mormon geography don't want to change their minds.

If the text of the Book of Mormon was clear and unambiguous, there would not be so many different opinions on the setting for the narrative. However, we're dealing with an ancient text, written by people from an entirely different culture, and translated into English while retaining archaic structures and terminology. It is not an easy task to achieve agreement on the geography passages.

It seems to be the Lord's will that we work this out on our own, "by study and also by faith" (D&C 88:118; 109:7, 14). We have abundant resources and decades of scholarly groundwork. We are all reading the same text. At the same time, we each read in light of our unique perspectives and insights and experiences.

So how do we reach consensus?

My first job out of law school was as a law clerk to the Chief Justice of the Supreme Court of New Mexico. Many of the cases we worked on involved interpretation of statutes and contracts. Judges consider the text as the starting point for interpretation, but if the language is ambiguous and the intent of the authors unclear, they look to extrinsic evidence of what the parties meant when they wrote the statute or contract.

In like manner, we have to recognize that many passages in the Book of Mormon are susceptible to a wide range of interpretations. These passages cannot be interpreted solely within the "four corners" of the document. Therefore, we should look at extrinsic evidence to see what the Book of Mormon means.

In the case of the Book of Mormon, the Bible gives context and background for many of the passages, such as the thirty-seven references to the Law of Moses. Whenever a passage in the Book of Mormon is unclear or ambiguous, it makes sense to see if the Bible helps explain and clarify the passage. Biblical usage of terms can help explain usage of those same terms in the Book of Mormon.

At the same time, the Book of Mormon verifies and clarifies the Bible. The *newer* scripture clarifies the *old*. The two books, together, help clarify one another. The two books of scripture are part of one whole.

In like manner, I propose that modern scriptures and teachings of Joseph Smith and his close associates help clarify the Book of Mormon. As an ancient record, the Book of Mormon text does not include any modern names or sites that can help us identify where events took place. But outside the text itself, the Lord *has* given us the location of at least two specific Book of Mormon sites that put pins in the map: Cumorah and Zarahemla.

All the standard works, along with the teachings and history of Joseph Smith and the Three Witnesses, are part of a whole and should be considered in the interpretation of the text.

Relevant extrinsic evidence includes dictionaries, both of English and Hebrew. We should look at sciences, including geology, geography, archaeology, and anthropology.

In considering specific verses in the next section, I draw upon these extrinsic sources and evidence to help understand what the text is actually saying. I seek to reconcile and integrate all the evidence available to us. In so doing, I hope to help facilitate achievement of a consensus.

Section 2 – Verse by Verse

Chapter 10 – 1 Nephi

THE FIRST 17 CHAPTERS OF 1 NEPHI CONTAIN SEVERAL references to distances and directions traveled by Lehi and his family between Jerusalem and the land on the Arabian peninsula they called Bountiful. These passages have been carefully analyzed by others and don't directly impact the geography of the new world.

However, it is important to note that Nephi used geographical terminology that carried over into the promised land in the new world. He wrote about *borders* and *wilderness* and he mentioned that he and his brethren went "*up* to the land of Jerusalem." (1 Nephi 3:9) *Up* refers to elevation, not traveling northward. Jerusalem is a steep climb up from the Dead Sea area, where Nephi and his brothers would have begun their ascent to the city.

The cardinal directions Nephi used (1 Nephi 16:13) lead us to assume Lehi's party arrived at the southeastern shore of the Arabian peninsula. The question is, which oceans did Lehi cross? If he sailed east, he would have crossed the Pacific and landed on the west coast of the Americas. If he sailed west, he would have crossed the Atlantic and landed on the east coast of the Americas.

---

1 Nephi 17

The text gives us little information on this question of which direction they sailed. In 1 Nephi 17:1, Nephi records that after Ishmael died and was buried in Nahom, "we did travel nearly eastward from that time forth." Some have interpreted this verse to mean that they also traveled eastward once they reached the water and built a ship. However, Nephi never explains in which direction they *sailed*. Verse 1 speaks specifically of their journey in the wilderness, not about their voyage across the ocean.[71]

Lehi's party sojourned in the wilderness for eight years before reaching the land they called Bountiful, from which they "beheld the sea, which we called Irreantum, which, being interpreted, is many waters." (1 Nephi 17:5)

Traveling "nearly eastward" from Nahom would put Lehi's group on the southeast coast of the Arabian peninsula, presumably somewhere in modern-day Oman, where Nephi could build a ship. This is the location proposed by Lynn M. Hilton, who described conditions in this area:

> That general locale turns out to be the south coast of the sultanate of Oman. This region is unique because it receives a lot of rain during the summer monsoon season when the southwest winds blow across the Arabian Sea, gathering moisture and pushing rain-laden clouds against the high mountains. From late May to early September, there is a more or less steady drizzle that turns the coastal area into a lush garden. This unique botanical region is bounded on the north by the desert and on the south by the sea... The important thing is that Nephi could have constructed his ship out of the reach of the pounding surf that characterizes the summer monsoon season.[72]

Nephi gives some additional information that may tell us when they left Bountiful. He says they entered the ship to leave "after we had prepared all things, much fruits and meat from the wilderness, and honey in abundance." (1 Nephi 18:6) To gather fruit, Nephi would have waited until after the September wet season when the fruit would ripen. In Israel, grains were typically harvested in the spring while fruits, including grapes, figs, pomegranates and olives, were harvested in the fall. Presumably Lehi's family followed this pattern. Perhaps they observed the Feast of the Tabernacles in late September to mid-October before leaving. This feast celebrates the fall harvest of fruits. In Oman, the first honey harvest is in June and July—too early for harvesting other fruits, and coinciding with pounding surf making a launch difficult—while the second is in October and November.[73]

I Nephi 18 tells us they sailed *with* the wind.

> 8. And it came to pass after we had all gone down into the ship, and had taken with us our provisions and things which had been commanded us, we did put forth into the sea and **were driven forth before the wind** towards the promised

land.... 22 And it came to pass that I, Nephi, did guide the ship, that we **sailed again** towards the promised land. 23 And it came to pass that **after we had sailed** for the space of many days we did arrive at the promised land...

Brother Hilton mentioned the unique seasonal weather feature of the sea off the Arabian coast: the cycle of seasonal monsoons that correspond with changes in ocean currents. From July through September, warming land in Asia causes the air to rise, which pulls air over the Indian Ocean north and east. Because the air flows from the southwest, this is called the Southwest monsoon season. Starting in November, the effect reverses, and the Northeast monsoon blows wind west and south.

The surface currents flow in the same direction as the wind. During the Southwest Monsoon, the current flows eastward, and during the Northeast Monsoon, the current flows west.[74] Accordingly, if Lehi left in the summer, the ship would have traveled eastward, making its way around India, through Indonesia, and across the Pacific. But if Lehi left in the late fall or winter, the ship traveled west and south around Africa, crossing the Atlantic.

Because Lehi's group harvested fruits and honey prior to leaving, they most likely left the coast of Oman in November or December. The ocean currents and the Northeast Monsoon would have taken them west toward the coast of Africa.

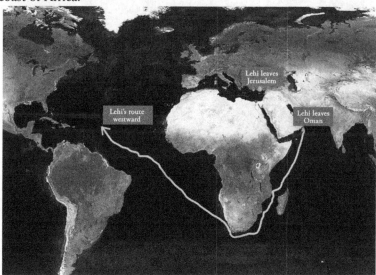

Figure 12 - crossing the Atlantic

Jonathan Neville

They would have followed the eastern African coast south, then turned west to cross the Atlantic.

The Atlantic crossing, including the circumnavigation of Africa, is shorter than any proposed Pacific crossing. Proximity to Africa offered Lehi's group multiple stops for supplies, including food and water, that they wouldn't have crossing the Pacific. The winds and ocean currents work for an Atlantic crossing, but make a Pacific crossing implausible.

The Mulekites, who presumably left from the coast of Israel or Lebanon, would also have crossed the Atlantic. Brother Sorenson agrees with that route, and he documented other evidence of transoceanic voyages.[75]

There is also historical evidence to support ancient voyages such as those of Lehi and the Mulekites. Around 600 B.C., Phoenician mariners circumnavigated Africa. Columbus crossed the Atlantic, using the same currents and winds as the ancient explorers did.

In 2008-2010, the Phoenicia, a ship reconstructed using 600 B.C. materials and technology, circumnavigated Africa. The currents and winds sent them across the Atlantic to within a few hundred miles of Florida before they managed to turn the ship around back to Africa.[76] This is the map of their route:

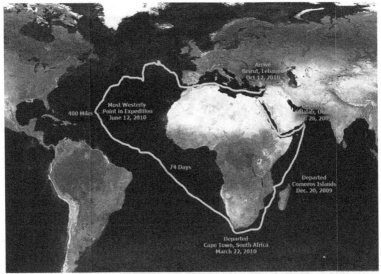

Figure 13 - Phoenicia voyage

The Phoenicia is an ideal test of the veracity of the Book of Mormon account. It shows not only that the materials and technology of 600 B.C. allowed construction of ocean-going vessels for both Lehi's group and the Mulekites, but that both groups could have crossed the Atlantic and landed in North America—coming from the east.

1 Nephi 18

Realizing that Lehi crossed the Atlantic is an important step, but that still leaves a wide range of possibilities for landing sites in the Americas.

Nephi records simply:

> And it came to pass that I, Nephi, did guide the ship, that we sailed again towards the promised land. And it came to pass that after we had sailed for the space of many days we did arrive at the promised land; and we went forth upon the land, and did pitch our tents; and we did call it the promised land. (1 Nephi 18:22-23)

This brief description emphasizes that they considered their new home a *promised land*; Nephi uses the term three times in this short passage. In the context of his otherwise brief record, this repetition demonstrates how important that aspect of the land was. Perhaps that was attributable to the conclusion of a long journey, but Nephi spends a lot of space on the plates emphasizing the promises and their link to the land.

Nephi's brevity leaves a lot of room for speculation about geography. How many days did the voyage take? Did they stop along the way? Did they disembark at the first land they saw, or were they guided by the Liahona to a particular location? What kind of terrain and fauna did they find when they landed? We wish we had answers to these questions, but we don't.

What we do have, though, is very useful. They landed about 589 B.C. Nephi explains that they planted their own seeds.

> And it came to pass that we did begin to till the earth, and we began to plant seeds; yea, we did put all our seeds into the earth, which we had brought from

the land of Jerusalem. And it came to pass that they did grow exceedingly; wherefore, we were blessed in abundance. (1 Nephi 18:24)

This passage conveys several important points. First, the Nephites engaged in agriculture, which means they did not subsist merely on wild plants and animals. This also means they did not encounter a significant indigenous civilization that had its own food supply.

Second, they found land they could farm, apparently without conflict with any existing civilization. They landed in an open, uninhabited—or lightly inhabited—area.

Third, the seeds they brought from the land of Jerusalem grew well. Nephi doesn't specify what crops they sowed or how long it took them to mature, but the success of the planting suggests that wherever the promised land was, the climate was not only amenable for the seeds from Jerusalem, but favorable to their growth. It's also interesting that after all those years in the wilderness of the Arabian peninsula, they kept the seeds from Jerusalem.

The Bible mentions over 125 plants, trees and herbs, including nuts, grains, fruits, and vegetables used for food, as well as fragrant plants and spices. Presumably Lehi brought seeds from Jerusalem that would be important for keeping the law of Moses, such as wheat and barley.

Given this information, it seems likely that Lehi would have landed in an area that shared features with Jerusalem. For example, Jerusalem is at 31.7833 degrees north latitude. The modern border between Alabama and Florida is 31 degrees north latitude, as is a portion of the boundary between Mississippi and Louisiana. A landing somewhere in that vicinity would be familiar to Lehi and his group in terms of solar and lunar events. Temperatures are comparable, with little risk of freezing. Wheat, small grains, and fruits and vegetables grow well in the Southeast. The Georgia/North Florida area receives more rainfall than Israel, which may account for Nephi's comment that the crops "did grow exceedingly."

For these reasons, the area around 31 degrees north latitude would make a good landing place for Lehi.[77] Figure 14 shows the general region of the landing, with two possible routes leading west and east of Florida. Nephi said he guided the ship using the compass (1 Nephi 18:21-22), so it's a question of where the compass led him. I propose the western side for a reason I'll explain in the next chapter, but anywhere in this area fits the text.

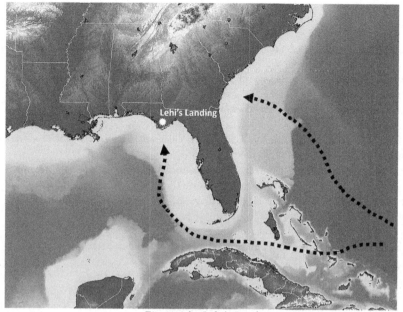

Figure 14 - Lehi's Landing

After they landed in about 589 B.C., Nephi reports that they "did pitch our tents" and they "journeyed in the wilderness." There is no hint of encountering an indigenous population; the term "wilderness" means an area uninhabited by humans and uncultivated, as when the children of Israel wandered for 40 years in the wilderness. Nephi's explorations were uninhibited. Lehi made this clear when he told his sons about the land of promise that "should be a land for the inheritance of my seed" (2 Nephi 1:5). This aspect of the promised land is discussed in the next chapter.

Nephi explains that:

> there were beasts in the forests of every kind, both the cow and the ox, and the ass and the horse, and the goat and the wild goat, and all manner of wild animals, which were for the use of men. And we did find all manner of ore, both of gold, and of silver, and of copper (1 Nephi 18:25).

These are all species found in North America,[78] as are the ores mentioned, so this is another good fit between the text and the real world. By contrast, the text never mentions species that are specific to Central America such as tapirs, monkeys, jaguars, etc.

81

Jonathan Neville

NOTES:

There are two rationales for a Pacific crossing: 1) to support a Mesoamerican setting and 2) to match the Frederick G. Williams/Orson Pratt theory of a landing in Chile, which has its own problems. The Pacific crossing is highly problematic from a practical standpoint. Even if one wants to adhere to one of the west coast theories, it is still more plausible that Lehi crossed the Atlantic. He could have circumnavigated South America to end up in Peru or Mesoamerica.

[72] Lynn M. Hilton, "In Search of Lehi's Trail—30 Years Later, *Journal of Book of Mormon Studies* 15/2 (2006): p. 7, available online here: http://bit.ly/Moroni32.

[73] "Beekeeping in Oman," the Honey Bee Research Department of the Ministry of Agriculture and Fisheries of the Sultanate of Oman (Food and Agriculture Organization of the United Nations, 2014), available online here: http://bit.ly/Moroni33.

[74] Chapter 11 (December 2006) http://bit.ly/Moroni34.

[75] John L. Sorenson and Carl L. Johannessen, "Scientific Evidence for Pre-Columbian Transoceanic Voyages to and from the Americas," available online here: http://bit.ly/Moroni35.

[76] See Phoenicia, the Phoeneican Shop Expedition, at this website: http://bit.ly/Moroni36.

[77] In early Church history, some people thought Lehi landed in Chile. The idea is based on a note written by Frederick G. Williams in the 1830s that claimed Lehi "landed on the continent of South America in Chile thirty degrees south Lattitude [sic]." Historians question the origin of the note. Orson and Parley Pratt seemed to accept it; Orson Pratt's footnotes in the 1879 Book of Mormon include note 8 to 1 Nephi 18:23 that Lehi's arrival in the promised land was "believed to be on the coast of Chili, So. America." A good analysis that rejects any link between Joseph Smith and the Williams claim about South America is found online here: http://bit.ly/Moroni37.

In my view, the specificity of "thirty degrees" latitude is fascinating. It is possible Williams heard Joseph Smith or Oliver Cowdery make a reference to thirty degrees latitude and assumed it was south because at the time, many people also assumed the Lamanites lived in South America (although there is no record that Joseph Smith ever said that).

[78] There are scientific debates about such issues as when horses went extinct in North America, but there is no question that horses were present anciently. Extinction dates are based on the latest remains found, so extinction is based on a lack of evidence and technically cannot be proven, only disproven. The longstanding assumption that horses used by Indians in North America were descended from horses brought by the Spanish conquerors is not well supported by the historical record. See Daniel Johnson, "'Hard' Evidence of Ancient American Horses," *BYU Studies Quarterly*, Vol. 54, No. 3 (2015), p. 149. That article unfortunately focuses on Mesoamerica, but most evidence of ancient horses is from North America, which is consistent with a North American setting.

Chapter 11 – 2 Nephi

⟶≫ ≪⟵

2 Nephi 1

AFTER MENTIONING THE LANDING IN THE PROMISED LAND and his explorations of the wilderness, Nephi focuses on his father Lehi.

Lehi gives blessings to his children that include prophecies about the future. He explains that "it is wisdom that this land should be kept as yet from the knowledge of other nations; for behold, many nations would overrun the land, that there would be no place for an inheritance" (2 Nephi 1:5, 8). Notice he refers to "nations" and not "people." This suggests there may have been people living in the area that were not organized into a level of civilization that could be described as a "nation." Archaeologists consider the people in the Florida area around 600 B.C. as hunter-gatherer bands.

There are archaeological sites in what is now the southeastern United States that predate 589 B.C. Some of these sites date back several thousand years; they could be evidence of the Adamite (pre-flood) civilizations, of the remnants of the Jaredite civilizations, or of other people who migrated to this area. The archaeological evidence is sparse, but archaeologists have identified cultural characteristics such as pottery types that help define cultures in the area such as the Deptford culture.[79]

One of the criticisms of the Book of Mormon has been unrealistic population numbers. For example, there are references to "wars" taking place when only "forty years had passed away" (2 Nephi 5:34). How could there have been enough people to have wars?

One demographic analysis of the text concludes "the Nephite population at the time of Nephi's death and during Jacob's ministry would have been small, measured in dozens and not hundreds of people."[80] This calculation is based on the three families who left Jerusalem that are enumerated in the text: Lehi's family, Ishmael's family, and Zoram, the servant of Laban, who married one of Ishmael's daughters. It seems unlikely that a few dozen people would have armed conflict characterized as "wars." John Sorenson points out that these wars "would have been nothing more than modest family-sized brawls unless local recruits supplemented the miniscule original numbers on both sides."[81]

In an effort to explain the discrepancy between the enumerated (small) population and the large population implied by having wars and building a temple, proponents of a Mesoamerican setting suggest that

> When the Book of Mormon peoples entered the not-empty New World, they entered a land that was not only populated, but which already boasted highly developed civilizations. The Book of Mormon does not explain Mesoamerican peoples—but Mesoamerican peoples help explain the Book of Mormon… With such a small Lehite population entering an established region with a significantly larger population, the most logical direction of cultural borrowing would have been from the established indigenous population to the small population that had originated in Jerusalem.[82]

This suggestion contradicts the text, in my opinion. I agree with the likelihood that the Nephites encountered indigenous people, but far from "cultural borrowing" from any "established indigenous population," Nephi keeps the law of Moses and is soon teaching his people how to build a temple, make weapons, etc., as we'll see in the next section.

Father Lehi's statement about "other nations" directly contradicts the idea that the Nephites landed among "highly developed civilizations" that existed in Mesoamerica. On the other hand, Lehi's statement is compatible with the various hunter/gatherer groups identified in the archaeological evidence in the southeastern United States at the time. Such groups would naturally be attracted to new arrivals who brought with them productive seeds for food, advanced technology for weapons and buildings, a written language and other benefits.

Another possibility for the relatively large population during Nephi's lifetime is that Lehi brought servants along with him. I consider this likely.

Erastus Snow noted that, "The Prophet Joseph informed us that… Ishmael was of the lineage of Ephraim, and that his sons married into Lehi's family, and Lehi's sons married Ishmael's daughters…these descendants of Manasseh and Ephraim grew together upon this American continent."[83]

In his analysis of Lehi's group, John Sorenson noted that "Nothing is said about Zoram's ancestry, but it seems statistically likely, given his bureaucratic/military role in Jerusalem, that he was a Jew, while both Lehi and Ishmael counted descent from Joseph."⁸⁴ This would make all of Lehi's group "Israelites, principally the descendants of Joseph," which is how Orson Pratt described them in his 1840 pamphlet.⁸⁵ However, Joseph Smith made a correction to this language when he wrote the Wentworth Letter. Joseph wrote, "They were principally Israelites, of the descendants of Joseph."⁸⁶ It is possible that Joseph Smith was referring to Zoram after all, clarifying he was not a Jew. He may have been referring to those who accompanied the Mulekites (presumably Phoenicians). But it is also possible that he was referring to others who accompanied Lehi.

Here are John Sorenson's comments on that topic.

> Were there servants? No mention is made of male or female servants, yet it is possible that there were some. At first glance, 1 Nephi 2:4 would seem to rule that out, since reference is made only to Lehi's taking "his family." Yet Near Eastern usage would not rule out including servants under that heading without specifically distinguishing them. Lehi's "great wealth" would seem to have called for at least female servants in the household. Nephi's hesitancy about even adding Zoram to their party would not apply in the case of family retainers, who would have known no other life than service to Lehi and Sariah and had no alternative place in society in the land of Jerusalem even if they dreamed of defecting. I do not consider it likely that there were such people along, but the door should not be shut on the possibility, for they might account for some genetic variety in the colony as well as providing additional hands for the construction of the ship when they reached Bountiful.

Finally, I note that Lynn M. Hilton has proposed in an unpublished paper that Laman and Lemuel took dark-skinned South Arabian women as second wives during the sojourn in Bountiful, thus accounting for the skin color attributed to the Lamanites in the promised land in America. That the party had social interaction with local inhabitants in Bountiful on the south Arabian coast does seem likely, even inevitable. Among other things, Nephi claims "neither did I build the ship after the manner of men" (1 Nephi 18:2), implying that he had knowledge of other ships which almost certainly would have existed on that coast. However, Jacob 3:5, which credits the Lamanites with a tradition of strict monogamy, goes against the Hilton suggestion, but Lehi could have picked up families, or single people who married Lehi's servants. We simply don't know.

I think it is likely Lehi brought servants. The journey from Jerusalem through the wilderness would have been arduous for any small group, but also dangerous. Lehi was a wealthy man, and likely accustomed to desert travel; in the context of the times, he would have had servants to assist him in his work, as well as to assist the household. Furthermore, it seems unlikely that Lehi would have sent all of his sons back to Jerusalem, leaving Lehi and Sariah and their daughters alone in the wilderness, if he did not have servants. Perhaps he also sent servants to accompany his sons on their trips to Jerusalem.

Joseph Smith said the group was "principally Israelites," so some of them were not. Apart from Zoram, the record gives no specifics on the identity of these non-Israelites. Had Zoram been the only exception, would Joseph have used the term "principally?" The term refers to rank or importance, not merely numbers, so even a significant number of non-Israelite servants would leave the group "principally Israelites."

Mesoamerican advocates have considered but rejected the notion that Lehi's party included servants or people from Arabia,[87] but I think that approach reflects a desire to show that Lehi landed among a sophisticated Mesoamerican population. In my view, that idea contradicts the text.

To summarize: I think Lehi brought servants and landed in a mostly uninhabited area in Florida, among a small population of hunter/gatherers who lacked a well-organized society.

2 Nephi 5:5-7

In Chapter 4, Lehi dies. Then, in chapter 5, Nephi separates from the Lamanites.

the Lord did warn me, that I, Nephi, should depart from them and flee into the wilderness, and all those who would go with me. Wherefore, I, Nephi, did take my family, and ... all those who would go with me... And we did ... journey in the wilderness for the space of many days. And after we had journeyed for the space of many days we did pitch our tents. (2 Nephi 5:5-7)

These verses don't tell us much about where Nephi went, other than "into the wilderness." He gives no directions or specific distances.

However, he gives an interesting clue. It was only *after* "we had journeyed for the space of many days" that "we did pitch our tents." This seems surprising. Nephi specified that they took their tents with them. Why did they wait until after they had journeyed for many days to pitch them?

One possibility is that the tents were semi-permanent; i.e., not the kind of think they would set up for one night's sleep. Maybe the tents were big and complex and would take a long time to set up or take down. Another possibility is that they were on the run from the Lamanites and could not stop, but that seems unlikely over "many days."

A third possibility that I find persuasive is that they were traveling by boat and simply stayed on the boats until they reached their destination.

It is common knowledge that ancient people tended to travel on or along rivers and waterways. This is particularly true where vegetation is dense and only the rivers offer a clear pathway. Rivers have the added advantage of a definite location. You can navigate them easily, provided you don't get lost by following the wrong tributary.

The people in Nephi's group would have been familiar with boats; after all, Nephi had built the ship on which they had all crossed the ocean, and indigenous people were familiar with the rivers. Although Sidon is the only river named in the text, other rivers are mentioned. Mormon explains that his work could not contain even "a hundredth part of the proceedings of this people... and their shipping and their building of ships." (Helaman 3:14) It seems unlikely that all of this activity took place on one river, and only after hundreds of years of history (the time period which Helaman covers).

Taking these factors into consideration, it would be surprising if Nephi and his people *did not* use boats to travel through the wilderness in the new world, particularly after he had been warned to put distance between him and his brothers. Dense vegetation covers Georgia and Alabama. Had he hacked a trail through the forest, his brothers could easily follow.

With these assumptions, I looked at maps to see what routes Nephi could have taken for his escape. Later in the text we learn that Nephi ascended to a higher elevation; the City of Nephi is always up from the place of their fathers' first inheritance. The highest locations in the area are in the Appalachian Mountains, such as in eastern Tennessee.

I found a river that leads from the coast to the mountains, which I consider a plausible candidate for Nephi's route to the land of Nephi.

Figure 15 is a proposed map with rivers displayed in white. The arrows depict Nephi's route.

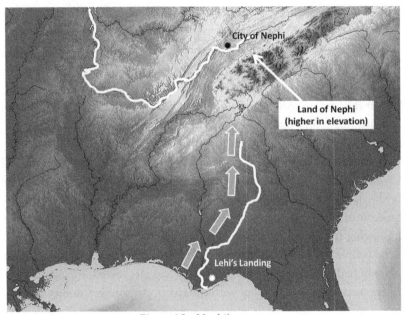

Figure 15 - Nephi's escape

2 Nephi 5:20-21

Once he had established his people in the new area, Nephi reflected on what had happened.

> Wherefore, the word of the Lord was fulfilled which he spake unto me, saying that: Inasmuch as they will not hearken unto thy words they shall be cut off from the presence of the Lord.... For behold, they had hardened their hearts against him, that they had become like unto a flint. (2 Nephi 5:20-21)

Hearts like flint. This is a surprising metaphor. Something must have triggered Nephi to compare his brothers' hearts to flint. No other scriptural passage makes this analogy (Later, Jacob quotes Isaiah, who uses flint in two passages, but neither of these relate to Nephi's metaphor. See 2 Nephi 7:7 and 15:28).

What made Nephi think of flint?

It turns out that the river in Georgia that I propose Nephi followed is named *Flint River.* The name comes from the abundance of flint in that riverbed, a source that has supplied Native Americans in the region for hundreds of years. Of course I'm not saying Nephi named this river, but had Nephi followed any other riverbed in the area, he may not have come across an abundance of high-quality flint and would have thought up a different metaphor to describe his brothers.

2 Nephi 5:10-15

When he describes the new territory he settles with his people, Nephi notes five specific things.

First, they kept the law of Moses (verse 10).

Second, they prospered with agricultural plants and animals (verse 11).

Third, they made weapons, including "many swords" (verse 14).

Fourth, they built a temple like Solomon's (verse 16).

Fifth, they built buildings with wood and particular ores:

15 And I did teach my people to build buildings, and to work in all manner of wood, and of iron, and of copper, and of brass, and of steel, and of gold, and of silver, and of precious ores, which were in great abundance.

This verse corroborates the theory that indigenous people had joined Nephi's group. Nephi listed those who accompanied him: "my family, and also Zoram and his family, and Sam, mine elder brother and his family, and Jacob and Joseph, my younger brethren, and also my sisters, and all those who would go with me" (2 Nephi 5:6). Everyone named here (including his sisters) would have been as familiar with how to build buildings and work in wood and metal as Nephi was. They would have learned all of this back in Arabia, or while crossing the ocean, or in the place of first landing.

The people Nephi would have needed to teach would be the indigenous hunter-gatherer people who joined him. The advanced knowledge Nephi describes here would have been a tremendous incentive for them to be counted among Nephi's people.

This passage also demonstrates that Lehi could not have landed among a major advanced civilization; they would have been teaching Nephi their culture and technology, not the other way around.

Note that Nephi does not say they "worked in" stone. The mountains of Tennessee have abundant forests with many species; it stands to reason Nephi would have them work in "all manner" of wood. Unfortunately, cultures who build in wood leave behind few traces after the passage of time.

This area also features an abundance of ores of the specific metals Nephi listed. In 1829, for example, there was a major gold rush in the southern Appalachian mountains of Georgia.[88] Over 15 million tons of copper ore were extracted from a copper mine in Ducktown, Tennessee, between 1899 and 1959. The copper ore contains gold and silver as well. Iron and zinc were also produced there. (Brass is an alloy of copper and zinc.)

There is archaeological evidence of human civilization in the area of Georgia and Tennessee dating from around 400 B.C. and earlier.[89] The scientific literature refers to the period between 1,000 BC and 1,000 A.D. as the "Woodland Period," and there is evidence of at least some mining during this period.[90] In his Journal,[91] published in 1542, Alvar Nunez Cabeza de Vaca describes his harrowing journey from Florida to the Pacific in 1527. Indians in Florida told him and his companions there was "much gold" in an area called Apalchen, the source for the name Appalachian.

None of this is proof that Nephi was there, but the evidence corroborates Nephi's account and makes Tennessee a plausible setting for these events.

2 Nephi 5:16

Nephi tells us he built a temple. The construction of a temple "after the manner of Solomon" is additional evidence that the Nephites maintained a

Hebrew culture, as opposed to adopting Mayan culture. It also raises an issue of archaeology in this area.

The Tennessee Valley Authority (TVA) was created to control the rivers in Tennessee and six other states. Thirty-two dams have been constructed, each of which has flooded river valleys that were once occupied. Archaeological surveys were performed before the flooding, including one called the Cox Mound in Norris Basin, which has been flooded since 1935. TVA recognized that "the flooding of large areas would cover with impounded water many sites showing evidence of man's prehistoric occupancy of the valley. Valuable evidence of prehistory would thus either be destroyed or forever placed beyond any possibility of investigation."[92]

A contemporary newspaper reported that "TVA archaeological workers today announced that they had unearthed an ancient Indian temple on the Indian river… The temple…is believed to have been built by a race which preceded the Cherokees in this section."[93] However, the TVA archaeologists documented their work and concluded that the remains were from the Mississippian culture.

As the TVA report acknowledged, these sites cannot be investigated now, so we have to rely on 80-year-old reports.

There are numerous archaeological sites in the area. For example, Old Stone Fort, located about 50 miles northwest of Chattanooga on the Duck River, "was first developed by the 'Owl Creek People' between 200 B.C. and 200 A.D.[94] There are indications that some of the sites in the area may have geospatial connections and alignments to astronomical events.[95]

Nephi says he instructed his people to work with wood; anything built from wood around 550 B.C. would be unlikely to survive, particularly in wet areas such as the southeastern United States. Sites featuring earth mounds are more likely to have survived, but these come later in the text—as they do in the archaeology of this area.

Archaeological work continues in the area. Leake Mounds is a site about 60 miles southeast of Chattanooga that was occupied from around 300 B.C.[96] Although the site was known since the 1890s, the detailed excavation didn't occur until 2004. As I indicated at the outset, this book focuses on the text, not the archaeology. There is abundant archaeological information about the areas I discuss, but more is being uncovered all the time.

NOTES

[79] Detailed discussion of archaeology is beyond the scope of this book but is discussed in the upcoming *Moroni's History*.

[80] James E. Smith, "How Many Nephites? The Book of Mormon at the Bar of Demography," in *Book of Mormon Authorship Revisited: The Evidence of Ancient Origins*, ed. Noel B. Reynolds (Provo, Utah: FARMS, 1997), p. 275.

[81] Sorenson, *Mormon's Codex*, p. 36.

[82] Brant Gardner, *Traditions of the Fathers*, pp. 153-4.

[83] Erastus Snow, "God's Peculiar People," *Journal of Discourses*, 23:184, available online at http://bit.ly/Moroni38.

[84] John Sorenson, "The Composition of Lehi's Family," in *By Study and Also by Faith*, (Neal A. Maxwell Institute), available online at http://bit.ly/Moroni39.

[85] Orson Pratt, *A[n] Interesting Account of Several Remarkable Visions*, p. 15, available online at http://bit.ly/Moroni40.

[86] The Wentworth letter was published in the 1 March 1842 *Times and Seasons*. The Historical Introduction in the Joseph Smith Papers explains that the letter echoes some wording from Pratt's pamphlet. The letter is available online at http://bit.ly/Moroni41.

[87] E.g., Brant Gardner, *Traditions of the Fathers*, p. 156.

[88] "Georgia Gold Rush," About North Georgia, http://bit.ly/Moroni42.

[89] The McClung Museum offers an overview here: http://bit.ly/Moroni43.

[90] See, e.g., http://bit.ly/Moroni44.

[91] *The Journey of Alvar Nunez Cabeza de Vaca*, American Journeys Collection, (Wisconsin Historical Society 2003), p. 12. The book in English translation is available online at http://bit.ly/Moroni45.

[92] William S. Webb, *An Archaeological Survey of the Norris Basin in Eastern Tennessee*, Smithsonian Institution Bureau of American Ethnology, Bulletin 118 (1938), p. xv, available online at http://bit.ly/Moroni46.

[93] *The Florence Times*, March 23, 1934, online here: http://bit.ly/Moroni47. For an analysis of the find, see Dr. Greg Little's report here: http://bit.ly/Moroni48.

[94] See http://bit.ly/Moroni49. A list of references assembled by an alliance of Creek, Choctaw and Seminole scholars is available here http://bit.ly/Moroni50.

[95] Alignments to solar events are suggested here: http://bit.ly/Moroni51.

[96] See maps and discussion at http://bit.ly/Moroni52.

Chapter 12 – Jacob and Enos

→»» ««←

JACOB DOESN'T OFFER MUCH IN THE WAY OF GEOGRAPHICAL information, but he does demonstrate familiarity with the Lamanites in Jacob 3:5-9. (In fact, he seems to be denouncing the Nephites' animosity toward the Lamanites, including racism and cultural denigration, as much as the other sins he accuses the Nephites of committing.)[97] This familiarity suggests the two groups were in close contact. Despite their differences, the Nephites and Lamanites were surely trading with each other.

Jacob 5

Jacob chapter 5 relates the allegory Zenos made about Israel and the Gentiles. The allegory demonstrates the scattering of Israel, the apostasy, and the gathering of Israel. No specific locations are mentioned, although the natural branches are hidden in the "nethermost part of the vineyard."[98]

One aspect of the allegory that is often overlooked is that when a branch of one plant is grafted onto the trunk of another, the branch retains its DNA. For example, any particular variety of apples we eat today is genetically identical to that variety when it was first discovered.[99]

This may have some bearing on the question of the DNA of Lehi and his descendants; i.e., maybe the parable suggests their DNA is not lost after all.

It is well known that the Hopewell Indians of the Midwestern United States, who lived in Book of Mormon time frames, had a particular type of DNA called Haplotype X2. This is Middle-Eastern DNA and is found among Native American Indian tribes from the Great Lakes region even today.[100] Most indigenous people of the Americas have DNA that is Asian in origin.

Jonathan Neville

Jacob 7

This chapter contains two important passages. First, Jacob discusses his confrontation with Sherem, a man of unknown origin whose presence raises a question about other groups in the area. The only description given of this man is in verse 1: "And now it came to pass after some years had passed away, there came a man among the people of Nephi, whose name was Sherem."

It's not clear whether Sherem was a former Nephite who had dissented, a Lamanite, or someone from another group altogether, but the text notes no problem with communication. The Book of Mormon Onomasticon, which offers derivations of the proper nouns used in the text, notes that "The observation has been made that the name SHEREM may not be Lehite."[101] The text says Sherem "had a perfect knowledge of the language of the people." I think Sherem was a well-educated Lamanite, which suggests a more sophisticated society that we often infer from the text. A possible connection is the site named Leake Mounds, which dates from around 300 BC and is not far from the Flint River in Georgia.

The second main point is that the Lamanites "sought by the power of their arms to destroy us continually" (verse 24). Jacob says the Nephites fortified against the Lamanites with their arms. It may be difficult to find archaeological evidence of wooden and earth fortification in this area of Tennessee from 500 B.C., but there may be evidence of ongoing, continual warfare. For example, farmers have found thousands of arrowheads in the areas, such as those found in Dade County, Georgia, and other locations that date to the Hopewell Woodland era. Can we expect to find more than arrowheads as evidence of inter-tribal warfare of the type described in the early period of Nephite history?

This brings up the larger question of expectations vs. reality in terms of archaeology. Archaeologists believe it was predominately a hunter-gatherer society that lived in the southeastern United States around 500 B.C.

Enos says the Lamanites

> were led by their evil nature that they became wild, and ferocious, and a blood-thirsty people, full of idolatry and filthiness; feeding upon beasts of prey; dwelling in tents, and wandering about in the wilderness with a short skin girdle about their loins and their heads shaven; and their skill was in the bow, and in

94

the cimeter, and the ax. And many of them did eat nothing save it was raw meat; and they were continually seeking to destroy us (Enos 1:20).

Such people leave behind little archaeological evidence. Evidence of conflict would consist of arrowheads and possibly some weapons; bones would long ago have been eaten or decomposed.

By contrast, the Nephites, according to Enos,

> did till the land, and raise all manner of grain, and of fruit, and flocks of herds, and flocks of all manner of cattle of every kind, and goats, and wild goats, and also many horses (Enos 1:21).

Should we expect to find evidence of ancient farms?

The earliest evidence of agriculture has been found in dry areas of the Fertile Crescent.[102] In Tennessee, archaeologists identify the Woodland Period (300 B.C. to A.D. 900) as the beginning of agricultural practices. Enos reports that the people raised all manner of grain and fruit. The archaeological record from this period includes remnants of

> hickory nuts, walnuts, butternuts, acorns, hazelnuts, beechnuts, chestnuts, grapes, persimmons, raspberries, blackberries, strawberries, blueberries, and honey locust pods....Practicing a more sedentary life and building more permanent dwellings than their forebears, Woodland peoples also demonstrated a preference for living near river flood plains....Agricultural practices began to emerge during these centuries. The Native Americans used both native and tropical plants. Seeds were cultivated from sunflowers, sumpweeds, and chenopodiums and taken from pigweeds, knotweeds, giant ragweeds, and maygrass."[103]

Again, the archaeological evidence is not proof of the Nephite civilization, but it is consistent with what the record says.

Jacob summarizes his life experience this way:

> the time passed away with us, and also our lives passed away like as it were unto us a dream, we being a lonesome and a solemn people, wanderers, cast out from Jerusalem, born in tribulation, in a wilderness, and hated of our brethren, which caused wars and contentions; wherefore, we did mourn out our days (Jacob 7:26).

Jonathan Neville

This passage corroborates a landing in a sparsely populated wilderness, where the ongoing conflict is with "our brethren" and not a vast pre-existing indigenous civilization.

NOTES:

[97] Some commentators have made a correlation between Jacob's denunciation in chapters 2 and 3 of the love of riches, pride and unchastity with Mesoamerican civilizations that had similar problems. See, e.g., Gardner, *Traditions of the Fathers*, pp. 197-201. I find that correlation illusory because the sins Jacob denounces are common to most, if not all, human societies—including ours in the present day. It's their universal application that makes them relevant. In fact, Brother Gardner writes, "Mesoamericans did not esteem these metals [gold and silver] as highly as did the Old World. For Mesoamericans, the highest value appears to have been placed on jade." The Book of Mormon never mentions jade, but it does often describe the value of gold and silver—further evidence that Nephite culture was not Mayan.

[98] A diagram is here: http://bit.ly/Moroni53.

[99] Michael Pollan, "The Call of the Wild Apple," *The New York Times*, November 5, 1998, online at http://bit.ly/Moroni54. Of course, cloning plants by grafting is different from sexual reproduction, but the allegory of the olive tree is based on preservation of lineage.

[100] A detailed discussion of the DNA issue is outside the scope of this book, but there is an essay on lds.org that addresses DNA. It is online here: http://bit.ly/Moroni55. In my view, the DNA link between the Middle-East and the Hopewell Indians deserves more study and analysis than this essay provides. This issue has been discussed at some length in the LDS literature, often with undue acrimony.

[101] See entry for Sherem here: http://bit.ly/Moroni56.

[102] Tia Ghose, "Evidence of Ancient Farming in Iran Discovered," *Live Science*, http://bit.ly/Moroni57.

[103] Carroll Van West, "Woodland Period," *The Tennessee Encyclopedia of History and Culture*, http://bit.ly/Moroni58.

Chapter 13 – Omni

—→≫ ≪←—

ALTHOUGH SHORT, THE BOOK OF OMNI CONTAINS critical geographical information that illuminates the rest of the book. Omni was the next-to-the-last book that Joseph translated. He and Oliver had moved to the Peter Whitmer farm in New York. They were days away from the manifestations to the Three Witnesses and the Eight Witnesses. It was the culmination of a difficult but thrilling process. People recorded that when Joseph and Oliver came downstairs after working on the translation, they glowed.

Oliver began working as scribe in Harmony, Pennsylvania, in April 1829 with what is now Mosiah 1. Historical documents suggest that Mosiah 1 was originally the third chapter of Mosiah; the first two chapters, and everything leading up to that, were part of the manuscript that Martin Harris lost. We don't know how much of what is contained in Omni was also contained in that lost manuscript, but it is remarkable how this brief book ties together several loose threads from the nearly 500 pages that follow it—and preceded it in the translation process.

Omni 1:12-14

After centuries living in the land of Nephi, king Mosiah was warned to flee, much like Nephi had been warned centuries earlier to flee from his brethren. The scripture records that Mosiah and his people

> departed out of the land into the wilderness, as many as would hearken unto the voice of the Lord; and they were led by many preachings and prophesyings. And they were admonished continually by the word of God; and they were led by the power of his arm, through the wilderness until they came down into the land which is called the land of Zarahemla. And they discovered a people, who were called the people of Zarahemla.

If the land of Nephi was in eastern Tennessee, and if Zarahemla was in Iowa across from Nauvoo as discussed in the first section of this book, how would Mosiah and his people get there? The text says they were guided through the wilderness, *down* into the *land* of Zarahemla. According to our interpretive key, the way one knows if he/she is ascending or descending is by comparison to a river.

The text does not say they came to the *city* of Zarahemla, but to the *land* of Zarahemla.

I propose they followed, or traveled upon, *Mosiah's river,* which we call today the Tennessee River. They would have traveled downstream (west and north) until they reached the Ohio River, and then downstream (west) to the Sidon River, which cuts through the land of Zarahemla. I propose that at the time Mosiah escaped, the land of Zarahemla embraced both shores of the upper Mississippi. This map depicts the scenario.

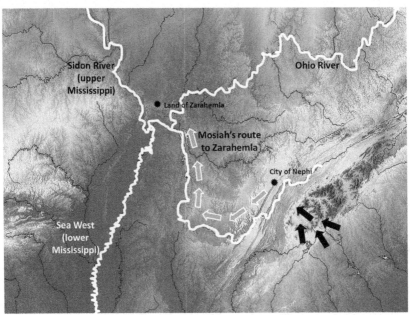

Figure 16 - Mosiah's escape route

The white arrows in the lower right are the Lamanites, encroaching from the south.

When Mosiah and his people discovered the people of Zarahemla, their leader, Zarahemla, rejoiced because Mosiah had "the plates of brass which contained the record of the Jews." These records had been maintained for nearly five hundred years by the time Mosiah reached Zarahemla, which explains why having a record on metal plates was so important.

Omni 1:12-19

At first, Mosiah and his people could not communicate with the people of Zarahemla with language because "their language had become corrupted and they had brought not records with them." As Mosiah soon found out, the people of Zarahemla—meaning their ancestors—came out from Jerusalem. Because Mosiah's ancestors, too, came out from Jerusalem, it may seem surprising that the two groups could not communicate. Scholars debate about how long it takes for languages to change, but another possibility is that the Mulekites—the common name for the people of Zarahemla—were brought to the New World by Phoencian sailors.[104] Perhaps the Mulekites adopted the Phoenician language or mixed it with their own. The use of Phoenician names such as Sidon and Isabel is further evidence of the Phoenician influence.[105]

Once he learned Mosiah's language, Zarahemla himself "gave a genealogy of his fathers, according to his memory." Unfortunately, we don't have that record. But it was presumably from Zarahemla that Mosiah learned about how Zarahemla's ancestors "came out from Jerusalem at the time that Zedekiah, king of Judah, was carried away captive into Babylon." Mulek was the son of Zedekiah who escaped captivity; hence the term *Mulekites*, which is actually not found in the scriptures.

Mulek and his companions "journeyed in the wilderness and were brought by the hand of the Lord across the great waters into the land where Mosiah discovered them and they had dwelt there from that time forth."

This verse tells us the Mulekites "journeyed in the wilderness" but doesn't reveal how long they journeyed or how far they went. They left Jerusalem, where Mulek's brothers had been killed and his father blinded before being

Jonathan Neville

taken captive, and reached a port. Most likely, they went to Egypt, since that is where his sisters and others found refuge (Jeremiah 43:6-7).

From Egypt, the Phoenicians would have transported Mulek and his group west through the Mediterranean, passing the Iberian Peninsula and across the Atlantic to the New World. They likely followed a route similar to that of Columbus and other explorers who left from the Mediterranean.

A key point here is that they were led by the Lord "into the land where Mosiah discovered them and they had dwelt there from that time forth." How would they have reached Iowa directly? And why would they have remained there for hundreds of years?

Figure 17 below depicts their course across the Atlantic Ocean. Figure 18 shows their route up the Mississippi to Iowa, across from Nauvoo.

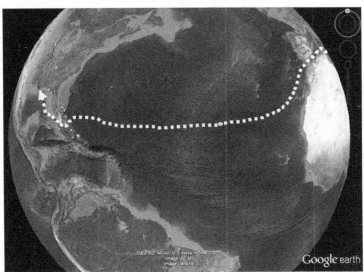

Figure 17 - Mulekite route across the Atlantic

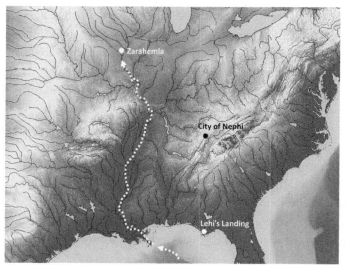

Figure 18 - Mulekite route up the Mississippi

There is a good reason why the Mulekites would have stopped in Iowa, across from Nauvoo. It is the first place up the Mississippi river from the Gulf Coast that, historically, was impassable for large ships, due to the Des Moines rapids located just south of there. Even in the 1840s, riverboats had to stop at the rapids, unload cargo, and then be dragged over the rapids before progressing north. (Now, a series of dams and locks makes the river navigable for barges and other large ships.)

The map shows another key point. The Mulekites could have easily sailed up the river without encountering the Nephites or the Lamanites, who were several hundred miles east. Furthermore, the Mulekites would have sailed right past other civilizations that likely existed in the area, descendants of Jaredites or other groups who had come to the continent.

The location in Iowa is ideal from several perspectives. First, being on the river provides plentiful water and facilitates commerce. Second, it is upriver from the Des Moines rapids, which provide a defensive barrier against river-borne invaders from the south. Third, the area has productive agricultural land. Ultimately, of course, it's where the Lord led them.

This geography helps clarify why the Nephites never encountered Zarahemla until Mosiah was prompted to flee from the land of Nephi. In our day, we might think people would explore freely, but anciently, the

101

wilderness was dangerous. There were wild beasts, unpredictable weather, the potential of getting lost, sicknesses, and no way to communicate over long distances. You were on your own in the wilderness. By contrast, there was safety in numbers and community. Farms provided food.

It required great faith for Lehi and his family to leave Jerusalem, let alone cross the ocean (which is why Nephi faced such resistance). In the new world, it required great faith for Nephi to flee from his brothers into the wilderness. Mosiah exercised great faith to leave the land of Nephi.

The dangers of exploration were demonstrated in the experience of the 43 scouts, whom Limhi sent to find the city of Zarahemla (Alma 8 and 21). They got lost and found Jaredite remains, which they incorrectly assumed was the site of Zarahemla. Because the experience of these scouts is often conflated with the journey of the Mulekites, I will address it here.

Omni 1:20-22

And it came to pass in the days of Mosiah there was a large stone brought unto him with engravings on it and he did interpret the engravings by the gift and power of God. And they gave an account of one Coriantumr and the slain of his people. And Coriantumr was discovered by the people of Zarahemla; and he dwelt with them for the space of nine moons. It also spake a few words concerning his fathers. And his first parents came out from the tower at the time the Lord confounded the language of the people and the severity of the Lord fell upon them according to his judgments which are just and their bones lay scattered in the land northward.

The sequence of events shows that Zarahemla had not mentioned Coriantumr or the Jaredites to Mosiah before the stone was brought forth. The parenthetical—"And Coriantumr was discovered by the people of Zarahemla; and he dwelt with them for the space of nine moons"—is ambiguous. The information could have been taken from the engravings, or perhaps the bringing of the stone prompted Zarahemla to tell Mosiah that his people had discovered Coriantumr. The text doesn't say when Coriantumr lived. It could have been during Zarahemla's lifetime or much earlier.[106]

Either way, there is no indication that the people of Zarahemla had themselves discovered any Jaredite remains. Everything Mosiah learned about the Jaredites at this point came from his translation of the engravings on the stone. This is important because it corroborates Amaleki's statement that the Lord led the Mulekites to the land where they settled and they never left that land. If they went directly to Iowa, then they never visited the land where the Jaredites lived and were ultimately destroyed—i.e., Cumorah.

The printed text does not retain the capitalization found in the printer's manuscript on the assumption that capitalization was random. The printer's manuscript capitalizes the word "Northward" here, suggesting it may be a proper noun. Some instances in the printer's manuscript capitalize *northward*, while others do not.

[NOTE: The account in Omni is straightforward, but some commentators have confused it with what happened when King Limhi sent a search party of 43 men who inadvertently discovered the Jaredites and their record in Mosiah 8:7-12. I will address that in the Mosiah chapter.]

What about Coriantumr? How did the people of Zarahemla discover him if they didn't discover the land where the Jaredites were destroyed? And where did the stone come from?

Ether, the final Jaredite prophet, had told Coriantumr that if he didn't repent, "he should only live to see the fulfilling of the prophecies which had been spoken concerning **another people receiving the land for their inheritance** and **Coriantumr should receive a burial by them** and every soul should be destroyed save it were Coriantumr." Ether 13:21. Just a few verses previously, Ether had also prophesied about the New Jerusalem.

> 2 For behold, they [the Jaredites] rejected all the words of Ether; for he truly told them of all things, from the beginning of man; and that after the waters had receded **from off the face of this land** it became a choice land above all other lands, a chosen land of the Lord; wherefore the Lord would have that all men should serve him who dwell upon the face thereof;
> 3 And that **it was the place of the New Jerusalem**, which should come down out of heaven, and the holy sanctuary of the Lord.
> 4 Behold, Ether saw the days of Christ, and he spake concerning a New Jerusalem **upon this land**. (Ether 13:2-4)

Jonathan Neville

As the sole survivor of the final battle, living all by himself in Cumorah (Ether having either died or declined to make contact), Coriantumr surely would have remembered Ether's prophecies. Ether correctly prophesied that Coriantumr would be the sole survivor; wouldn't Coriantumr therefore believe that the New Jerusalem would come? Ether had referred to it coming to "this land" which was "a chosen land," just as he told Coriantumr that "another people" would receive "the land for their inheritance." Coriantumr could reasonably conclude that the site of the New Jerusalem would be where he would meet the new people who were to receive the land for their inheritance.

From D&C 84:1-5, we know the New Jerusalem will be "in the western boundaries of the State of Missouri." How would Coriantumr get there from Cumorah?

One route would be to travel south on the Allegheny River to the Ohio River, then south and west to the Mississippi River on his way to the Missouri River, which leads directly to the New Jerusalem. Along the way, probably while on the Mississippi, he was apparently found by the people of Zarahemla, who took him in for nine months before he died.

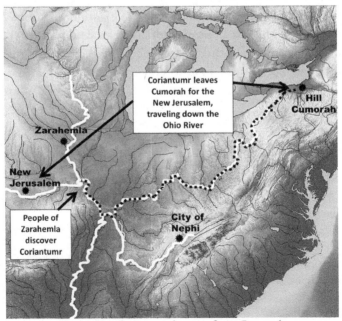

Figure 19 - Coriantumr's route from Cumorah

As for the stone, I think Coriantumr carved it during those nine months he lived with the people of Zarahemla. There is no indication in Omni that Coriantumr communicated with the people. They would have had completely different languages. Unlike the situation with Mosiah, who at least shared a common Israelite ancestry and culture with the people of Zarahemla, nothing about Coriantumr's Jaredite culture would be familiar. The people of Zarahemla did not keep records and apparently had no writing system, since Zarahemla recounted his genealogy by memory. Coriantumr, having seen another of Ether's prophecies fulfilled—that he would see another people receive the land for their inheritance—would have wanted to leave a record of his people and his own life. Engraving a stone would probably be the only method available to do so. (Even if he knew Ether kept a record, Coriantumr would have no way of knowing what became of Ether's plates.) Coriantumr knew the people of Zarahemla wouldn't understand his engravings, but figured that eventually, someone would decipher it.

His hopes were realized when Mosiah arrived.

Jonathan Neville

NOTES

[104] John Sorenson wrote, "It is very likely that non-Jews were in the crew of the vessel that brought Zedekiah's son Mulek to the New World (see Omni 1:15-16). A purely Israelite crew recruited in the Palestine homeland would have been possible during some periods, but at the time Mulek's party left, all the Mediterranean ports of the kingdom of Judah were in Bablylonian hands. Most likely the crew of the ship (there could have been more than one, of course) were 'Phoenician,' itself a historical category that was by no means homogenous." John L. Sorenson, "When Lehi's Party Arrived in the Land, Did They Find Others," *Journal of Book of Mormon Studies*, Vol. 1 Fall 1992 (Provo, Utah, FARMS), 13.

[105] Hugh Nibley noted that Sidon is the name of the Phoenician harbor in what is now Lebanon. The city still bears that name. Of course, the name also appears in the Old Testament as part of a border description (Genesis 10:19). Isabel, the harlot Alma chastised his son Corianton for visiting in Alma 39:3, is also "the name of the Patroness of Harlots in the religion of the Phoenicians." Nibley, "The Book of Mormon: Forty Years After," in The Prophetic Book of Mormon (Deseret Book/FARMS 1992) available online at http://bit.ly/Moroni59. Siron is another possible Phoenician influence. The Book of Mormon Onomasticon notes, "Given the possibility of Phoenician influence on the Mulekites who first settled the land around ZARAHEMLA,[1] this GN [given name] may be identical to the biblically attested Phoenician name for Mount Hermon, namely, śiryôn (Deuteronomy 3:9 and Psalms 29:6), Sirion in KJV (JH, JAT).[2]. Notice also the similar biblical word siryôn which in Jeremiah 46:4 and 51:3 is a type of body armor (JH). http://bit.ly/Moroni60

[106] Estimates for the final battle of the Jaredites range from 580 B.C. to 400 B.C. (Sorenson, An Ancient American Setting, p. 119) or as late as 200 B.C. (Gardner, Traditions of the Fathers, p. 391). This question is addressed in the Mosiah and Ether chapters.

Chapter 14 – Words of Mormon

-->>> <<<-

THE SHORT BOOK TITLED "WORDS OF MORMON" doesn't contain much information about geography, but it does indicate that "the armies of the Lamanites came down out of the land of Nephi" (verse 13) to battle against the people of king Benjamin. This is a confirmation that the land of Nephi was higher in elevation, and is consistent with the Lamanites coming north down the Tennessee River (Mosiah's river) to attack the Nephites, starting with southern Illinois.

King Benjamin's armies "did contend against their enemies until they had slain many thousands of the Lamanites"(verse 14). This suggests the numbers were fewer "tens of thousands" that we read about later in Alma, Helaman, 3 Nephi and Mormon.

"And it came to pass that they did contend against the Lamanites until they had driven them out of all the lands of their inheritance" (verse 14). This is an example of how pronouns can be confusing. "Their inheritance" could refer to either the Nephites' inheritance or the Lamanites' inheritance. Presumably in this context it refers to the Nephites' lands of inheritance, meaning the land of Zarahemla and not the land of Nephi.

Chapter 15 – Mosiah

—➤≫ ≪←-

Mosiah 1 – Language

KING BENJAMIN TAUGHT HIS SONS THE IMPORTANCE of language, but apparently the writing system was difficult. Lehi could read the engravings on the brass plates because he "had been taught in the language of the Egyptians" (verse 4), and yet the plates contained the Hebrew Torah. One needed to understand the "learning" of the Jews and the "language" of the Egyptians (1 Nephi 1:2).

> King Benjamin wanted his three sons to become 'men of understanding,' so he 'caused that they should be taught in all the language of his fathers, . . . that they might know concerning the prophecies which had been spoken by the mouths of their fathers.' (Mosiah 1:2). The expression "in all the language" can only mean that different degrees of mastery were possible. He wanted the princes to master the system to the maximum degree, not to have just a superficial knowledge... The substantial time investment required to attain mastery of the texts explains the later observation that "some were ignorant because of their poverty, and others did receive great learning because of their riches" (3 Nephi 6:12). Unlike Benjamin's princes, the Nephite poor could not afford the years of study, nor the mentors, needed to master full literacy.[107]

Without a written language, "even our fathers would have dwindled in unbelief, and we should have been like unto our brethren, the Lamanites, who know nothing concerning these things or even do not believe them when they are taught them because of the traditions of their fathers, which are not correct" (verse 5).

Benjamin's declaration indicates that the Lamanites, like the Mulekites before Mosiah taught them, did not have a written language. This is consistent with the experience in North America, where there is little evidence of written language, and inconsistent with Mesoamerica, where there is abundant evidence of written language.

Mosiah 1 – Temple Sermon

In verse 10, Benjamin tells his son Mosiah

My son, I would that ye should make a proclamation throughout all this land among all this people, or the people of Zarahemla, and the people of Mosiah who dwell in the land, that thereby they may be gathered together; for on the morrow I shall proclaim unto this my people out of mine own mouth that thou art a king and a ruler over this people, whom the Lord our God hath given us.

Some commentators have interpreted this to mean the people had only one day to assemble, so the population must have been low in numbers and confined to a small territory, like a city-state. This is one possible interpretation; according to the Oxford English Dictionary, *morrow* can mean *morning* or *the following day*. But the term can also mean *the time immediately following a particular event*. In this case, the particular event is the gathering of the people. Viewed this way, verse 10 means King Benjamin will speak to the people on the morning or the day after the people are gathered together, *not* on the day after he is speaking to Mosiah.

This makes sense; even using modern communications in Salt Lake Valley, it would be difficult to get everyone together on a single day's notice. It is also significant that the scripture says the proclamation went unto "all the people" but it doesn't say "all the people" gathered; just "the people" gathered. By implication, not "all the people" responded. Many would be expected to stay home. Those who attended brought only sacrificial animals (Mosiah 2:1), leaving other animals that would need to be tended. Crops in the fields would have to be watched over. Defensive positions would need to be manned. There would be sick people, elderly people, and infants who would likely not travel.

One demographic analysis suggests the population of Zarahemla could have ranged from 300,000 to 1.5 million people in 87 B.C., about 40 years after Benjamin's address.[108] It is unlikely such a large group would assemble at the temple, so the distinction between "all the people" being notified and merely "the people" gathering makes sense. John Sorenson suggests an assembly of 20-25,000 people could be addressed in the open.[109] This seems like a reasonable estimate.

Mosiah 2

Verses 1 and 2 suggest the territory was large and organized into smaller units.

> 1. And it came to pass that after Mosiah had done as his father had commanded him, and had made a proclamation throughout all the land, that the people gathered themselves together throughout all the land, that they might go up to the temple to hear the words which king Benjamin should speak unto them.
> 2. And there were a great number, even so many that they did not number them; for they had multiplied exceedingly and waxed great in the land.

The people "gathered themselves together" in their communities so they could go up to the temple. The number was more than they could count. The number was so great they could not fit within "the walls of the temple."

The text does not otherwise describe the temple, but Nephi reported that he built a temple "after the manner of the temple of Solomon." This was in the land of Nephi hundreds of years before King Benjamin's time, but presumably the Nephites retained some elements of that design.

The temple of Solomon was surrounded by walls. The building itself was 90 feet long and 30 feet wide. Here is a diagram of Solomon's temple platform.[110]

The area was extended by King Herod until it included about 37 acres in a trapezoid. Herod's temple is included in the model of the city of Jerusalem now on display in that city.

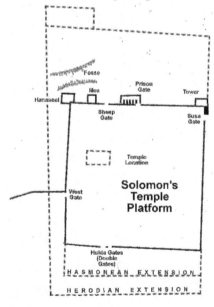

Figure 20 - Solomon's Temple Platform

Figure 21 - Temple Mount in Jerusalem

By comparison, a few miles north of Chillicothe, Ohio, there is an example of an ancient temple mound surrounded by walls that may be similar to the site where King Benjamin's people assembled. The walls enclose 32 acres, although Ephraim Squier, who documented the site, noted that "It is possible that a fourth wall originally bounded the enclosure on the west, which has been destroyed by the river, in its encroachments."[111]

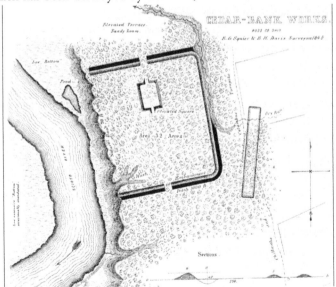

Figure 22 - Temple Mound in Ohio

The mound labeled "elevated square" inside is 250 feet long by 150 feet wide. A temple the size of Solomon's could easily fit on top of the elevated square, with walls along the edges of the elevated area forming the walls of the temple. The larger enclosure would define the larger sacred space.

It is interesting to note that outside Solomon's temple there was a "brazen sea" or round vessel of water 10 cubits in diameter (15 feet) that rested on the backs of twelve sculpted oxen. There was also a square altar outside the temple.[112] The theme of circles and squares is present in many Hopewell sites. The Cedar-bank works in Ohio also include a circle and square, although much larger than those associated with Solomon's temple.

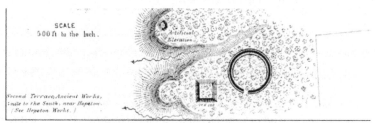

Figure 23 - Circle and Square in Ohio

Mosiah 2-6

Previously I noted that when Nephi taught his people to build a temple like Solomon's, he was demonstrating that the Hebrew culture he brought to the New World persisted. It was not swallowed up or absorbed by Mayan culture. King Benjamin's speech is more evidence of that.

Years of research have identified many threads of evidence in the Book of Mormon that tie back into the observance of ancient Israelite festivals. While traces of several preexilic Israelite festivals have been found in various places in the Book of Mormon, no source has been more fertile than King Benjamin's speech.[113]

To the extent that indigenous people joined with the Nephites (and the Lamanites), King Benjamin's speech is more evidence that the Nephite culture prevailed over the hunter/gatherer societies the may have encountered. This further corroborates the North American setting.

Jonathan Neville

Mosiah 7-8

These chapters introduce the critical history of Limhi and his descendants. Amaleki had concluded the book of Omni by mentioning that his brother went with "a certain number who went up into the wilderness to return to the land of Nephi." He reported there was a rebellion, and fifty men returned to the land of Zarahemla, where they "took others to a considerable number" and took their journey into the wilderness.

Mosiah 7:1 explains that the new king Mosiah

> was desirous to know concerning the people who went up to dwell in the land of Lehi-Nephi, or in the city of Lehi-Nephi; for his people had heard nothing from them from the time they left the land of Zarahemla; therefore, they wearied him with their teasings.
> 2 And it came to pass that king Mosiah granted that sixteen of their strong men might go up to the land of Lehi-Nephi, to inquire concerning their brethren.
> 3 And it came to pass that on the morrow they started to go up, having with them one Ammon, he being a strong and mighty man, and a descendant of Zarahemla; and he was also their leader.

In Omni, Amaleki wrote that the group went up to the land of Nephi. The different name here—it is spelled LehiNephi without a hyphen in the printer's manuscript—is generally accepted to mean the same place.

> This city may have been identical to the city formerly known simply as NEPHI, which had been settled by NEPHI I and his people during the 6th c. BC (2 Nephi 5:8). It is possible that the LAMANITES, who were not friendly with NEPHI, renamed the site LEHI after MOSIAH I and his people had left. Thus, it would have been called simply LEHI by the LAMANITES when ZENIFF and his people arrived. Thus, too, when ZENIFF and the returning NEPHITES arrived (Mosiah 9:1, 6, 8), they may have wished to refer to the site by its original designation, NEPHI, but out of deference to the LAMANITE king, whom they accepted as their nominal leader, they settled for a compromise.[114]

The Index to the Triple Combination also equates the two names.[115] I accept this explanation in my analysis, but recognize the two terms could refer to different places.

114

Ammon plays a key role in the account of the people of Limhi. As a descendant of Zarahemla, he presumably had never been to the Land of LehiNephi. The next verses explain the consequences.

> 4 And now, they knew not the course they should travel in the wilderness to go up to the land of Lehi-Nephi; therefore they wandered many days in the wilderness, even forty days did they wander.
> 5 And when they had wandered forty days they came to a hill, which is north of the land of Shilom, and there they pitched their tents.

If it seems strange that Mosiah would send them off into the wilderness without directions and without a guide, I agree. However, the text suggests something more specific. According to the Cambridge dictionary, a "course" is "the particular path something such as an aircraft or ship takes as it moves, or the path along which a river flows."[116]

According to my proposed map, the course for Ammon to follow would be easy—until he reaches the point where he has to "go up to the land of LehiNephi." At that point, he has to go up the Ohio River and then turn right at the Tennessee River and follow the correct tributaries. Finding the correct course on an unknown and unmarked river can be very difficult.

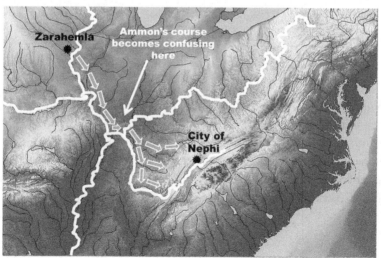

Figure 24 - Ammon's course becomes confusing

Jonathan Neville

Later in the text we will see that it was about a 20-day trip from the city of Nephi to Zarahemla (although that is not necessarily a direct route). The text says it took Ammon 40 days. One reason for the extra time could be Ammon's exploration of various tributaries to find the correct ones.

However, Ammon didn't arrive directly in the city of Nephi. Instead, verse 5 says "they came to a hill, which is north of the land of Shilom, and there they pitched their tents.

On modern maps, the river systems have been altered by the TVA. The following map from 1853[117] shows the pre-TVA setting. Of course, this map may not reflect conditions as of 121 B.C. when Ammon made his journey, but it gives an idea of what he might have faced.

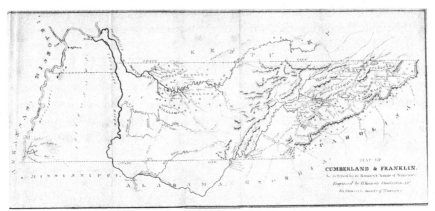

Figure 25 - 1853 Map of Tennessee Rivers

A close-up shows how Ammon could have proceeded up the Tennessee River and taken a fork to the Elk River or Duck River and proceeded overland to the hills overlooking the valleys to the south and east. Or he could have taken the Cumberland River to the Cany (Caney) Fork. There are several valleys in southeastern Tennessee that match the description in the text. Chattanooga is in the bottom right of this close up.

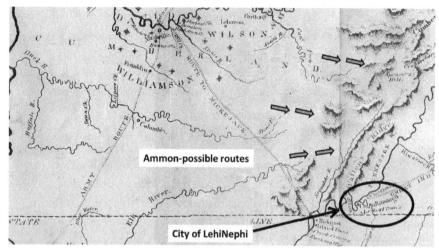

Figure 26 - 1853 map close up

Ammon and his three brethren, Ameleki, Helem and Hem, were arrested by the king's guard and taken to prison, presumably in the city of LehiNephi. The king was Limhi, the son of Noah, who was the son of Zeniff who left Zarahemla to inherit the land. In verse 10, Limhi said, "I desire to know the cause whereby ye were so bold as to come near the walls of the city, when I, myself, was with my guards without the gate?"

The walls are not described, but they could be mounds of earth, mounds topped with wooden pickets, or stone.

When Ammon explains he, too, is a descendant of Zarahemla, King Limhi was "exceedingly glad" and has his guards retrieve Ammon's brethren whom he left on the hill north of Shilom.

Verse 16 includes a curious statement: "they had suffered hunger, thirst, and fatigue." The Book of Mormon mentions people suffering from thirst in the desert or in prison, but only in two cases, here and in Alma 17:5, do people suffer "hunger, thirst and fatigue." If they had been traveling up a river, how could they suffer thirst? The likely answer is they were hiding on the hill, far above the water. Perhaps they had seen the arrest of Ammon and the others and were afraid to descend the hill.

There was no shortage of food and drink in the city; Limhi provided both for them. By around 121 B.C., the main crops were apparently corn and barley, both of which are found in ancient North America: "we at this time do pay tribute to the king of the Lamanites to the amount of one half of our corn and our barley and even our grain of every kind." (Mosiah 7:22)

The next day—on the morrow—king Limhi sent a proclamation among all his people. When they had gathered—the text doesn't say how long that process took—he recited the history of his people and promised an escape.

Mosiah 8

When Limhi finished speaking, Ammon told the people about what had happened in Zarahemla while they had been gone. He read the plates on which Limhi recorded his peoples' history. Then Limhi asked if Ammon could interpret languages. Ammon told him he could not. Then Limhi explained why he asked.

He had sent 43 "of my people" to take a journey to search for Zarahemla and get help to escape from the bondage of the Lamanites. Limhi explained:

8 And they were lost in the wilderness for the space of many days, yet they were diligent, and found not the land of Zarahemla but returned to this land, having traveled in a land among many waters, having discovered a land which was covered with bones of men, and of beasts, and was also covered with ruins of buildings of every kind, having discovered a land which had been peopled with a people who were as numerous as the hosts of Israel.

9 And for a testimony that the things that they had said are true they have brought twenty-four plates which are filled with engravings, and they are of pure gold.

These are the plates that Moroni eventually translated as the Book of Ether. They describe what happened to the Jaredites. Moroni wrote about the people in "this north country" where he was engraving the plates, which was near Cumorah where the final great battle between Shiz and Coriantumr took place.

Limhi's 43 people made a mistake; instead of reaching Zarahemla, they traveled to an area where the Jaredites had died in large numbers. When we look at the map, it's pretty easy to see how the 43 people, leaving from the City of Nephi, made such an error.

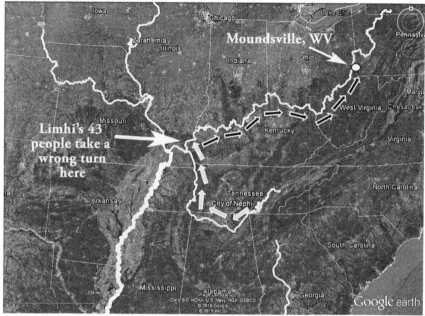

Figure 27 - Limhi's 43 explorers' wrong turn

For whatever reason, Limhi's 43 people did not have precise enough directions to avoid getting lost "for many days." Presumably they knew Zarahemla was on the east bank of the river Sidon, and they knew they would eventually reach the river Sidon when they traveled downstream on Mosiah's river (the Tennessee River). At that point, they would have to turn right and go north. The error they made was turning up the Ohio River instead of continuing downstream about 40 miles until they reached the river Sidon (today's upper Mississippi River).

Traveling upstream on the Ohio and Allegheny Rivers would take them along the southern border of modern-day Ohio through Pennsylvania and eventually to western New York. The route would not take them all the way to Cumorah, but we expect that from the text. Once they landed, the 43 people saw "ruins of buildings of every kind," and the Book of Mormon text does not claim the Jaredites built buildings[118] near Cumorah. Presumably 43 explorers stopped at the first major city they found, which turned out to be a scene of Jaredite destruction instead of Zarahemla.

Jonathan Neville

One candidate[119] for such a site is the Grave Creek Flats in Moundsville, West Virginia. As surveyed in the 1800s, the site featured a large mound in the lowlands and hilltop lookout points.

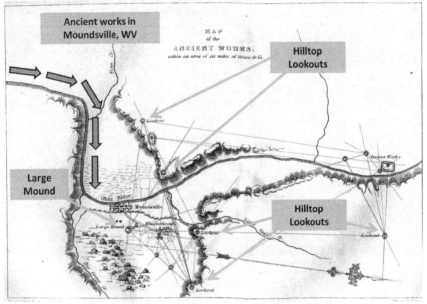

Figure 28 - Moundsville, WV

This particular Adena mound is dated circa 300 B.C. to 200 B.C., but the Adena was much older, and as the National Park Service noted, "the destructive forces of settlement eliminated all but a few of the hundreds of earthworks which were spread across the roughly 2000 acre terrace known as the Grave Creek Flats." [120]

The Adena culture dates from about 1,000-1,400 B.C. to 200 B.C.,[121] which corresponds to part of the Jaredite history.[122] This culture is identified by their distinctive mounds, art, small stone tablets, and pottery. The Grave Creek mound itself dates to a period about 80-180 years earlier than the arrival of 43 explorers circa 121 B.C. The text does not tell us when the final battle of the Jaredites took place.

In Omni, Amaleki explains that Coriantumr lived nine months with the Mulekites, so the destruction probably happened sometime after about 580 B.C. (unless Coriantumr lived an unusually long time after the final battle).

One Book of Mormon scholar proposes "200 B.C. as an approximate death date for Coriantumr and his contemporary Ether and therefore as a plausible anchor for the generational chronology"[123] which would match the evidence from Grave Creek. Working backward from that time means the Jaredites would have originated around 1,100 B.C., which also matches the appearance of the Adena culture. The 43 explorers found human and animal bones, as well as rusting weapons, presumably on the surface. This suggests the destruction had not happened many decades before the discovery.

Once Limhi's people found the plates among the ruins, they successfully returned to the borders of the land of Nephi.

The account of these 43 explorers is mentioned three times in the text. First, Mosiah 8 relates the story in the context of Ammon's appearance. Next, Mosiah 21 provides a slightly different account. Finally, Alma 22:30-31 refer to the incident. The story is important because of the record of the Jaredites, but it also plays a significant role in Book of Mormon geography.

Limhi's 43 explorers

Because it has led to one of the most significant errors regarding Book of Mormon geography, the account of Limhi's 43 explorers requires some additional explanation.

Alma 22 is the text's most extensive description of Book of Mormon geography. Verses 30 and 31 contain a critical passage:

> 30. And it bordered upon the land which they called Desolation, it being so far northward that it came into the land which had been peopled and been destroyed, of whose bones we have spoken, which was discovered by the people of Zarahemla, it being the place of their first landing.
> 31 And they came from there up into the south wilderness.

Based on these verses, some authors have claimed that the Mulekites (the people of Zarahemla), when they crossed the ocean from the Middle-East, made landfall on a sea coast in the land northward. From there, these authors claim the Mulekites traveled south into the land southward and up in elevation because of Alma 22:31. (Some also claim they then founded their capital, Zarahemla, in the land southward because of Mormon 1:6, a point I'll address in the chapter on Mormon.) Some further infer this means the Sidon flowed downhill toward the north.

In my view, this interpretation is an error—albeit a widely shared one. Look again at the passage without punctuation, as it was originally:

> 30 And it bordered upon the land which they called Desolation it being so far northward that it came into the land **which had been peopled and [had] been destroyed** of whose bones we have spoken which was discovered by the people of Zarahemla it being the place of their first landing and they came from there up into the south wilderness...

I inserted [had] in verse 30 based on Royal Skousen's conclusion that the word was in the original text but inadvertently omitted during publication.[124] It's an important detail, as we'll see.

(Another important point is ascertaining the antecedent(s) for the pronoun "it" throughout the passage, but I'll skip that for now.)

Mormon makes a fascinating allusion when he writes "of whose bones we have spoken." There are two references to these bones that precede this verse (not counting what Mormon might have written in the lost manuscript). The first we considered in Mosiah 8:7-12, which is a quotation from King Limhi's conversation with Ammon. Verse 8 says

> 8 And they were lost in the wilderness for the space of many days, yet they were diligent, and found not the land of Zarahemla but returned to this land, having traveled in a land among many waters, having discovered a land which was covered with bones of men, and of beasts, and was also covered with ruins of buildings of every kind, having discovered a land which had been peopled with a people who were as numerous as the hosts of Israel.

The second account of the 43-person search party is in Mosiah 21:25-27, which was taken directly from "The Record of Zeniff" as explained in the introduction to Mosiah 9.

> 25 Now king Limhi had sent, previous to the coming of Ammon, a small number of men [43] to search for the land of Zarahemla; but they could not find it, and they were lost in the wilderness.
> 26 Nevertheless, they did find a land which had been peopled; yea, a land which was covered with dry bones; yea, **a land which had been peopled and which**

had been destroyed; and they, having supposed it to be the land of Zarahemla, returned to the land of Nephi, having arrived in the borders of the land not many days before the coming of Ammon.

27 And they brought a record with them, even a record of the people whose bones they had found; and it was engraven on plates of ore.

The correction noted by Royal Skousen helps to make clear that in Alma 22:30, Mormon was directly quoting from Mosiah 21:26.

Mosiah 21:26- "a land which had been peopled and which had been destroyed"
Alma 22:30 – "the land which had been peopled and had been destroyed"

This quotation was not coincidental; Skousen has pointed out that Mormon was very deliberate and consistent in his use of "systematic phraseology" or repetitive verbiage.[125] The only thing missing from the direct quotation is the second *which* from Mosiah 21.

In addition, the definite pronoun "the" in Alma 22:30 shows Mormon is referring to a specific land; i.e., the one described in Mosiah 21:26.

The only record of "the people of Zarahemla" finding this land is in the accounts in Mosiah 8 and 21. Recall that in Omni, Mosiah translated the stone and that was the first time Zarahemla and his people learned about the Jaredites. Prior to that, Coriantumr had lived with them for nine months but was apparently unable to communicate with them. Mosiah's translation of the stone took place well before Limhi's 43 explorers discovered the plates.

Could the "small number [43] of men" king Limhi sent actually be the "the people of Zarahemla" that Mormon referred to in Alma 22?

The scriptures indicate yes.

King Limhi was the grandson of Zeniff. Zeniff described his background in Mosiah 9:1 this way: "I Zeniff having been taught in all the language of the Nephites and having had a knowledge of the land of Nephi or of the land of our fathers' first inheritance…" This shows he was among the people of Zarahemla who were taught in the language of Mosiah (the language of the Nephites) (Omni 1:18). The passage indicates he learned about the land of Nephi but had not previously been there. That Zeniff calls it "the land of our fathers' first inheritance" does not necessarily mean Zeniff *himself* was a Nephite; instead, it reflects the reality that "the people of Zarahemla and of Mosiah did unite together" and that he therefore felt entitled "to possess the land of their inheritance" along with others from Zarahemla. That Zeniff had not come from the land of Nephi with Mosiah is evident from his surprise when he first encountered the Lamanites. He writes, "when I saw that which was good among them I was desirous that they should not be destroyed." Mosiah 9:1.

From this we can infer that Zeniff was one of the "people of Zarahemla," as were those who accompanied him on the trip to the land of Nephi. This is corroborated by Ammon, who stated "I am Ammon and am a descendant of Zarahemla and have come up out of the land of Zarahemla to inquire concerning our brethren whom Zeniff brought up out of that land" (Mosiah 7:13). Ammon was not a biological Nephite, and neither were at least some of his "brethren" who accompanied Zeniff. See also Mosiah 1:8-9.

Consequently, the "small number of men" Limhi sent to search for Zarahemla were themselves "people of Zarahemla." Mormon accurately characterized them as the "people of Zarahemla" in Alma 22:30.

Mormon adds the comment "it being the place of their first landing."

Many have inferred that this refers to the first landing of the Mulekites on their way from the Old World, but we've already seen Mormon wasn't writing about that group; he was writing about the "people of Zarahemla" sent by Limhi. As discussed above, this group of 43 people simply took a wrong turn and ascended the wrong river. Because they were searching for Zarahemla, the first place they would land would be where they thought there was a city. Their place of first landing was the land which "had been peopled and had been destroyed."

They went ashore and searched the area. At some point, they found the Jaredite record, and "they returned to the land of Nephi having arrived in the borders of the land not many days before the coming of Ammon" (Mosiah 21:26), or, as Mormon expressed it on Alma 22, "they came from there up into the south wilderness." To people coming from the north, the south wilderness and the borders of the land of Nephi would be the same thing. On the map, they traveled down the Ohio River to Mosiah's River and then upstream to the borders of the land of Nephi—up in elevation.

Another corroboration of this interpretation is Amaleki's explanation that the people of Zarahemla who came out from Jerusalem never discovered the land which "had been people and had been destroyed." They learned about that land for the first time from Mosiah's translation of the large stone.

When Mosiah encountered the people of Zarahemla, they had no records of their own. Zarahemla learned Mosiah's language and then gave Mosiah "a genealogy of his fathers, according to his memory." Presumably this is how "Mosiah discovered that the people of Zarahemla came out from Jerusalem at the time that Zedekiah, king of Judah, was carried away captive into Babylon." (Omni 1:15) Only later was the large stone with engravings on it brought to Mosiah.

It was the engravings, not Zarahemla, that "gave an account of one Coriantumr and the slain of his people," including the explanation that "the severity of the Lord fell upon them according to his judgments which are just and their bones law scattered in the land northward." The text does not state or imply that the people knew about the Jaredites other than through Mosiah's translation of the engravings on the stone.

As discussed in the chapter on Omni, Coriantumr lived among the people for nine moons, but there is no indication that he communicated with them (apart from carving the large stone). Amaleki's explanation indicates that the people of Zarahemla learned about the Jaredites history from Mosiah's translation, not from their own experience.

This raises the question of why Zeniff's search party didn't recognize the bones as the land described on the stone. It's likely they didn't know about Mosiah's translation, or at least not the details. Maybe the stone didn't give enough details even if they had heard the translation. At any rate, they fully expected to find Zarahemla. As a new generation, they had never seen Zarahemla itself, and they knew so little about what to expect that they thought the devastated Jaredite scene was Zarahemla.

There is further corroboration of this interpretation. Ameleki pointed out that the people of Zarahemla "came out from Jerusalem… and they journeyed in the wilderness and were brought by the hand of the Lord across the great waters into the land where Mosiah discovered them and they had dwelt there from that time forth." If, when Mormon mentioned the place of first landing in Alma 22:30, he was referring to the group who came out from Jerusalem, then they would have still been there, living where the Jaredites had been destroyed. However, the people who "came out from Jerusalem" went directly to the land of Zarahemla and never left. They didn't land in one place and then go to another.

Jonathan Neville

Instead, it was the "people of Zarahemla"—the 43-person search party sent by King Limhi—who found the Jaredite land and who left that place and went up into the south wilderness in the land of Nephi, where they gave the plates to Limhi.

Mosiah 9-10

Mosiah 9 is the beginning of the record of Zeniff. He explains how he obtained the land of LehiNephi and the land of Shilom from the Lamanite king. Perhaps Zeniff's self-described zealousness blinded him, but in retrospect, as he wrote his record, he realized that "it was the cunning and the craftiness of king Laman, to bring my people into bondage, that he yielded up the land that we might possess it" (verse 10). The map of the area shows why the Lamanite King would agree to Zeniff's proposal. The Lamanites had Zeniff surrounded. The only way out was down the river— another reason why the 43 explorers would have traveled by boat, perhaps slipping out by night in canoes to evade the Lamanite guards.

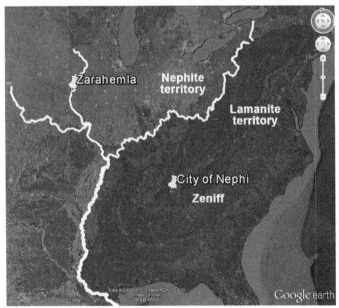

Figure 29 - Zeniff surrounded

The detail map below shows several potential candidates for the land of Shilom and the land of Lehi-Nephi. In the city of Lehi-Nephi and the city of Shilom, the people tilled the ground "with all manner of seeds, with seeds of corn, and of wheat, and of barley, and with neas, and with sheum, and with seeds of all manner of fruits" (Mosiah 9:9). Even today, the Chattanooga area has a long growing season and fertile soils.

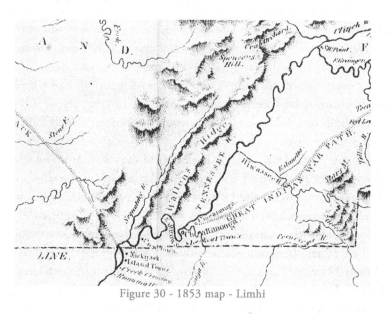
Figure 30 - 1853 map - Limhi

In verse 14, Limhi's people were watering their flocks "away on the south of the land of Shilom" when a "numerous host of Lamanites came upon them." The Nephites fled to the city of Nephi. If the land of Shilom was in the long valley west of Wallens Ridge, the people would be on the south to water their flocks, because that's where the river was. Lamanites could "come upon them" from the north, west, or south. The Nephites could then flee to the city of Nephi—Chattanooga—for protection.

In Mosiah 10:8, the Lamanites "came up upon the north of the land of Shilom." This would make sense because of the ridges on the north. Zeniff and his men "did go up to battle against the Lamanites," meaning they went up the hills to meet them.

Jonathan Neville

Mosiah 11, 19-22

Mosiah 11:12 relates that King Noah, Zeniff's son, built "a very high tower, even so high that he could stand upon the top thereof and overlook the land of Shilom, and also the land of Shemlon, which was possessed by the Lamanites, and he could look over all the land round about."

If Noah wanted to look over all the land round about, there could hardly be a better place to do so than Lookout Mountain which rises out of the river valley above Chattanooga to a height of almost 2,400 feet. On clear days, mountains 100 miles away are visible from the summit.

The tower was near the temple, but there is no description of where the temple was. It may have been enclosed in walls within the city, or it may have been built on a high place, which would explain why Noah built his tower near the temple.

In Mosiah 19, Gideon chased King Noah to the tower, from which Noah saw "the army of the Lamanites were within the borders of the land" (verse 6). It is unlikely a tower could be high enough to provide such a panoramic view unless it was built on a high place, such as Lookout Mountain.

If the Book of Mormon did not take place in or around Chattanooga, it had to have taken place somewhere with similar topographical features.

Mosiah 22 describes the escape of king Limhi and his people. They give wine to the Lamanite guards, and when the guards are drunk, they escape at night out the "back pass, through the back wall, on the back side of the city." The text gives no hint of direction, but it does explain that "they went round about the land of Shilom in the wilderness, and bent their course towards the land of Zarahemla, being led by Ammon and his brethren." This means Limhi's people went to Zarahemla following the route Ammon took.

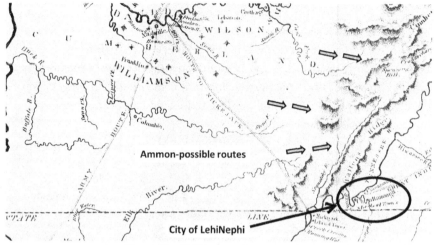

Ammon-possible routes

City of LehiNephi

Figure 31 - 1853 map - Ammon routes

The Lamanites would not have expected this, so apparently there were no guards along that route. A Lamanite army pursued Limhi's people for two days, but then lost their tracks, probably at a river. This suggests that Limhi's people traveled overland for a while before reaching a river, which is consistent with the proposed route Ammon took when he followed a river to its source and then crossed land to reach the hills overlooking the land of Shilom.

With the Lamanite army in pursuit, it seems unlikely that the people of Limhi could have built boats quickly enough to accommodate all the people, their animals, and their provisions. Perhaps they walked down the river far enough to hide their tracks and then continued overland. The text implies the journey took a long time: "after being many days in the wilderness they arrived in the land of Zarahemla" (Mosiah 22:13).

Mosiah 18, 23-24

These chapters focus on Alma. When Alma "fled from the servants of king Noah" (Mosiah 18:1), he didn't go far. He "went about privately among the people" to teach the gospel. Those who believed him went to the "place which was called Mormon, having received its name from the king,

Jonathan Neville

being in the borders of the land having been infested, by times or at seasons by wild beasts" (Mosiah 18:4).

The place of Mormon seems unusual, being close enough to the city of LehiNephi for Alma to go about privately teaching, yet also in the borders infested by wild beasts. One possible location is the mountain ranges east of Chattanooga, which are natural borders and would harbor migrating or hibernating animals such as bears.

Verse 5 offers more description of the place Mormon:

> 5 Now, there was in Mormon a fountain of pure water, and Alma resorted thither, there being near the water a thicket of small trees, where he did hide himself in the daytime from the searches of the king.

There are plentiful natural springs in this area of Tennessee, some of which are tourist attractions today. The "thicket of small trees" suggests this particular fountain had been cleared, possibly to be developed as a water source.

Eventually, the king found out where Alma was assembling with his followers. The Lord warned Alma that the king's army was coming, so he took his congregation of about 450 people and "departed into the wilderness" (Mosiah 18:34) with their tents and families, as well as their flocks and grain (Mosiah 23:1).

Although the text does not give us directional information, it seems likely that Alma would move in the direction of Zarahemla—north and west—instead of deeper into Lamanite territory.

They "fled eight days' journey into the wilderness and they came to a land, yeah even a very beautiful and pleasant land, a land of pure water" (Mosiah 23 3-4). They called the land Helam and "they built a city, which they called the city of Helam" (Mosiah 23: 19-20).

There are many places in Tennessee that fit this description. One candidate that has been preserved and can be visited today is Pinson Mounds, located approximately 200 miles northeast of Chattanooga and 28 miles from the Tennessee River. The 400-acre site is elevated above wetlands and a river that form its southern border. Over 30 mounds were constructed here over a long period of time. The probable age of some features is between about 100 B.C. and A.D. 260,[126] a reasonable fit for Alma's early development in about 145 B.C. As is typical of many sites, mounds were added and developed in later years. The site includes the "second-tallest mound in the United States (Sauls Mound, at 72 feet) and a circular earthen enclosure similar to earthworks found in the Ohio Valley."[127]

Could Alma and his people travel 200 miles in 8 days? That's an average of 25 miles per day, or about 8-10 hours of walking at 2.5 to 3 miles per hour. Because they were fleeing from the Lamanites, this seems a reasonable estimate, even for a large group with animals.

About 20 to 24 years later, though, the army of Lamanites that was chasing Limhi's people came across the land of Helam. Alma surrendered to the army.

An initially strange thing about this account is that this army chased the people of Limhi for two days before losing their tracks, at which point "they were lost in the wilderness" (Mosiah 22:16). How could they become lost after two days when they were following tracks? Couldn't they have simply turned around and made their way back to LehiNephi?

One possible answer is they feared being killed by the king of the Lamanites if they returned empty-handed. We learn in Mosiah 23 that they "had followed after the people of king Limhi" and "had been lost in the wilderness for many days" (Mosiah 23:30). This suggests they did not stop the pursuit of Limhi when they lost the tracks. Maybe they continued down the river. Every fork in a river is a problem, of course.

At some point, the Lamanites stumbled upon the priests of king Noah, led by Amulon. Amulon and his brethren joined the Lamanites, but for some reason, Amulon also didn't know the way back to the land of Nephi.

Continuing with the proposed geography, if the Lamanites had chased king Limhi's people to the Duck River, they would have eventually reached the Tennessee River at a point about 30 miles downriver from a point due east of Pinson Mounds. The Lamanites "were traveling in the wilderness in search of the land of Nephi when they discovered the land of Helam" (Mosiah 23:35). Perhaps they didn't recognize the Tennessee River as the way back to the land of Nephi so they followed tributaries into the land of Helam. Alma had no problem showing them "the way that led to the land of Nephi" (Mosiah 23:37), which suggests the "way" was obvious, even though the Lamanites had missed it. What obvious way could there be other than a

Jonathan Neville

river? Alma would simply have to take the Lamanite army to the Tennessee River and explain that way back was upriver.

Of course, this is merely one of many scenarios possible in this area of the country. There are many other rivers and archaeological sites in Tennessee where the events described in the text could have taken place. Pinson Mounds is plausible, based on the text; other plausible alternatives would likely be about the same distance northwest from the city of Nephi.

Amulon and language

The Lamanite king, Laman, made Amulon the king and ruler over Alma's people in the land of Helam. The king also "appointed teachers of the brethren of Amulon in every land which was possessed by his people, and thus the language of Nephi began to be taught among all the people of the Lamanites" (Mosiah 24:4).

The text specifies that Amulon taught a written language; "they taught them that they should keep their record and that they might write one to another" (Mosiah 24:6). This implies that the Lamanites did not previously have a written language, which is consistent with the archaeological record in North America, where there is little evidence of a written language. Nothing in the text suggests or implies that the Lamanites wrote in a permanent medium, such as on metal plates or stone.

In fact, the text specifies that Amulon did not teach them anything about God. This is a stark contrast to the Mayan glyphs that described dozens of dieties. Instead, the Lamanites used language for economic purposes: "the Lamanites began to increase in riches and began to trade one with another and wax great" (Mosiah 24:7).

Alma's escape

Facing oppression from Amulon and his Lamanite overseers, Alma and his people prayed for deliverance. When the Lord promised to deliver them, Alma and his people gathered their flocks and grain overnight.

And in the morning the Lord caused a deep sleep to come upon the Lamanites, yean, and all their task-masters were in a profound sleep. And Alma and his

132

people departed into the wilderness and when they had traveled all day they pitched their tents in a valley (Mosiah 24:19-20).

They didn't stay long, the Lord warned Alma that the Lamanites had awakened and were in pursuit. The text explains that Alma and his people "departed out of the valley and took their journey into the wilderness. And after they had been in the wilderness twelve days they arrived in the land of Zarahemla" (Mosiah 24:24-5).

The text doesn't indicate where in the land of Zarahemla they arrived. Using Pinson Mounds as an example, the site is about 400 miles from the proposed city of Zarahemla in Iowa, but only about 125 miles from the proposed head of Sidon in what is now southern Illinois. When Alma and his people left the valley, they could have traveled faster or slower than they did when they left the place of Mormon, leaving any estimate of distance pure conjecture.

Mosiah 25-27

After the arrival of Alma and Limhi and their respective people, king Mosiah "caused that all the people should be gathered together" (Mosiah 25:1). No census numbers are provided in the text; we're told merely that there were more descendants of Mulek than of Nephi, and there were more than twice as many Lamanites.

The disparity in population sizes could be attributable to a combination of several factors, including differences in fertility rates, dissensions from the Nephites (as in the case of Amulon), and more absorption of indigenous people by the Lamanites, who controlled a much larger territory.

The text says that all the people of Nephi and all the people of Zarahemla "were assembled together" (Mosiah 25:4). This raises the same issue presented by the gather for King Benjamin's address; i.e., did every individual attend, or did groups send representatives? Verse 7 refers to Mosiah's "people who tarried in the land." The passage implies some of Mosiah's people did not tarry in the land. Does that mean some of them left after Mosiah's speech? More likely, the archaic connotation of tarry, meaning a temporary stay or sojourn, applies here, which would mean some people didn't come to the assembly.

Verse 12 points out that some of the people who came with Alma were children of Amulon and his brethren. Because their mothers were Lamanites, they were half-Lamanite. They renounced their fathers and became Nephites.

The people gathered to hear Mosiah divided themselves into "large bodies" so Alma could preach the gospel to them (Mosiah 25:15). Alma baptized the people of Limhi and then established seven "churches throughout all the land of Zarahemla" (Mosiah 25:19, 23). Again, no population numbers are given, nor do we know how far apart these churches were.[128] The text speaks in generalities:

> And there began to be much peace again in the land; and the people began to be very numerous, and began to scatter abroad upon the face of the earth, yea, on the north and on the south, on the east and on the west, building large cities and villages in all quarters of the land. And the Lord did visit them and prosper them, and they became a large and wealthy people. (Mosiah 27: 6-7)

What is the distinction between a city and a village?

Although the Book of Mormon distinguishes between *villages* and *cities* (and, beginning around AD 363, *towns*), the text never clarifies the distinction. The 1828 Webster's dictionary defines "city" as: "In a general sense, a large town; a large number of houses and inhabitants, established in one place. In a more appropriate sense, a corporate town."[129] The same dictionary defines a "village" as "A small assemblage of houses, less than a town or city, and inhabited chiefly by farmers and other laboring people."[130] In England, the lack of a market distinguishes a village from a town.

This suggests a plausible meaning of the term *city*; i.e., a *village* is where farmers live, while a *city* is where not only farmers but tradespeople, merchants, and government officials live. The only mention of a "market" in the text is in connection with a city: "the highway which led to the chief market, which was in the city of Zarahemla." (Helaman 7:10)

Perhaps a Book of Mormon city was defined by architecture, such as a city wall or barrier. Or it could be a formal administrative designation—a "corporate town." This could be analogous to modern usage, whereby a city is technically defined by its formal incorporated area. The largest city in California in terms of territory—California City—encompasses over 200 square miles but actually has a small population (14,000 people).

A city need not have a large population. "Many ancient cities had only modest populations, however (often under 5,000 persons)."[131] When Lehi left Jerusalem, the city had a population of only about 25,000 people.[132]

Roger Kennedy discussed the terms "city" and "building" this way.

> Our English noun *city* comes from the Latin... city carries from its demographic root the implication of intention. A city was the consequence of a purpose. Perhaps it is not so much a noun as the outcome a verb; not a location but a phenomenon. A city was where a relatively large number of citizens congregated... In the Middle Ages, in the British Isles, a city became a place in which a potent religious leader such as a bishop was headquartered.[133]

The cities described by the text fit Kennedy's concept quite well. There is no requirement for massive stone temples and palaces. Such are never mentioned in the text. The only palace described in the text was Noah's, and it was made "of fine wood," not stone (Mosiah 11:9).

Possibly the term *city* includes elements of an advanced civilization, which would require evidence of advanced mathematics, knowledge of astronomy, including solar and lunar cycles, and public works large enough to require organization and coordinated effort. These are present in the major earthworks in the Midwestern United States.

The Nephites built "large cities and villages in all quarters of the land" (Mosiah 27:6), but the text does not describe the boundaries of "the land" at this point. Certainly at this point the Nephite civilization was expanding in population and territory, but it likely was centered around Zarahemla and along the Sidon River and its nearby tributaries, as proposed in Figure 32.

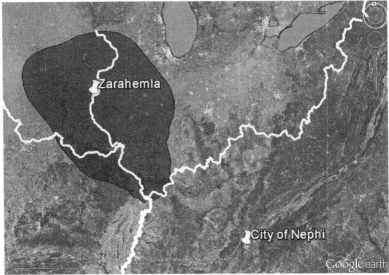

Figure 32 - Land of Zarahemla

In several places, the text in Alma uses the phrases "east of Sidon," "east of the river Sidon," and "west of the river Sidon." This usage demonstrates that many Nephite cities bordered the river Sidon.

Mosiah 28-29

The sons of Mosiah, who had rebelled against the Church but then repented, "traveled throughout all the land of Zarahemla and among all the people who were under the reign of king Mosiah" (Mosiah 27:35), preaching the gospel. They went to their father and asked if they could "go up to the land of Nephi that they might preach the things which they had heard and that they might impart the word of God to their brethren the Lamanites" (Mosiah 28:1).

The map shows why they would "go up" to the land of Nephi; they would have to travel up the Tennessee River to reach the area. After inquiring of the Lord, Mosiah granted their wish and they left.

Because his sons departed to teach the Lamanites and none of his sons wanted to be King, Mosiah gave the records to Alma, the son of Alma. Among the records were the plates found by "the people of Limhi" (his 43 explorers). Mosiah had translated these Jaredite plates and shared the knowledge with his people.

Now, instead of asking the people to gather—presumably their numbers had continued to increase and the territory had expanded—Mosiah sought the will of the people through correspondence. They wanted Mosiah's son Aaron to be king, but Mosiah didn't want to ask Aaron to return from his mission. Instead, he established a system of judges to rule the people.

The people "assembled themselves together in bodies throughout the land, to cast in their voices concerning who should be their judges... and they were exceedingly rejoiced because of the liberty which had been granted unto them" (Mosiah 29:39). This was 509 years from the time Lehi left Jerusalem, or about 91 B.C.

Jonathan Neville

NOTES

[107] John L. Sorenson, *Mormon's Codex*, p. 216-218.

[108] James E. Smith, "How Many Nephites? The Book of Mormon at the Bar of Demography," in *Book of Mormon Authorship Revisited: The Evidence of Ancient Origins*, ed. Noel B. Reynolds (Provo, Utah: FARMS, 1997), p. 281.

[109] Sorenson, Ancient American Setting, p. 157.

[110] http://bit.ly/Moroni61. For a comparison of the temples of Solomon, Herod, and Ezekiel, see the diagram here: http://bit.ly/Moroni62.

[111] Ephraim G. Squier and Edwin H. Davis, *Ancient Monuments of the Mississippi Valley*, (Smithsonian Institution Press, 1848, 1998), p. 53.

[112] A depiction of these is available here: http://bit.ly/Moroni63.

[113] Terrence L. Szink and John W. Welch, "King Benjamin's Speech in the Context of Ancient Israelite Festivals," in *King Benjamin's Speech*, Ed. by John W. Welch and Stephen D. Ricks, (FARMS, Provo, Utah, 1998), p. 147.

[114] Book of Mormon Onomasticon, "Lehi-Nephi," available online here: http://bit.ly/Moroni64.

[115] Index to the Triple Combination, "Lehi-Nephi, City of and Land of," available online at http://bit.ly/Moroni65.

[116] Cambridge dictionary, "course," online at http://bit.ly/Moroni66. The term is used in connection with water in Alma 37:44 (the compass "would point unto them a straight course to the promised land") and Alma 63:6 (Nephites "took their course northward" in Hagoth's ships). In Moses 6:34, "rivers shall turn from their course." Twice the term is used to refer to a direction or route through the desert wilderness (1 Nephi 16:33 and Alma 37:39), and the sea is compared to a desert wilderness (Isaiah 21:1, alternate translations).

[117] Ramsey's *Annals of Tennessee to the End of the Eighteenth Century* (1853), Map of Cumerland and Franklin, online at http://bit.ly/Moroni67.

[118] The definition of a "building" is key. Dr. Roger Kennedy, the former director of the Smithsonian's American History Museum, explained it this way: "*Build* and *building* are also very old words, often used in this book as they were when the English language was being invented, to denote earthen structures. About 1150, when the word *build* was first employed in English, it referred to the construction of an earthen grave.... So when we refer to the earthworks of the Ohio and Mississippi Valleys as *buildings* no one should be surprised. Roger G. Kennedy, *Hidden Cities: The Discovery and Loss of Ancient North American Civilization* (The Free Press, New York, 1994), p.vii.

[119] I'm not saying Moundsville is the site, but it is one of the only remaining sites that can be evaluated. Zarahemla was on the west bank of Sidon, and Moundsville is on the east bank of the Ohio River, but the text never says the place the 43 explorers found was on the west bank. They apparently knew so little about Zarahemla that even the existence of the Jaredite records in a different language they couldn't read didn't dissuade them from their conclusion they had found Zarahemla.

[120] Grave Creek Mound, National Park Service, National Register of Historic Places, available at http://bit.ly/Moroni68.

---

[121] Estimates vary considerably; "The point of origin of Adena man with his mound-building traits cannot yet be demonstrated." William S. Webb, *The Adena People*, (Univ. of Tennessee Press, 1974), p. 317. Societies develop new practices, sometimes gradually. 1400 B.C. is taken from *The People of the Mountain*, National Park Service, available here: http://bit.ly/Moroni69.

[122] I recognize that some critics, such as proponents of a Mesoamerican setting, claim that "The Book of Mormon requires that the Jaredites not be in the same area, but rather in the lands north of the Nephites and Lamanites" (FairMormon.org). However, Moroni specified that his account involved those destroyed "upon the face of this north country." The text is silent about people who may have been living elsewhere. Ether spoke of the New Jerusalem "upon this land," which we know refers to Missouri. Ether also describes the war "upon all the face of the land." That it ended in the north country—at Cumorah in New York—does not mean the Jaredites left the rest of the land vacant.

[123] Brant Gardner, *Traditions of the Fathers*, p. 391. Although Gardner advocates a Mesoamerican setting, his chronological analysis of the Jaredites has a solid foundation in the text.

[124] Royal Skousen, Analysis of Textual Variants, Part Four, p. 2066.

[125] Royal Skousen, editor, *The Book of Mormon: The Earliest Text*, Yale University Press: New Haven, 2009, Editor's Preface, p. xlv. Elsewhere, Skousen points out that we "have discovered the systematic nature of the text because of the occasional error." Skousen, "Changes in the Book of Mormon," *Interpreter: A Journal of Mormon Scripture* 11(2014), p. 172, online at http://bit.ly/Moroni70. The omission of [had] in Alma 22:30 is another example of how an error pointed to the systematic phraseology. Skousen concludes that "The systematic nature of the original text supports the theory that the text was revealed to Joseph Smith word for word." Skousen, "The Systematic Text of the Book of Mormon," *Journal of the Book of Mormon and Other Restoration Scripture*, Vol. 11, No. 2 (2002), p. 66. Online at http://bit.ly/Moroni71.

[126] Robert C. Mainfort, Jr., *Pinson Mounds: Middle Woodland Ceremonialsim in the Midsouth* (University of Arkansas Press, Fayetteville, 2013), p. 197.

[127] Robert C. Mainfort, Jr., and Mary L. Kwas, "Pinson Mounds State Archaeological Park," *The Tennessee Encyclopedia of History and Culture*, online at http://bit.ly/Moroni72.

[128] Some commentators have proposed specific sites for these seven churches in Mesoamerica. The best analysis I'm aware of is an article titled "The Church in Zarahemla," here: http://bit.ly/Moroni73. That article provides a detailed scriptural analysis and plausible assumptions, but suffers from the flaw that the "face of the land" in this Mesoamerican area has never changed.

[129] "city." *Noah Webster's 1828 American Dictionary of the English Language*. http://bit.ly/Moroni74 (8 February 2015).

[130] Ibid, "village."

[131] Michael E. Smith, "Ancient Cities," *The Encyclopedia of Urban Studies* (R. Hutchison, ed., Sage, 2009): 24. Available at http://bit.ly/Moroni75.

Jonathan Neville

---

[132] John W. Welch and Robert D. Hunt, "Culturegram: Jerusalem 600 B.C.," *Glimpses of Lehi's Jerusalem* (Foundation for Ancient Research and Mormon Studies (FARMS), Provo, Utah 2004): 5.

[133] Kennedy, *Ancient Cities*, p. vii.

Chapter 16 – Alma

-->>> <<<--

THE BOOK OF ALMA PROVIDES CONSIDERABLE INFORMATION about Book of Mormon geography. As discussed in Chapter 7, Alma 22 contains an overview of the lands of the Nephites and the Lamanites that is useful for explaining the general setting of the wars the text describes. It also helps clarify the events from 1 Nephi through Mosiah.

In most cases, the description of geography is vague, leading to a variety of possible interpretations. My main objective is to offer an overall framework for Book of Mormon events; I think the text does not provide enough information for anyone to specify exactly what happened where. (That is why the two pins from modern revelation—Cumorah and Zarahemla—are so essential.) That said, there are plausible locations for many events that I will propose in this chapter.

Three more things to remember.

First, Mormon and Moroni lived centuries after the events in Alma took place, and although Mormon as a child and later as a military leader traversed the country from the Cumorah area to Zarahemla and back again, he did not necessarily visit every location of which he wrote. That may be one reason why he referred to place names without providing any geographic information.

Second, there was tremendous destruction prior to the Savior's visit to America. The text says "the whole face of the land was changed" (3 Nephi 8:12). This phrase is significant, because there are few places in the world where the "whole *face* of the land" can be changed while leaving the overall geography recognizable. The river valleys in the Midwest, however, have long demonstrated not only how this is possible, but how it has actually happened in recorded history. I'll explain that in more detail in the chapter on 3 Nephi, but for now it's important to recognize that even those areas

Jonathan Neville

Mormon personally visited would have changed substantially from Alma's time period.

Today, we are another 1700 years removed from Mormon's lifetime.

To give an idea of how the "face of the land" changes in this area, a geological investigation of the Mississippi River alluvial valley was conducted in 1944 by the Mississippi River Commission. They produced a map showing 27 changes in the river's course, through 1944.[134]

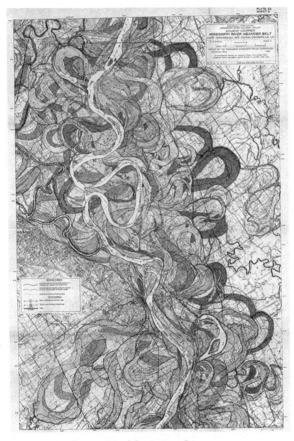

Figure 33 - Mississippi River courses

Any proposed Book of Mormon map derived from current maps or satellite images cannot possibly represent the river as it was in 100 B.C. As the map of changes shows, normal variation alone has completely changed "the face of the land" over the last few centuries. In modern times, states bordering the Mississippi have litigated changes to their boundaries caused by the shifting river. These cases have risen to the U.S. Supreme Court. The exceptional type of destruction described in 3 Nephi made the variation between the days of Alma and the days of Mormon and Moroni even more dramatic.

142

Therefore, the locations proposed in this chapter are merely examples of how the events could have taken place in Alma's day. In the chapter on 3 Nephi, I discuss the real-world setting of the destruction in more detail.

The third thing to remember is that there are pins in the map beyond Cumorah and Zarahemla. Although the Book of Mormon does not specify the location of the New Jerusalem, the Doctrine and Covenants does. Zelph's Mound is the mound in Illinois where Joseph Smith had a vision of the man whose bones were found, who was a warrior in the final battles of the Nephites and Lamanites.[135] Joseph Smith designated Huntsville, Missouri, as the location of ancient Manti according to two accounts.[136] My purpose here is not to settle that debate but to see if a Missouri location is consistent with the rest of the geography. I think it is.

Zelph's Mound, Adam-ondi-Ahman, and the New Jerusalem do not correspond to specific sites in the Book of Mormon, but their location in the Midwestern United States suggests doctrinal and geographic connection with the Nephites. To put this point in context, I've placed these sites as pins on the map, shown with modern boundaries for context.

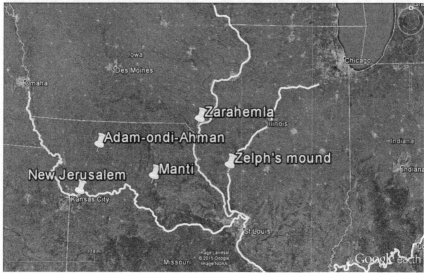

Figure 34 - Zelph's mound

Jonathan Neville

Geographic overview of Alma.

The Book of Alma uses a lot of place names that can be difficult to keep straight. The text also distinguishes between *cities* and *lands*; i.e., the *city* of Zarahemla vs the *land* of Zarahemla. In my analysis, I assume designation of a *land* means either the area administered by the government located in the city of the same name, or the area in the general proximity of the city of the same name.[137]

In Figure 35, I show the proposed setting for some of the major cities and lands mentioned in Alma circa 120-90 B.C. Obviously, these are rough approximations. Most of the occupied areas would have been along the rivers. The Nephites and Lamanites would have stationed guards along the border—the narrow strip of wilderness—between their two lands, but they would have had areas of wilderness in which no one lived.

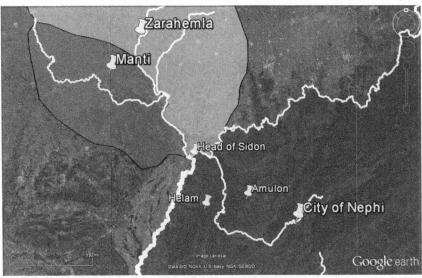

Figure 35 - Lands circa 120-90 B.C.

Figure 36 depicts Alma 22, the territory after the Nephites expanded eastward.

144

Figure 36 - Lands circa 90-77 B.C.

Figure 37 shows the same setting with modern borders.

Figure 37 - Lands in modern times

Jonathan Neville

As previously discussed, the location of Helam is merely an example for illustrative purposes, based on a single archaeological site that dates to the correct time frame. I chose it because it can be visited today. There are other sites in the area (as well as many that have been destroyed) that could also fit the text. Amulon is also an example, based on the proposed escape route of Limhi's people.

The text provides more detail about the Nephite territory, particularly regarding communities near the River Sidon. Much of the action in Alma takes place along this river. Several archaeological sites dating to this time period have been found in the area; the shifting rivers have likely flooded or buried many other sites.

The following diagram[138] depicts a few known sites and shows the relative location of Zarahemla and Nauvoo.

Iowa Hopewell Sites
500BC to 100BC

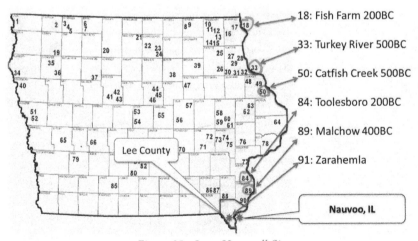

18: Fish Farm 200BC

33: Turkey River 500BC

50: Catfish Creek 500BC

84: Toolesboro 200BC

89: Malchow 400BC

91: Zarahemla

Nauvoo, IL

Figure 38 - Iowa Hopewell Sites

Today, the Toolesboro site has seven burial mounds, but anciently there were more that have been destroyed in modern times.[139]

A marker at the Malchow site shows occupation dates of 400 B.C. to 400 A.D., which is a good fit for the Mulekites and Nephites.

An example of the challenge of archaeology in this area is the recovery of the steamboat Arabia, which I discuss in the chapter on 3 Nephi.

Figure 39 - The Malchow Mounds

Alma 1

Chapter 1 introduces Nehor, whose philosophy and followers appear repeatedly in Alma. Nehor murdered Gideon and was brought before Alma to be judged. This occurred "in the first year of the reign of Alma in the judgment-seat" (Alma 1:2), but the text does not say where these events occurred. Nehor went "about among the people," which implies he was somewhere in the land of Zarahemla, but not necessarily in the city itself.

The text doesn't say that Alma was in the city of Zarahemla when he sentenced Nehor to death. The only geographic information given is that the people "carried him upon the top of the hill Manti... and there he suffered an ignominious death" (Alma 1:15).

The lack of information makes it impossible to tell if the hill Manti[140] was near the land or city Manti. I think that's unlikely, although Alma could have been traveling a circuit through the land of Zarahemla, acting as judge in various parts of the land. The land of Manti is first mentioned in Alma 17:1, which takes place about 77 B.C., suggesting that Manti was occupied well after Alma became the chief judge. It seems more likely that there was a hill in or near the city of Zarahemla named Manti.

Alma 2

The next reported challenge Alma faced came in the fifth year of his judgeship. A follower of Nehor named Amlici desired to be king and demanded an election. When he lost, his supporters made him their king and he started an armed rebellion against the government in Zarahemla.

Alma, as chief judge and governor, led the Nephite armies against the Amlicites, who had come "upon the hill Amnihu, which was east of the river Sidon, which ran by the land of Zarahemla" (Alma 2:15). The text does not give north/south directions relative to the city of Zarahemla, but the later context suggests the hill Amnihu was south. How far south is unknowable.

The account seems to say that the entire battle lasted one day, but I think this is an erroneous conclusion.

17 And they began to slay the Amlicites upon the hill east of Sidon. And the Amlicites did contend with the Nephites with great strength, insomuch that many of the Nephites did fall before the Amlicites.

18 Nevertheless the Lord did strengthen the hand of the Nephites, that they slew the Amlicites with great slaughter, that they began to flee before them.

19 And it came to pass that the Nephites did pursue the Amlicites all that day, and did slay them with much slaughter,

According to verse 19, the Nephites killed 12,532 Amlicites while losing 6,562 Nephites. These are massive numbers for a single day of battle, especially using swords, cimeters, bows, arrows, stones and slings. Even at Antietam, the deadliest one-day battle in the Civil War, only 3,650 people were killed (2,100 Union and 1,550 Confederate).[141] The practical reality of such a battle leads me to propose that the battle at Amnihu lasted for several days, and it was only when the Amlicites began retreating that the Nephites pursued them for an entire day.

Presumably Alma pursued the Amlicites southward, because the Amlicites joined up with the Lamanites, who would have been coming from the land of Nephi to the south. Alma stopped in the valley of Gideon and his people pitched their tents for the night. One wonders how the army brought tents when they were engaged in hand-to-hand combat all day, chasing the enemy. Tents were not mentioned in their preparation (Alma 2:12). I infer their supplies were brought to them from the rear.

The next few verses have engendered a common misperception about this geography, so I'll quote them in full.

21 And Alma sent spies to follow the remnant of the Amlicites, that he might know of their plans and their plots, whereby he might guard himself against them, that he might preserve his people from being destroyed.

22 Now those whom he had sent out to watch the camp of the Amlicites were called Zeram, and Amnor, and Manti, and Limher; these were they who went out with their men to watch the camp of the Amlicites.

23 And it came to pass that on the morrow they returned into the camp of the Nephites in great haste, being greatly astonished, and struck with much fear, saying:

24 Behold, we followed the camp of the Amlicites, and to our great astonishment, in the land of Minon, above the land of Zarahemla, in the course of the land of Nephi, we saw a numerous host of the Lamanites; and behold, the Amlicites have joined them;

25 And they are upon our brethren in that land; and they are fleeing before them with their flocks, and their wives, and their children, towards our city; and except we make haste they obtain possession of our city, and our fathers, and our wives, and our children be slain.

This all happened at night, so it is not clear how the spies observed this. Perhaps there was a full moon, or maybe the Amlicites and the Lamanite army had torches.

Figure 40 shows the relative position of the named sites.[142]

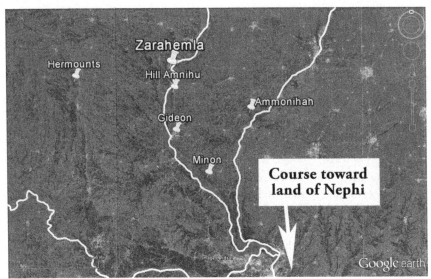

Figure 40 - Alma 2 sites

The main geographic clue is "in the course of the land of Nephi." As discussed previously when Ammon did not know the course to go up to the land of LehiNephi (Mosiah 7:4), a course is a way or path. In this case, "the course of the land of Nephi" would have been the river Sidon itself, which was the path or way out of Zarahemla, leading toward the land of Nephi. This tells us the spies followed the Amlicites south along the river.

The phrase "above the land of Zarahemla" is unique in the text; no other *geographic* information refers to one place being "above" another. When used to describe land, the term is always used *qualitatively*; e.g., "a land which is choice above all other lands" (1 Nephi 2:20). If the term is used consistently here, it would mean Minon was a "more choice" land than Zarahemla, which might be one reason the spies were so astonished to see it being plundered. Alternatively, it could be a unique usage, intended to mean that the land of Minon was higher in elevation than the land of Zarahemla, which is why I placed it in the hilly area between the Mississippi and Illinois rivers on the map above.

Another possibility is that the land of Minon was on the west side of the river Sidon and that the spies made their observations by looking across the river. There are hilly areas on that side, as well.

When the spies told Alma he needed to "make haste," they could have meant make haste to reach the city and set up defenses, or make haste to intercept the Lamanites. The next verses suggest the Nephites were going to try to outrun the Lamanites, but couldn't do it.

> 26 And it came to pass that the people of Nephi took their tents, and departed out of the valley of Gideon towards their city, which was the city of Zarahemla. 27 And behold, as they were crossing the river Sidon, the Lamanites and the Amlicites, being as numerous almost, as it were, as the sands of the sea, came upon them to destroy them.

Because the Lamanites "came upon" the Nephites as the Nephites were crossing the river, the Lamanites had to be behind the Nephites, following them into the river.

An interesting feature of the Mississippi River is the numerous islands that form in the channel. Here's an example.

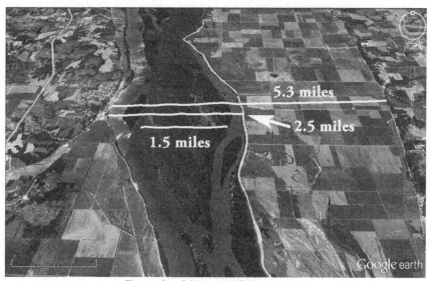

Figure 41 - Mississippi River crossing

This section of the river, located just north of my proposed Gideon, is 2.5 miles wide, from bank to bank. The island in the channel is about 1.5 miles wide at its widest point. What is now farmland to the east (right) of the

151

current river is part of the historic channel, which is over five miles wide. (Now the river is controlled by dams and locks.)

With this in mind, the description in Alma of a battle taking place while crossing the river makes perfect sense. Alma, strengthened by his faith, killed Amlici with his sword. The scripture describes what happened next.

> 32 And he also contended with the king of the Lamanites; but the king of the Lamanites fled back from before Alma and sent his guards to contend with Alma.
> 33 But Alma, with his guards, contended with the guards of the king of the Lamanites until he slew and drove them back.
> 34 And thus he cleared the ground, or rather the bank, which was on the west of the river Sidon, throwing the bodies of the Lamanites who had been slain into the waters of Sidon, that thereby his people might have room to cross and contend with the Lamanites and the Amlicites on the west side of the river Sidon.
> 35 And it came to pass that when they had all crossed the river Sidon that the Lamanites and the Amlicites began to flee before them, notwithstanding they were so numerous that they could not be numbered.
> 36 And they fled before the Nephites towards the wilderness which was west and north, away beyond the borders of the land; and the Nephites did pursue them with their might, and did slay them.
> 37 Yea, they were met on every hand, and slain and driven, until they were scattered on the west, and on the north, until they had reached the wilderness, which was called Hermounts; and it was that part of the wilderness which was infested by wild and ravenous beasts.
> 38 And it came to pass that many died in the wilderness of their wounds, and were devoured by those beasts and also the vultures of the air; and their bones have been found, and have been heaped up on the earth.

There are a lot of strange aspects of this account. The Lamanites and Amlicites originally attacked from the south, having come from the direction of "the course of the land of Nephi." Yet when they start losing the battle, the Lamanites and Amlicites are chased to the west and north—exactly the opposite direction. It's understandable that the Nephites would want to chase them to Hermounts, where the wild beasts would help finish them off, but why would the Lamanites not just retreat back from where they came?

As I read this, Alma was crossing the river when the Lamanites attacked. The battle ensued on the river; i.e., on one of these islands in the middle of the river. Alma then cleared the west bank of the island so his people could "have room to cross and contend with the [enemy] on the west side of the river" (Alma 2:34). This fits the text, which distinguishes between the "ground, or rather the bank, which was on the west of the river"—the ground Alma cleared—and the "west side of the river," where Alma wanted to fight the battle.

The scripture says "when they had all crossed the river Sidon," which I take to mean all the combatants, not just all the Nephites. Alma wisely saw that he had to lure the Lamanites to the west side; the last thing he would want is the Lamanites and Amlicites to return where they came from. Once he got them on the west bank, he could prevent them from returning home. Instead, he scattered them on the west and north.

The sequence and location of these events are shown on the map below.

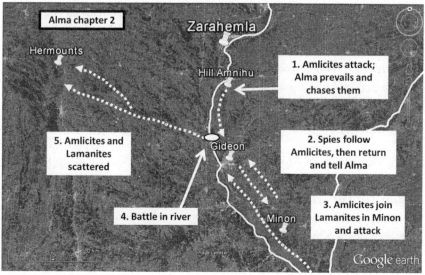

Figure 42 - Alma 2 - Amlicite battles

The scattering and death of the Amlicites and Lamanites who attacked Alma's army was not the end of the wars caused by Nehor's teachings. Nehor and Amlici developed a following prior to their deaths, and this became one of the main causes of the wars between the Nephites and the Lamanites.

Jonathan Neville

Nehor/Amlici Ideology

Nehor's teachings resembled many of the things we hear today. He advocated a paid clergy whose income would depend on their popularity. He claimed people had no need to fear nor tremble because all mankind would be saved at the last day, "and, in the end, all men should have eternal life." He was "lifted up in the pride of his heart," and he wore "very costly apparel." After his death, Amlici and others perpetuated Nehor's philosophy. They strongly opposed the Nephite church and missionaries, and they manipulated the Lamanites into several battles with the Nephites.

Later in Alma, another group appears calling themselves the Amalekites. However, from close analysis of variant spellings in the original manuscript and the printer's manuscript, Royal Skousen has proposed that the term *Amalekites* (Alma chapters 21-27, 43) should have been spelled *Amlicites,* and that *Amlicites* should be pronounced as *Amlikites*.[143] This helps to clarify that the Nehor/Amlici influence persisted in the history and that the Amalekites were not a separate group of dissenters.

Therefore, Nehor's teachings were the cause of many of the wars documented in Alma.

Nehor/Amlici Chronology

The chronology of Amlici and his followers is a little difficult to follow in the text because some of the back story is not explained until later chapters in Alma.144 For example, Skousen also points out that although the sons of Mosiah spent 14 years on their mission, we have a record of only a few of the later years of their ministry.

Here is an overall chronology from 91 B.C. to 74 B.C.

91 B.C. The sons of Mosiah go up to the Lamanite territory to preach the gospel.

91 B.C. Nehor spreads priestcraft and kills Gideon. Alma sentences him to death. He is killed at the hill Manti, but Nehor's followers continue spread his teachings in Zarahemla and in the lands of Amulon and Helam (Amulon being the priest of Noah who abused Alma's people in Helam). The people living there are identified as Lamanites, Amulonites and Amlicites (Amalekites). Amlici becomes a leader among the Nehors (Alma 21: 1-3).

87 B.C. In Ammoniah, Amlici seeks to become king in Zarahemla. The people vote on the matter and Amlici loses, but his followers—the Amlicites—make them their king. The Amlicites attack Zarahemla but Alma kills Amlici. (An detailed analysis of this battle follows this chronology.)

Circa 87-81 B.C. Ammon separates from the other sons of Mosiah and goes to the city of Jerusalem, where he preaches to the Amlicites. They refuse to listen so he leaves for the village of Ani-Anti (Alma 21: 1-11).

82 B.C. Alma preaches in Ammoniah, a city dominated by the Nehors. Alma is rejected, returns and meets Amulek. Alma and Amulek preach again, are imprisoned, and are delivered.

Circa 87-77 B.C. Some of the Lamanites accept the gospel, become the Anti-Nephi-Lehies (likely meaning "the ones of Nephi and Lehi"[145]). The Amlicites and Amulonites, still after the order of the Nehors, are not converted (Alma 23).

Circa 87-77 B.C. The Amlicites and Amulonites provoke the remaining Lamanites to attack the Anti-Nephi-Lehies, who refuse to fight (Alma 24).

Circa 87-77 B.C. Lamanites take revenge on the Amlicites and Nehorites in Ammonihah and destroy the city (Alma 25:2), but fail in battles against other Nephites.

77 B.C. The Amlicites again attack the Anti-Nephi-Lehies, but Ammon leads them to safety (Alma 27).

74 B.C. Amlicites join with the Zoramites in Antionum to lead another Lamanite army (Alma 43:6) but Moroni defeats them (Alma 43:29-54) and the Amlicites are never heard of again.

Alma 3

The first verse illustrates the importance of burial among the Nephites; they didn't return to their lands until "after they had finished burying their dead." They did the same for their enemies they had chased into Hermounts, of whom the text reports, "their bones have been found and have been heaped up on the earth" (Alma 2:38). Such burial mounds are common among the Hopewell people. Zelph's mound, discussed above, is an example. Many other such mounds have survived in Iowa, Illinois, and surrounding sites today.

However, the Nephites didn't bury the bodies of the Lamanites and Amlicites who they killed on the bank of the river Sidon. These they "cast into the waters of Sidon and behold their bones are in the depths of the sea

Jonathan Neville

and they are many" (Alma 3:3). This verse equates the "waters of Sidon" with the sea and could be figurative or could describe how the bodies floated downriver to the Sea West (the lower Mississippi).

The war had a significant impact on the people of Zarahemla:

> 2 Now many women and children had been slain with the sword, and also many of their flocks and their herds; and also many of their fields of grain were destroyed, for they were trodden down by the hosts of men.

The text mentions women and children being killed only in the land of Minon, the area that was "above the land of Zarahemla." Perhaps this means Minon was the breadbasket for the people generally, the most productive agricultural area, which would be consistent with the use of the term "above" in his context. Alternatively, we can infer that women and children were also killed in the area between the hill Amnihu and Gideon, or that the battle was more extensive than the narrative indicates. Because the text specified that 12,532 Amlicites and 6,562 Nephites died at Amnihu, but the numbers of dead at the river battle were too large to count, it could be that the war covered far more territory than the record indicates.

But the Lamanites came back for more—or for retaliation.

> 20 Now it came to pass that not many days after the battle which was fought in the land of Zarahemla, by the Lamanites and the Amlicites, that there was another army of the Lamanites came in upon the people of Nephi, in the same place where the first army met the Amlicites.
> 21 And it came to pass that there was an army sent to drive them out of their land.
> 22 Now Alma himself being afflicted with a wound did not go up to battle at this time against the Lamanites;
> 23 But he sent up a numerous army against them; and they went up and slew many of the Lamanites, and drove the remainder of them out of the borders of their land.

Tens of thousands of people died in these wars (Alma 3:26).

The Lamanite invaders followed the same route as their predecessors, coming north from the land of Nephi along the river. The Nephites apparently had not fortified the southern border, or at least not very well. This would become a major issue in the next few decades.

Alma 4-15

Those who survived initially experienced a religious revival, but soon thereafter, the people became to be prosperous and prideful. Wickedness of the church led Alma to resign as chief judge to preach the gospel and "reclaim" the people (Alma 4:19). He went on a mission, starting in the city of Zarahemla (Alma 5-6), then visiting Gideon (Alma 6-7), Melek (Alma 8:3-6), Ammoniah (Alma 8-14), and Sidom (Alma 15). His mission is shown on the map below.

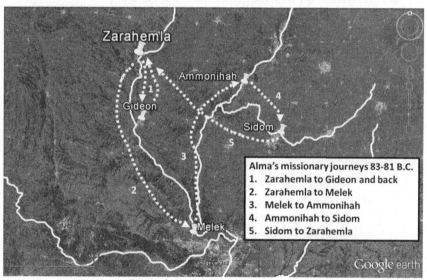

Figure 43 - Alma's missionary journeys

These proposed sites fit the general descriptions on the text and correspond to the following modern cities. Although the Book of Mormon mentions only the Sidon River by name, other rivers are implied when people travel "over" from one place to another. Ancient people generally lived along rivers for obvious reasons.

Gideon – Quincy, IL, on the east bank of the Mississippi River, home of Indian Mounds Park.

Melek – St. Charles area north of St. Louis, on the west bank of the Mississippi River. St. Louis was once known as Mound City because of the dozens of Indian mounds that once were located there. Big Mound was 319 feet long, 158 feet wide, and 34 feet high. It was destroyed in the 1860s when its dirt was used to build the railroad along the Mississippi River.

Ammonihah – Havana, IL, on the Illinois River adjacent to Fulton County. "There are over 3,000 Indian mounds and village sites in Fulton County, the highest such concentration in the Midwest."[146] Not far from here is Dickson Mounds.

Sidom – Springfield, IL, a site on the Sangamon River that was settled by trappers and traders for its strategic location and good soil.

Alma 16

Alma 16 relates how a Lamanite army destroys Ammonihah, thereby telling us more about the geography of the area. I assume the Lamanites traveled upon or along the rivers; these verses don't say how they traveled, but the Lamanites moved too fast for the Nephites to respond.

> 2 For behold, the armies of the Lamanites had come in upon the wilderness side, into the borders of the land, even into the city of Ammonihah, and began to slay the people and destroy the city.
> 3 And now it came to pass, before the Nephites could raise a sufficient army to drive them out of the land, they had destroyed the people who were in the city of Ammonihah, and also some around the borders of Noah, and taken others captive into the wilderness.

The Nephites wanted to rescue the captives. Zoram, the chief captain of the Nephite armies, asked Alma if the Lord wanted him to go into the wilderness to find them. Alma replied that "Behold, the Lamanites will cross the river Sidon in the south wilderness, away up beyond the borders of the land of Manti. And behold there shall ye meet them, on the east of the river Sidon, and there the Lord will deliver unto thee thy brethren who have been taken captive by the Lamanites" (Alma 16:6).

The text doesn't say where the meeting between Zoram and Alma took place, but it seems unlikely it was in Zarahemla. The Lamanites had already destroyed Ammoniah and taken the captives, and they had acted quickly. It seems unlikely that Zoram could have chased them down unless the Lamanites had decided to stay put in the south wilderness for some reason. However, no Lamanite city is mentioned. Maybe they were raiding additional Nephite villages in the area.

I suggest that Alma and Zoram were in the land of Manti, and that's why Alma told Zoram he'd have to go "beyond the borders of the land of Manti." Alma had finished the previous year in Zarahemla, after having visited Ammoniah and Sidom (Alma 15). The Lamanite invasion occurred on the fifth day of the second month of the eleventh year, giving Alma and Amulek time to recuperate before leaving again to preach throughout all the land. Although the text does not explicitly state as much, perhaps Zoram traveled with Alma as a sort of body guard after Alma and Amulek had been imprisoned in Ammoniah. Later, in 77 B.C., Alma is on his way from Gideon to the land of Manti when he meets the sons of Mosiah on their way to Zarahemla (Alma 17:1-3). Presumably this was one of several visits, but at least it shows Alma did visit Manti.

Verse 1 also says "there was a cry of war heard throughout the land." This might imply a very small territory indeed, if a literal cry was heard this way. A more likely interpretation is that the Nephites were communicating over long distances the way the Native American Indians did—with line-of-sight communication from one hilltop or mound to another. In this manner, news of the raid on Ammonihah could travel quickly, wherever Alma and Zoram happened to be.

According to our geography, Ammonihah is already on the east side of Sidon, so how, if the Lamanites cross the river Sidon in the south wilderness, will they be on the east of the river?

The answer is in the detailed geography of where the Illinois River (along which Ammoniah and Noah are located) meets the Mississippi River. The Lamanites, traveling south on or along the Illinois River with their captives, intersect or cross the Mississippi River.

Zoram doesn't cross the river; he crosses *over* it.

Jonathan Neville

7 And it came to pass that Zoram and his sons **crossed over** the river Sidon, with their armies, and marched away beyond the borders of Manti into the south wilderness, which was on the east side of the river Sidon.

8 And they came upon the armies of the Lamanites, and the Lamanites were scattered and driven into the wilderness; and they took their brethren who had been taken captive by the Lamanites, and there was not one soul of them had been lost that were taken captive. And they were brought by their brethren to possess their own lands.

These events are depicted in this map, which shows two possible routes of Zoram in black. It seems unlikely that he could catch the Lamanites if he crossed the river at Zarahemla and marched all the way down. Instead, I propose he went down the Missouri River, crossed Sidon there, and then marched into the wilderness to intercept the Lamanites.

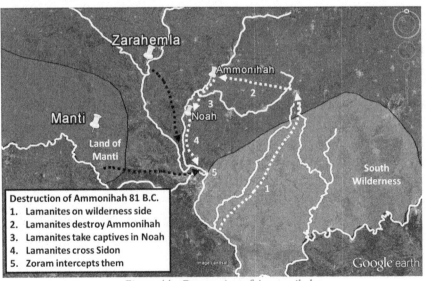

Figure 44 - Destruction of Ammonihah

Alma 17-26

The sons of Mosiah went to preach to the Lamanites. "And it came to pass when they had arrived in the borders of the land of the Lamanites, that they separated themselves and departed one from another" (Mosiah 17:13). The text says nothing about their means of travel, but I propose they did this by taking different rivers and tributaries.

The text gives little description of the geography to go by. The cities and lands are named but not identified by directions or distances. There are dozens of locations in Tennessee and surrounding states that would fit the text. It is possible that ongoing archaeological research may provide new information that could help identify more specific sites that fit the text, but many ancient sites have been destroyed, some covered with modern cities and other developments.

The Lamanites had their hearts "set upon riches, or upon gold and silver and precious stones" (Mosiah 17:14), the only time such stones are mentioned in the text. The precious metals are among those listed by Nephi when he founded his city, so they likely came from the area around the proposed city of Nephi.

The sons of Mosiah had great success with the Lamanites in the land of Ishmael. Their converts took the name Anti-Nephi-Lehi, meaning "one of Nephi-Lehi."

The Amlicites, Amulonites and Lamanites in the lands of Amulon, Helam, and Jerusalem became angry against the converts and prepared to fight against them. The Anti-Nephi-Lehies covenanted not to kill, so they submitted to their attackers, allowing themselves to be killed. Eventually the chagrin of their Lamanite foes led to the destruction of Ammonihah.

Alma 27-28

Ammon persuaded the Anti-Nephi-Lehies to follow him to the land of Zarahemla. When they reached the wilderness that divided the land of Nephi from the land of Zarahemla, the people stayed near the borders while Ammon went to the city of Zarahemla to arrange for a land for his converts. On both sides of the Mississippi in that area, there are hills that provide natural defensive positions.

Along the way, Ammon met Alma, who was traveling from Gideon to Manti (Alma 27:16-20). This suggests that Ammon went the along the normal "course" from the land of Nephi to the city of Zarahemla, which would be along the rivers.

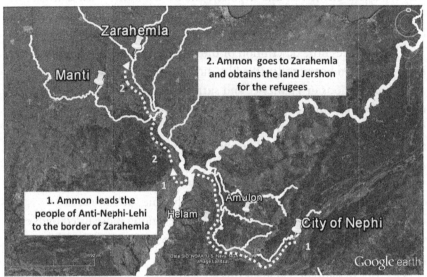

Figure 45 - Ammon and Anti-Nephi-Lehies

To get from Zarahemla to Manti, which is located on a tributary of the Missouri River, Alma could have traveled overland, which would be a shorter distance. However, river travel allows much easier transport of supplies. The encounter between Alma and the sons of Mosiah makes sense if they were all traveling by river.

Alma accompanied Ammon back to the city of Zarahemla. After hearing Ammon's request, the chief judge sent a proclamation seeking the voice of the people.

> 22 And it came to pass that the voice of the people came, saying: Behold, we will give up the land of Jershon, which is on the east by the sea, which joins the land Bountiful, which is on the south of the land Bountiful; and this land Jershon is the land which we will give unto our brethren for an inheritance.

> 23 And behold, we will set our armies between the land Jershon and the land Nephi, that we may protect our brethren in the land Jershon; and this we do for our brethren, on account of their fear to take up arms against their brethren lest they should commit sin; and this their great fear came because of their sore repentance which they had, on account of their many murders and their awful wickedness.

24 And now behold, this will we do unto our brethren, that they may inherit the land Jershon; and we will guard them from their enemies with our armies, on condition that they will give us a portion of their substance to assist us that we may maintain our armies.

This is an important geographical passage that is susceptible to multiple interpretations. Although it is the first time the name Jershon is mentioned, subsequent references help explain its location.

The name Jershon may be derived from the Hebrew root meaning "to inherit."[147] This might explain why the "voice of the people" described where the land was. In most cases, the names of lands are mentioned without geographical information because the people keeping the record would know the location of the named land. Here, the people give a description, which suggests it was a new land, designated for an inheritance for these immigrants.

Here is the text as given in the printer's manuscript:

The land of Jershon which is on the east by the sea which joins the land bountiful which is on the south of the land bountiful.

Here is the passage in parallel structure.

1. The land of Jershon
2. which is on the east by the sea
3. which joins the land bountiful
4. which is on the south of the land bountiful

This structure clarifies that each *which* clause modifies Jershon.

Line two raises these questions: East of what? What sea?

To this point, there has been no mention in the text of a sea east, apart from Mormon's editorial insertion in Alma 22, which he added centuries after the events he is relating. There is no indication in the text that in 77 B.C. the Nephites had explored much outside of the corridor of the Sidon and Mosiah rivers (Mississippi and Tennessee Rivers, respectively). Except for Limhi's 43 explorers (his people of Zarahemla), there is no record of anyone having visited the land of the Jaredites.

So what would people living in Zarahemla in around 77 B.C. think of as *east* in terms of territory? References in this time frame are always to *east* or *west* of the Sidon River; i.e., east and west are significant primarily in relation to the river.

The text changes the normal usage here; instead of a river, the people refer to the sea: "on the east by the sea." As I discussed previously, the Hebrew term "sea" includes "a mighty river." Because Jershon is of Hebrew derivation, the use of Hebrew to interpret the term *sea* is consistent. Consequently, I propose the people are making a distinction between the river Sidon, which flows south past Zarahemla, and the river *after* it is joined by the Illinois and Missouri Rivers, when it becomes much larger—a "mighty river," or a *sea*.

Line three explains that Jershon "joins" the land bountiful, which probably means "adjacent to" in this context. Notice that in the printer's manuscript, the name *Jershon* is capitalized but the word *bountiful* is not. Other references to the land Bountiful, both in the Arabian Peninsula (1 Nephi) and in the promised land (Alma 50-55, Helaman 1-5, 3 Nephi 3, 11) capitalize the word as a proper noun. Maybe this is just an error on the part of Oliver Cowdery, but it is also possible that the term is being used as an adjective, not as a proper noun. Not only is it possible, but it makes sense.

As shown on the map below, the area where Ammon would have left the Anti-Nephi-Lehies is lower Illinois. The area is known today as "Little Egypt" because in 1831, northern Illinois suffered from an unusually long and cold winter, a late spring, and a killing frost on September 10. Southern Illinois was not affected, so the corn production from the area kept the north from starvation. People remembered the Biblical story of the sons of Jacob going to Egypt to buy corn, and made the comparison with southern Illinois.[148] Perhaps similar situations arose in Nephite times. This would explain why the people of Zarahemla would use the adjective *bountiful* to describe the area that Jershon joins.

Line four of the parallel structure specifies that Jershon is south of the land bountiful, which makes strategic sense. This was the area in which the Lamanites had taken the captives from the land of Noah before Zoram rescued them.

In addition, the "voice of the people" recognized that the Anti-Nephi-Lehies had repented, but not without citing the offenses: "this their great fear came because of their sore repentance which they had on account of their many murders and their awful wickedness" (Alma 27:23).

In modern times, is it not understandable that the people of Zarahemla might not want to bring these new immigrants—refugees, really—into the heart of the land? Wouldn't it make sense to have them inhabit a buffer zone and have them pay for their own defense? As verse 24 explains, "we will guard them from their enemies with our armies on condition that they will give us a portion of their substance to assist us that we may maintain our armies." This was a win-win; i.e., the Anti-Nephi-Lehies obtained a land for their inheritance, but the Nephites obtained a militarized buffer zone, paid for by the Anti-Nephi-Lehies.

Verse 26 tells us where Ammon had kept the people while they waited for him to return. "And they went down into the land of Jershon and took possession of the land of Jershon."

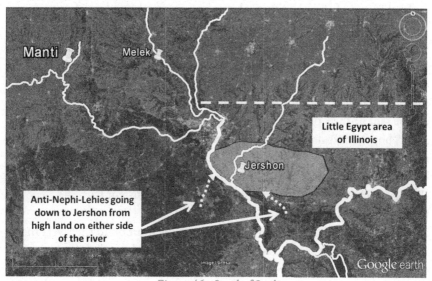

Figure 46 - Land of Jershon

Alma 28:1-3 explains what happened next. I break it out for easier reading.

Jonathan Neville

1 And now it came to pass that

i) after the people of Ammon were established in the land of Jershon, and
ii) a church also established in the land of Jershon, and
iii) the armies of the Nephites were set round about the land of Jershon, yea, in all the borders round about the land of Zarahemla;
iv) behold the armies of the Lamanites had followed their brethren into the wilderness.

2 And thus there was a tremendous battle; yea, even such an one as never had been known among all the people in the land from the time Lehi left Jerusalem; yea, and tens of thousands of the Lamanites were slain and scattered abroad.

3 Yea, and also there was a tremendous slaughter among the people of Nephi; nevertheless, the Lamanites were driven and scattered, and the people of Nephi returned again to their land.

In this area of Illinois, about where the southern boundary of my proposed land of Jershon is, a series of ancient stone forts form a line across the peninsula. Archaeologists have found artifacts that suggest the area was occupied by seasonal hunters dating back to 600 A.D., but that activity doesn't explain the stone walls and other apparent fortifications. "Despite significant archaeological work at those sites, nothing irrefutably conclusive can be said of their purpose."[149] No burial sites have been found in the area so far, but the text doesn't explain where these battles took place. The stone forts in Illinois may have served more as staging areas or early warning barricades than as forts in the traditional sense. Still, the stone forts in Illinois, many of which can be visited today, are consistent with the proposed setting of Jershon.

Because the Lamanites followed the people of Ammon to the rivers that formed the boundary between the lands of Nephi and Zarahemla, many of the battles may have occurred along the waterfront. Numerous burial mounds once existed along the river boundaries of southern Illinois, although few have been preserved. Alma 28:11 says, "the bodies of many thousands are moldering in heaps upon the face of the earth," an apt description.

Alma 30-33

In about 76 B.C., Korihor appears in the land of Zarahemla, preaching against the gospel, "leading away the hearts of many, causing them to lift up their heads in their wickedness" (Alma 30:18). He visits the land of Jershon, but the people of Ammon "were more wise than many of the Nephites for they took him and bound him and carried him before Ammon who was a high priest over that people" (Alma 30:20). Ammon banishes Korihor, so he goes to Gideon to teach. The high priest there, Giddonah, sends him up the river to Alma in Zarahemla, where he is stuck dumb.

Eventually Korihor makes his way to the land of Antionum, where the Zoramites had settled after separating themselves from the Nephites. After the Zoramites kill Korihor, Alma decides to go on a mission to the land. This is about 74 B.C.

The geography is outlined in Alma 31:3, which looks like this in parallel format:

Now the Zoramites had gathered themselves together in a land
which they called Antionum,
which was east of the land of Zarahemla,
which lay nearly bordering upon the seashore,
which was south of the land of Jershon,
which also bordered upon the wilderness south,
 - which wilderness was full of the Lamanites.

The Book of Mormon Onomasticon suggests the name Antionum "may derive from the gold antion (Alma 11:19), the most valuable unit of Nephite money... It is a fitting name for the Zoramite city of pride and wealth (Alma 31:3ff).[150]

The description parallels that of the land of Jershon, except Antionum is not actually bordering the seashore, and it borders the wilderness south, meaning the Ohio River. This is also the area that the Nephites had fortified prior to the huge battle with the Lamanites. I infer from this that Antionum was not in the highlands where the stone forts are, but was in the lowlands along the Ohio River.

Jonathan Neville

This location makes practical sense. It is in a strategic location along the river, which would contribute to economic prosperity. (Another impressive site, Kincaid Mounds, is located in this area and can be visited today, although current dating there goes back only to 1,050 A.D.[151]) If the area had been occupied prior to the war of 77 B.C., it was likely vacated during that war.

The setting on the Ohio River—part of the narrow strip of wilderness separating the land of Zarahemla from the land of Nephi—also explains why "the Nephites greatly feared that the Zormites would enter into a correspondence with the Lamanites and that it would be the means of great loss on the part of the Nephites" (Alma 31:3).

The wealthy Zoramites rejected Alma's message, but the more humble people respond. Alma, Amulek and the other missionaries "came over into the land of Jershon" (Alma 35:2), likely meaning they crossed the highlands where the stone forts are. In response, the Zoramites exiled those who believed Alma's teachings. Then their leader changed his mind and demanded that the people of Ammon return those who had been cast out of Antionum. Instead, the people of Ammon welcomed the refugees and gave them lands for their inheritance (Alma 35:9).

This response "did stir up the Zoramites to anger against the people of Ammon and they began to mix with the Lamanites and to stir them up also to anger against them. And thus the Zoramites and the Lamanites began to make preparations for war against the people of Ammon, and also against the Nephites. (Alma 35:10-11).

The people of Ammon had covenanted not to fight, so they left Jershon and "came over into the land of Melek" (Alma 35:13), leaving the converted Zoramites in Jershon, along with the armies of the Nephites, to fight against the Lamanites. Alma and the missionaries returned to Zarahemla. These movements are shown on the map below.

168

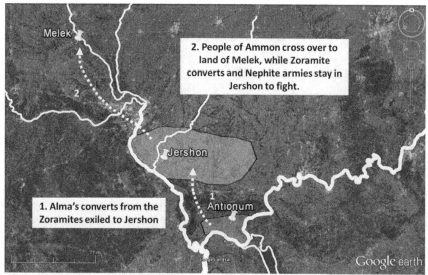

Figure 47 - Zoramite converts exiled

Alma 43-44

Chapter 43 resumes the account of the wars between the Nephites and the Lamanites. The Nephites gathered their armies in the land of Jershon, while the Lamanites came into the land of Antionum. All the leaders of the Lamanites were Amlicites (Amalekites) and Zoramites.

Captain Moroni met the Lamanites "in the borders of Jershon" (Alma 43:18), but when the Lamanites saw that the Nephites were better armed and protected with breastplates and arm-shields and thick clothing, their leaders "departed out of the land of Antionum into the wilderness, and took their journey round about in the wilderness, away by the head of the river Sidon, that they might come into the land of Manti and take possession of the land" (Alma 43:25).

From the Lamanite perspective, this made sense. Moroni had fortified the land of Jershon, and presumably the sea, or mighty river, it bordered. The Lamanites could do an end run around Jershon, past the productive (bountiful) farmland into the wilderness north, and then cross the Sidon to reach Manti.

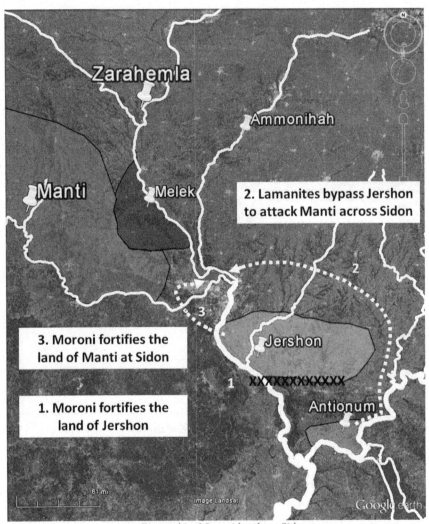

Figure 48 - Moroni battle at Sidon

The confrontation between Moroni and the Lamanites is another battle in and near the river. Moroni "found by his spies which course the Lamanites were to take" (Alma 43:30).

> 31 Therefore, he divided his army and brought a part over into the valley, and concealed them on the east, and on the south of the hill Riplah;

32 And the remainder he concealed in the west valley, on the west of the river Sidon, and so down into the borders of the land Manti.

33 And thus having placed his army according to his desire, he was prepared to meet them.

34 And it came to pass that the Lamanites came up on the north of the hill, where a part of the army of Moroni was concealed.

35 And as the Lamanites had passed the hill Riplah, and came into the valley, and began to cross the river Sidon, the army which was concealed on the south of the hill, which was led by a man whose name was Lehi, and he led his army forth and encircled the Lamanites about on the east in their rear.

36 And it came to pass that the Lamanites, when they saw the Nephites coming upon them in their rear, turned them about and began to contend with the army of Lehi.

The Nephites were better armed and protected, so "the Lamanites became frightened because of the great destruction among them even until they began to flee towards the river Sidon… and they were driven by Lehi into the waters of Sidon and Lehi retained his armies upon the bank of the river Sidon that they should not cross" (Alma 43:39-40).

Moroni had stationed the rest of his army "in the valley on the other side of the river Sidon" (Alma 43:41). When his men began to "fall upon" the Lamanites and to slay them, "the Lamanites did flee again before them towards the land of Manti and they were met again by the armies of Moroni" (Alma 43:41-2).

All of this was taking place near the "head of Sidon," because that is where the Lamanites planned to attack.

The passage describes a river that is a significant barrier, with a hill and bank on the east side and a large valley on the west side. Armies can cross it (at least at some times of the year), but it is a significant barrier. This cannot be "headwaters" as some commentators have proposed.

Another requirement: there must be a way out of the valley toward the land of Manti.

One place that fits this description nicely is where the Missouri River meets the Mississippi. On the east bank, there are hills. The west bank is a wide valley, with access to the north and west toward what would have been the land of Manti.

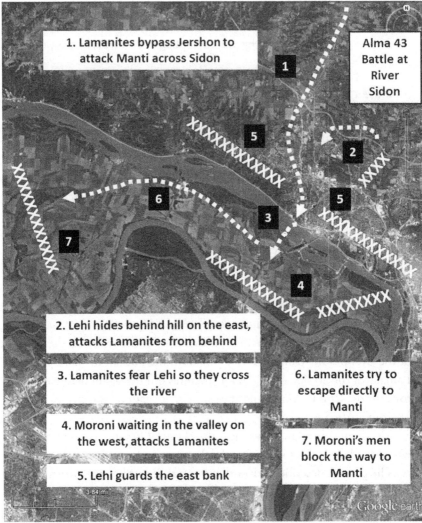

1. Lamanites bypass Jershon to attack Manti across Sidon

Alma 43 Battle at River Sidon

2. Lehi hides behind hill on the east, attacks Lamanites from behind

3. Lamanites fear Lehi so they cross the river

4. Moroni waiting in the valley on the west, attacks Lamanites

5. Lehi guards the east bank

6. Lamanites try to escape directly to Manti

7. Moroni's men block the way to Manti

Figure 49 - Alma 43 – Battle at River Sidon (modern St. Louis)

At this point, the Lamanites were surrounded. Moroni offered a truce, but Zerahemnah, the Lamanite leader, refused to enter a covenant of peace. Moroni resumed the battle until "Zerahemnah, when he saw that they were all about to be destroyed, cried mightily unto Moroni, promising that he would covenant and also his people with them, if they would spare the

remainder of their lives, that they would never come to war against them"
(Alma 44:19).

As before with the Amlicites, "they did cast their dead into the waters of
Sidon and they have gone forth and are buried in the depths of the sea"
(Alma 44:22).

Alma 45-62

The rest of the Book of Alma describes the wars between the Nephites
and the Lamanites from about 73 B.C. to about 57 B.C. The Nephite
civilization was expanding eastward, as described by Mormon in Alma 22. It
was during this period that the Nephites expanded into the east, including to
areas where the Jaredites had lived.

One author has identified around one hundred instances of armed
conflict described in the text.[152] In fact, as John W. Welch has pointed out,

> One powerful dimension of historicity of the Book of Mormon is the sheer
> complexity of the record. The amazing achievement of the Book of Mormon is
> not the fact that it is a big book containing numerous chapters on warfare, but
> the stark reality that those chapters are complicated and consistent. They present
> an involved military history that presupposes, reflects, and visualizes an entire
> civilization and its worldview on warfare.... Another indicator of historicity is
> realism. The human and social events recorded in the Book of Mormon are
> realistic. They make sense in light of the way people and nations in fact
> behave.[153]

Placing the Book of Mormon events in North America enhances the
historicity of the account because the text lines up so well with the real-world
geography.

There were two major fronts involved with these wars. The
western/southern front was along the Sidon corridor. The eastern/northern
front focused on the small neck of land between the land southward and the
land northward, the area in western New York where the narrow strip of
wilderness—the river systems—ends. Control of this area gave access to the
interior of the Nephite territory in Ohio.

It is tempting to play war games and identify particular sites as Book of
Mormon locations,[154] but there are dozens of potential archaeological sites in

North America to consider, and many more that have been obliterated. The text names some locations and provides vague geographical references, but also says "they also began in that same year to build many cities on the north" (Alma 50:15). The land northward includes everything north of the narrow strip of wilderness, including Ohio and New York.

Figure 50 depicts some of the mounds and enclosures in Ohio.[155]

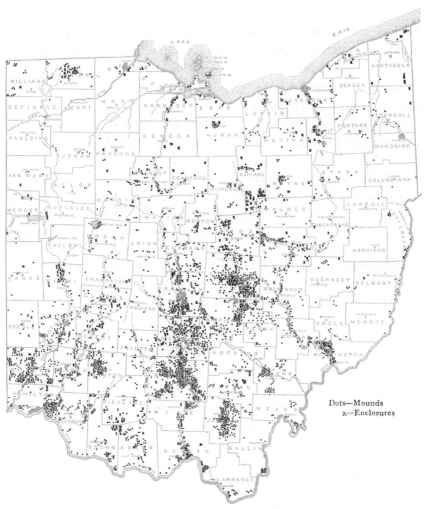

Dots—Mounds
x—Enclosures

Figure 50 - Mounds in Ohio

Several of the cities in the Book of Mormon are described as being near the sea. Figure 51 shows a few known ancient sites located in and around Cleveland, Ohio, at the edge of the sea (Lake Erie). Kirtland is in the upper right corner. Two thousand years ago, in Nephite times, the Great Lakes were higher than they are today, which would put the Kirtland area close to the shoreline.

Additional archaeological exploration in this area may yet uncover more relevant information. With the limited information we have now, we could plausibly place a Book of Mormon city in the Kirtland area.

Figure 51 - Ancient sites near Kirtland

Of all the places on Earth, the Lord chose Kirtland, Ohio, as the site for the first temple of this dispensation and the site for the restoration of the Priesthood keys by Moses, Elias, and Elijah. The Lord himself appeared here to Joseph Smith and Oliver Cowdery (D&C 110). Was the site where Joseph built the temple just a random location, chosen because it was on a hill, or does it have more significance?

Ohio is the proposed area for the land of Bountiful, and it was at the temple in the land of Bountiful where the Lord appeared to the Nephites after his resurrection. That's not to say that Kirtland was the site of that ancient temple, but I think it is possible that the Kirtland site is important not only in modern Church history, but in Book of Mormon history.

Challenge of war gaming

One way to illustrate the challenge of trying to locate Book of Mormon sites without any pins in the map is to look at what has taken place in Central America. Figure 52 shows six proposed sites for Zarahemla.[156]

Figure 52 - Zarahemlas proposed

Other researchers have proposed additional sites in Mesoamerica, each with their pros and cons.

Even with the Cumorah pin in New York and the Zarahemla pin in Iowa, locating other Book of Mormon sites remains a matter of opinion based on evaluation of the various criteria. The overall point of the North American geography is to harmonize all the evidence and to realize that Moroni's America is the promised land.

That said, I will address a few of the passages in the war chapters.

Mounds and fortifications

As you read the war chapters, notice how often Moroni uses dirt and earth to fortify positions. The text describes the earthworks in the Midwestern United States so well that early detractors insisted Joseph Smith was describing these sites, although he had never visited them in person. He had seen the Nephite civilization in vision, but that is an explanation his critics could never accept.

I have visited many of these sites myself, and I encourage you to visit them if you get a chance. Pictures alone don't convey the massive size of some of the few earthworks that still remain from Nephite times. Many of the most impressive sites are long gone, preserved only in the drawings of Squire and Davis in their 1848 book, *Ancient Monuments of the Mississippi Valley*, which I've mentioned before.[157]

I will highlight one example from Alma 49 to give an idea of what exists in North America.

Alma 46

This chapter tells about Captain Moroni raising the title of liberty. One can imagine Mormon selecting this incident because of Moroni's powerful prayer "for the blessings of liberty to rest upon his brethren, so long as there should a band of Christians remain to possess the land" (Alma 46:13). That would resonate for Mormon, who tried in vain to persuade his own people to repent. And, of course, it has significance for those who live in America today.

And it came to pass that when he had poured out his soul to God, he named all the land which was south of the land Desolation, yea, and in fine, all the land, both on the north and on the south—A chosen land, and the land of liberty.

And he said: Surely God shall not suffer that we, who are despised because we take upon us the name of Christ, shall be trodden down and destroyed, until we bring it upon us by our own transgressions. (Alma 46:17-18)

This passage can be interpreted two ways. Maybe Moroni meant to name only the land south of the land Desolation as "a chosen land, and the land of liberty." By saying "all the land, both on the north and on the south," he would be referring to the greater land of Zarahemla and the land of Nephi, intending to inspire and liberate all the "seed of Jacob" (Alma 46:23) who lived on the promised land. This would include Nephites and Lamanites.

Alternatively, he could have meant only the land of Zarahemla, which was south of the land Desolation, and he said "both on the north and on the south" to show that he sought a united Zarahemla.

Finally, he could have meant not only the land south of Desolation, but all the land, including Desolation.

I favor the first interpretation because I think Moroni was describing what I now call Moroni's America—a chosen land, and the land of liberty.

If so, we should consider whether the covenant Moroni and his people entered is still applicable today: "Now this was the covenant which they made, and they cast their garments at the feet of Moroni, saying: We covenant with our God, that we shall be destroyed, even as our brethren in the land northward, if we shall fall into transgression; yea, he may cast us at the feet of our enemies, even as we have cast our garments at thy feet to be trodden under foot, if we shall fall into transgression." (Alma 46:22).

Alma 49-50

In Alma 49, the Lamanites approach the land of Ammonihah. Mormon describes some of the defensive structures and strategies that Captain Moroni employed. Some of these were built to protect cities; others were strategic defensive positions manned by the army to protect the borders. There were also "small forts, or places of resort" (Alma 48:8). Here are verses from Alma 49.

2. And behold, the city had been rebuilt, and Moroni had stationed an army by the borders of the city, and **they had cast up dirt round about** to shield them from the arrows and the stones of the Lamanites; for behold, they fought with stones and with arrows.

4. But behold, how great was their disappointment; for behold, the Nephites had **dug up a ridge of earth round about them**, which was so high that the Lamanites could not cast their stones and their arrows at them that they might take effect, neither could they come upon them save it was by their place of entrance. (Alma 49:2, 4)

18 Now behold, the Lamanites could not get into their forts of security by any other way save by the entrance, because of **the highness of the bank** which had been thrown up, and **the depth of the ditch** which had been dug round about, save it were by the entrance.

A site in southwest Ohio, near Hamilton,[158] fits this description. Squier and Davis describe the location as being the summit of a hill about 250 feet high. "It is surrounded at all points, except a narrow space at the north, by deep ravines, presenting steep and almost in accessible declivities. The descent towards the north is gradual; and from that direction, the hill is easy of access."[159] The interior of the fortification rises in elevation so that from the top, occupants can overlook the entire adjacent countryside.

This fortified hill is not unique in this area. Squier and Davis explain:

In the vicinity of this work, are a number of others occupying the valley; no less than six of large size occur within a distance of six miles down the river. The character of this structure is too obvious to admit of doubt. The position which it occupies is naturally strong, and no mean degree of skill is employed in its artificial defences. Every avenue is strongly guarded. The principle approach, the only point easy of access, or capable of successful assault, is rendered doubly secure. A mound, used perhaps as an alarm post, is placed at about one-fourth of the distance down the ascent; a crescent wall crosses the isthmus, leaving but narrow passages between its ends and the steeps on either hand. Next comes the principal wall of the enclosure. In event of an attack, even though both these defences were carried, there still remains a series of walls so complicated as inevitably to distract and bewilder the assailants, thus giving a marked advantage to the defenders.[160]

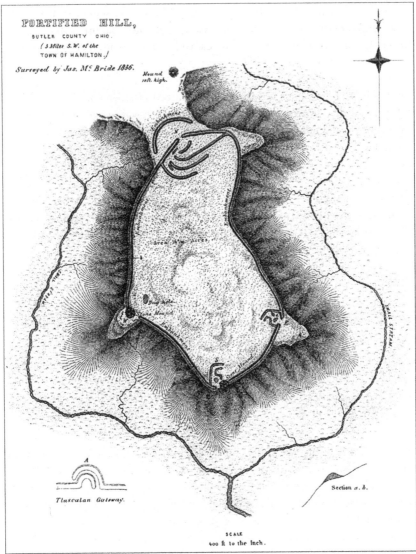

Figure 53 - Fortified Hill, Ohio

Notice how the "place of entrance" is set up to force intruders through a maze of well-defended positions. This is the type of "place of resort" where civilians could be protected with a minimal force, while the army could watch over the surrounding area.

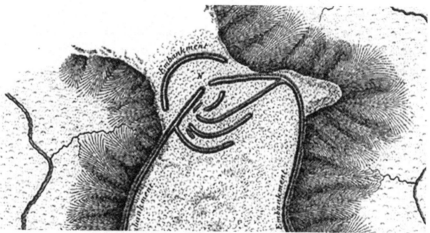

Figure 54 - Place of Entrance

The steep banks at the southern part of the fortification contain similar mazes.

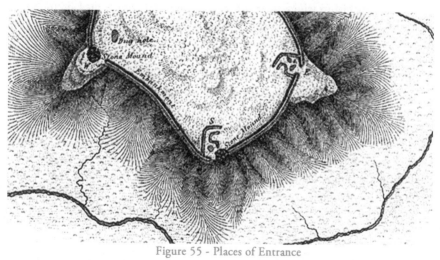

Figure 55 - Places of Entrance

There is not enough information in the text to identify this as a particular Nephite location, but it illustrates a manner of building defenses that the text describes. This site was surveyed in 1836, well after the Book of Mormon was published.

In Alma 50, Moroni continued preparations for war, causing his armies "that they should commence in digging up heaps of earth round about all the cities" (Alma 50:1). They built "works of timbers" on top of the ridges of earth, with a frame of pickets and towers.

With fortifications in place, Moroni took the offensive. Perhaps he saw this as a partial fulfillment of the title of liberty; i.e., he sought to liberate all the remnant of the seed of Joseph.

> 7 And it came to pass that Moroni caused that his armies should go forth into the east wilderness; yea, and they went forth and drove all the Lamanites who were in the east wilderness into their own lands, which were south of the land of Zarahemla.

> 8 And the land of Nephi did run in a straight course from the east sea to the west.

> 9 And it came to pass that when Moroni had driven all the Lamanites out of the east wilderness, which was north of the lands of their own possessions, he caused that the inhabitants who were in the land of Zarahemla and in the land round about should go forth into the east wilderness, even to the borders by the seashore, and possess the land.

> 10 And he also placed armies on the south, in the borders of their possessions, and caused them to erect fortifications that they might secure their armies and their people from the hands of their enemies.

> 11 And thus he cut off all the strongholds of the Lamanites in the east wilderness, yea, and also on the west, fortifying the line between the Nephites and the Lamanites, between the land of Zarahemla and the land of Nephi, from the west sea, running by the head of the river Sidon—the Nephites possessing all the land northward, yea, even all the land which was northward of the land Bountiful, according to their pleasure.

A key point here is that the east wilderness was "north of the lands of their own possessions." This is true whether he refers to the Nephites or the Lamanites; i.e., the east wilderness was south of the narrow strip of wilderness, but because the Ohio and Allegheny rivers flow from the north, the east wilderness is actually north of much of the land of Zarahemla (including the land Bountiful).

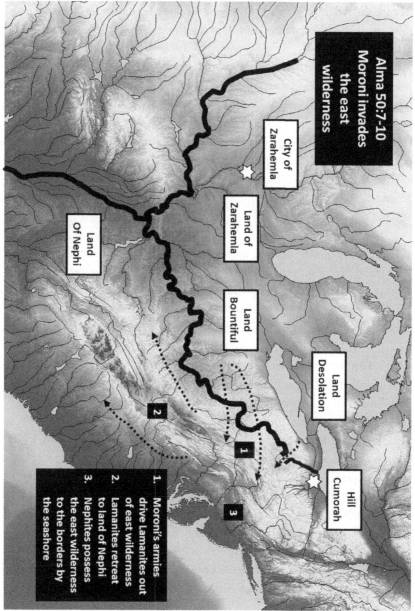

Figure 56 - Alma 50

When Moroni drove the Lamanites down to the land of Nephi, south of Zarahemla, he extended Nephite territory all the way east to the seashore, in this case the Atlantic. At that point, the land of the Lamanites ran in a straight east/west line instead of following the narrow strip of wilderness northeast.

When Moroni "cut off all the strongholds of the Lamanites in the east wilderness," it was a smart strategic move because it removed the vulnerability from the small neck of land between the rivers that formed the narrow strip of wilderness. He was then able to fortify the rest of the narrow strip, the "line between the Nephites and the Lamanites, between the land of Zarahemla and the land of Nephi, from the west sea running by the head of the river Sidon" (Alma 50:11).

Alma 51-62

These chapters describe the battles between the Nephites and Lamanites, the political problems among the Nephites, and Moroni's eventual victory. The war was fought in to major fronts. The southwestern front was in the land of Manti, where Helaman's army, including the 2,000 stripling warriors, fought the Lamanites who had gained ground by the west sea south (Alma 53:8). Moroni fought mainly in the east, in the land Bountiful, but he had to return to Gideon to rescue Pahoran and restore him to the judgment-seat in Zarahemla (Alma 62:6-8).

As I mentioned, these chapters can be mapped with several variations depending on the assumptions one wants to make. It's important to remember that these events took place about 62-57 B.C., with centuries of Nephite civilization and warfare yet ahead before the final battles that culminated in Cumorah. Even by the time Mormon and Moroni wrote, these sites would have been historical locations with little evidence of the original battles, the way Revolutionary and Civil War sites are to us today.

Nevertheless, it is possible that someday we will be able to identify a particular archaeological site as the city of Nephihah. (Alma 62:18-30). The text tells us the city is near the "plains of Nephihah," which I infer is among the plains of the Nephites Joseph Smith observed in Ohio, Indiana or

Illinois. Which of the dozens or hundreds of ancient sites in those states might be Nephihah awaits further research.

Ultimately, Moroni did defeat the Lamanites and "drive them out of the land" (Alma 62:38).

Mormon concludes his account of the wars with important insights:

39 And thus ended the thirty and first year of the reign of the judges over the people of Nephi; and thus they had had wars, and bloodsheds, and famine, and affliction, for the space of many years.

40 And there had been murders, and contentions, and dissensions, and all manner of iniquity among the people of Nephi; nevertheless for the righteous' sake, yea, because of the prayers of the righteous, they were spared.

41 But behold, because of the exceedingly great length of the war between the Nephites and the Lamanites many had become hardened, because of the exceedingly great length of the war; and many were softened because of their afflictions, insomuch that they did humble themselves before God, even in the depth of humility.

Alma 63

In the 37th year, "there was a large company of men, even to the amount of five thousand and four hundred men, with their wives and their children, departed out of the land of Zarahemla into the land which was northward." This would make a group of 10-20,000, depending on family size. The text does not explain whether these people sailed north or traveled overland. It doesn't even specify from where in the land of Zarahemla they left. All we know is that the land was "northward" from Zarahemla.

Whether they sailed or hiked, it seems unlikely that such a large group would veer far from a river. At a minimum, they would need a constant supply of water. The text says nothing about herds or grain; presumably the people would prefer fresh sources of food from fishing.

Two rivers they could follow north are the Illinois and Mississippi Rivers and their tributaries. Because the text does not say they left from the city of Zarahemla (on the west bank of the Mississippi), it seems more likely they would follow the Illinois River out of the land. This would have led them in

Jonathan Neville

proximity to the southern part of Lake Michigan and the Michigan peninsula.

The text suggests this northward migration piqued the curiosity of a man named Hagoth.

> 5 And it came to pass that Hagoth, he being an exceedingly curious man, therefore he went forth and built him an exceedingly large ship, on the borders of the land Bountiful, by the land Desolation, and launched it forth into the west sea, by the narrow neck which led into the land northward.

> 6 And behold, there were many of the Nephites who did enter therein and did sail forth with much provisions, and also many women and children; and they took their course northward. And thus ended the thirty and seventh year.

The story of Hagoth shows the Nephites were proficient in shipbuilding, as Mormon implies in Helaman 3:14. Mormon does not mention Hagoth because he built a ship; he mentioned Hagoth because he built an *exceedingly large* ship. Because the entire civilization was founded by seafarers, it would be more surprising if the Nephites did *not* use ships than if they did, and Hagoth demonstrates that they knew how to build ships.

One wonders why he built such a large ship and which Nephites became passengers. Given the sequence of events, it is possible that the "large company of men" sailed north on the Illinois River, reaching the source. They would continue overland to the "land which was northward" where they reached the west sea and sent word back to Hagoth. Then Hagoth came north and built an "exceedingly large ship" to accommodate "many of the Nephites" who had gone northward.

Why did all these people go northward? One reason could be natural expansion; i.e., the Nephite population was growing and the Lamanites occupied all the land south of Zarahemla. The east (Bountiful) was already populated. The west may have been less appealing. Another reason could be economic opportunity in the north, perhaps associated with the abundant copper on the Keweenaw Peninsula where hundreds of ancient mines have been found.[161]

The text says Hagoth built his ship "on the borders of the land Bountiful by the land Desolation." This implies he constructed it inland, presumably in a protected area that would be deep enough, like on a river or inlet. From the construction site, he "launched it forth into the west sea by the narrow neck which led into the land northward."

This passage is susceptible to more than one meaning. Of course, a "narrow neck" can be either water or land, and the text doesn't explain which it is in this case (unlike Ether 10:20, which specifies a "narrow neck of land").

I discussed the various "narrow" features in the geography in Chapter 6. The Oxford English Dictionary includes these definitions of *neck*:

5. d. A pass between hills or mountains; the narrow part of a mountain pass.
5. e. A narrow channel or inlet of water; the narrow part of a sound, etc.
7. a. A narrow piece of land with water on each side; an isthmus or narrow promontory.
7. b. A narrow stretch of wood, pasture, ice, etc.

No mountains or woods are mentioned in Alma 63, so presumably we are dealing with 1) a narrow channel or inlet of water; 2) the narrow part of a sound; 3) an isthmus; 4) or a narrow promontory.

A common interpretation treats *by* as a synonym of *near*, i.e., Hagoth launched his ship into the west sea *near* the narrow neck, and the narrow neck leads into the land northward. This interpretation assumes the neck was a neck of land, but it's not clear how a neck of *land* would lead *into* a larger land mass. A neck of land would lead *to* a larger land mass, but not *into* one. This interpretation also raises the question of why the narrow neck is associated with the launch, but not the construction, of the ship. That is, Hagoth built the ship *by* the land Desolation but launched it *by* the narrow neck that led into the land northward.

A second interpretation assumes that because Hagoth built the ship inland, the narrow neck could be the neck of a river that led *into*—meaning penetrated—the land northward.

A third possibility is that the narrow neck was a waterway—a narrow channel or inlet—by means of which he launched his ship into the sea. In this case, the relative pronoun *which* would refer back to the west sea; i.e., the west sea leads into the land northward.

Yet another interpretation would have the launching itself constitute what led into the land northward. A comma after neck would clarify this meaning; i.e., "launched it forth into the west sea by the narrow neck, which led into the land northward."

This interpretation is somewhat corroborated by the sequence of events. Hagoth built the ship by the land Desolation, launched it into the west sea, then picked up his passengers and took their course northward. Clearly, the west sea led into the land northward; it's only a question of whether, and how, the narrow neck did also.

The text distinguishes between the land northward and the land Desolation. Again, this reflects the relative nature of these terms. Often in the text, the land Desolation is northward. Here, the frame of reference is near the land Desolation where Hagoth built his ship. Consequently, the land northward in these passages is *north* of Desolation.

Verse 7 points out that the first ship returned "and set out again to the land northward." That seems inconsistent with the idea that Hagoth's departure point was close to the land northward, which would be the case if it was next to a narrow neck that led into that land. His passengers were boarding a ship in the west sea because that *sea* led into the land northward, not because the narrow neck did.

There are several places along Lake Michigan that would qualify as a "narrow neck" under the definitions given. The lake today is at around 577 feet above sea level. There are areas such as Benton Harbor where the land is only a few feet higher than the lake. In ancient times, when the lake was higher, the harbor would have been much bigger than it is today, surrounded by peninsulas—narrow necks.[162] It would be a good place to build an exceedingly large ship, and then launch it into the west sea.

This all becomes clearer by referencing the map in Figure 57.

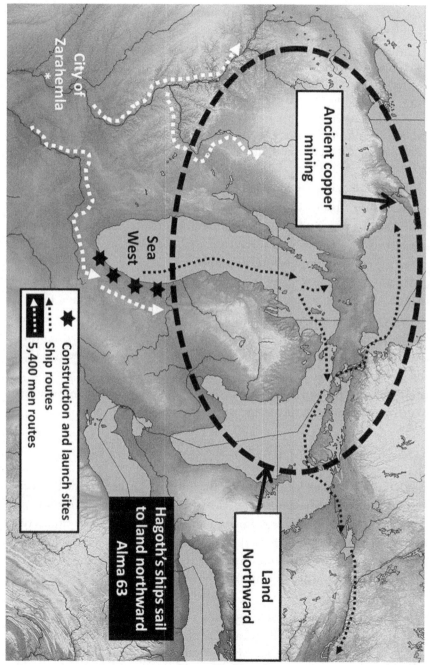

Figure 57 - Hagoth

Jonathan Neville

Hagoth was not satisfied with only one ship.

7 And in the thirty and eighth year, this man built other ships. And the first ship did also return, and many more people did enter into it; and they also took much provisions, and set out again to the land northward.

8 And it came to pass that they were never heard of more. And we suppose that they were drowned in the depths of the sea. And it came to pass that one other ship also did sail forth; and whither she did go we know not.

The text does not say in what month of the thirty-seventh year Hagoth launched his first ship, or in what month it returned in the thirty-eighth year. The first ship could have been gone an entire year, only a few months, or nearly two years. I assume it returned after about a year, only because Hagoth built other ships before it returned.

At any rate, the first voyage was successful. Either the ship sailed for six months, discovered something worth exploring, and turned around for supplies for an even longer expedition, or it spent some period of time—a winter, perhaps—at its destination before returning. It may have dropped off passengers at various locations, such as the mining areas in northern Michigan, and then continued exploring. There was at least one permanent community in the land northward because Alma's son Corianton went forth to deliver provisions to the people who had settled there (Alma 63:10).

Polynesia

One aspect of the Hagoth verses is the link that has been made between Hagoth and the Polynesian people. Although the text says the Nephites thought Hagoth's people were drowned at sea, there are LDS traditions that Hagoth's people went to Japan, Hawaii, and Polynesian Islands.[163]

Without commenting on the merits of these traditions, is the North American setting consistent with them?

The answer is yes.

Although the common view regarding Hagoth is that he launched his boats directly into the Pacific Ocean (i.e., the west sea), his ships could have arrived in the Pacific from Lake Michigan also. Figure 50 shows a northeast waterway that leads to the St. Lawrence Seaway. From there, a ship could

190

navigate to the Pacific by going south around South America or north through the Northwest passage and down through the Bering Strait.

In a 1976 talk to the Samoans, President Kimball referred to the scattering of Israel in connection with the Polynesians. He said, "Some of them remained in America and went from Alaska to the southern point."[164] That could be consistent with the Northwest Passage route.

Other traditions refer to the ancestors of the Maoris coming from "the joining of two waters."[165] Although Matthew Cowley and others interpreted that phrase to refer to the "narrow neck of land between two bodies of water," meaning Central America, the two waters do not join there. Two waters join at the southern tip of South America: the Atlantic and the Pacific.

The North American setting doesn't establish the Hagoth-Polynesia link, but it doesn't contradict it, either.

NOTES

---

[134] One source has compiled these maps into a composite image of much of the Mississippi River. It is online here: http://bit.ly/Moroni76.

[135] The Zelph's Mound incident has generated considerable debate, mainly because Mesoamerican advocates seek to discredit the account. During Zion's camp, some of the men spotted a large mound along the Illinois River with a stone altar on the top. Joseph Smith and some of his brethren ascended the large mound where they dug up a large skeleton. Several accounts were written. Here is what Wilford Woodruff wrote:

While on our travels we visited many of the mounds which were flung up by the ancient inhabitants of this continent probably by the Nephites & Lamanites. We visited one of those Mounds and several of the brethren dug into it and took from it the bones of a man.

We visited one of those Mounds: considerd to be 300 feet above the level of the Illinois river. Three persons dug into the mound & found a body. Elder Milton Holmes took the arrow out of the back bones that killed Zelph & brought it with some of the bones in to the camp. I visited the same mound with Jesse J. Smith. Who the other persons were that dug in to the mound & found the body I am undecided.

Brother Joseph had a vission respecting the person. He said he was a white Lamanite. The curs was taken from him or at least in part. He was killed in battle with an arrow. The arrow was found among his ribs. One of his thigh bones was broken. This was done by a stone flung from a sling in battle years before his death. His name was Zelph. Some of his bones were brought into the Camp and the thigh bone which was broken was put into my waggon and I carried it to Missouri. Zelph was a large thick set man and a man of God. He was a warrior under the great prophet /Onandagus/ that was known from the hill Camorah /or east sea/ to the Rocky mountains. The above knowledge Joseph receieved in a vision. (spelling original)

For more information, see Donald Q. Cannon, "Zelph Revisited," in *Church History Regional Studies-Illinois*, BYU Department of Church History and Doctrine, 97-109, available online here: http://bit.ly/Moroni77. Note that Woodruff uses the Book of Mormon term "east sea" in proximity to the Hill Camorah [Cumorah].

[136] The Manti accounts are susceptible to various interpretations. For a discussion of the controversy regarding the Manti accounts, see bookofmormonwars.blogspot.com.

[137] Some commentators claim the lands named after the cities must have been relatively small, but I don't think the text sets forth any such limitation.

[138] Diagram and photo of Malchow courtesy of Wayne May.

[139] See the National Park Service report here http://bit.ly/Moroni78 and a teachers guide from the State Historical Society of Iowa here http://bit.ly/Moroni79.

[140] The name "Manti" is of uncertain origin, but possibly related to an Egyptian prince in Upper Egypt circa 650 B.C., as explained in the Book of Mormon Onomasticon here http://bit.ly/Moroni80. It is used four ways in the text:
1. Hill of, on which NEHOR is executed, 1st cent. B.C. (Alma 1:15)
2. NEPHITE soldier sent to watch AMLICITES, 1st cent. B.C. (Alma 2:22)

3. NEPHITE land of, on southern border with LAMANITES (Alma 16:6, 7; 17:1; 22:27; 43:22, 24, 25, 32, 42; 59:6).

4. NEPHITE city of, chief city of land of Manti (56:14; 57:22; 58:1, 13, 25, 26, 27, 28, 39).

[141] Total casualties were higher; this is just the number of men killed. http://bit.ly/Moroni81. By comparison, 7,550 were killed at Gettysburg over three days.

[142] Notice there is no mention of crossing any river in these verses. Some commentators claim the Amlicites and spies crossed the Sidon River to the west bank, and then the spies crossed back over to the east bank to return to Alma. It probably doesn't make much difference, but I think the text would mention two river crossings.

[143] Royal Skousen, *Analysis of Textual Variants of the Book of Mormon* Part 3 (Provo, Utah: FARMS, 2007), p. 1605, Discussion of Alma 2:11-12.

[144] Kirk Magleby sorted out the chronology on his blog here: http://bit.ly/Moroni82. I don't follow his chronology exactly, but it was a helpful starting point. I highly recommend his blog, http://bookofmormonresources.blogspot.com/ for its excellent scholarship and analysis (apart from the references to Mesoamerica).

[145] See "Anti-Nephi-Lehi" in the Book of Mormon Onomasticon, http://bit.ly/Moroni83.

[146] Dan Guillory, "The Dilemma of Dickson Mounds," http://bit.ly/Moroni84.

[147] "Jershon," Book of Mormon Onomasticon, http://bit.ly/Moroni85.

[148] Judge Andrew D. Duff, "Egypt," *Springhouse Magazine*, from *The Golconda Weekly*, Nov. 23, 1871, http://bit.ly/Moroni86.

[149] Joe McFarland, "Wall of Mystery," http://bit.ly/Moroni87.

[150] "Antionum," Book of Mormon Onomasticon, http://bit.ly/Moroni88.

[151] Directions and information are available here. http://bit.ly/Moroni89.

[152] John L. Sorenson, Appendix: Annals of the Nephite wars, in "Seasonality of Warfare in the Book of Mormon and in Mesoamerica," in *Warfare in the Book of Mormon*, edited by Stephen D. Ricks and William J. Hamblin (Deseret Book Company and FARMS, 1990), p. pp. 462-474. Available online at http://bit.ly/Moroni90. This is an excellent resource for studying the wars, with the caveat that the comparisons to Mesoamerica detract from the analysis. For example, Sorenson identifies a "seasonal pattern for fighting" that he thinks reflects seasons in Mesoamerica. He shows wars being fought in the 10th through 5th months, but not at all in months 6-9. If the Nephites used a Jewish calendar, this would mean they fought from February through August (April is usually the first month), but not at all in September through December. That's a perfect fit for the fall harvest in North America; i.e., you need people working in the fields, not fighting, in the fall.

[153] John W. Welch, "Why Study Warfare in the Book of Mormon?" in *Warfare in the Book of Mormon*, p. 17.

[154] There are numerous books and web pages that have mapped out the various invasions and defensive actions. A good example is Map 9 in Sorenson's book Mormon's Codex. I've done that myself and I was tempted to include a map here, but there are many candidates for Book of Mormon sites, and many that formerly existed but have been destroyed. My objective in this book was to provide an overview of the North American setting. I'm working on a more detailed book that incorporates specific archaeological sites.

---

[155] D. Case, *The Scioto Hopewell and Their Neighbors* (Springer Science + Business Media, 2008), Figure 7.2 Ohio Mounds and Enclosures, available online at http://bit.ly/Moroni91.

[156] Map adapted from "Zarahemla ca. 1955," Book of Mormon Resources.blogspot.com, http://bit.ly/Moroni148.

[157] There are abundant online resources that document the moundbuilders, including the National Park Service here: http://www.nps.gov/mwac/index.htm. For an LDS perspective, see the books and articles by Wayne May and Rod Meldrum. Unfortunately, many LDS scholars have focused on Mesoamerica instead of North America. Hopefully this will change in the future.

[158] The site can be seen on google maps here: http://bit.ly/Moroni143.

[159] Squier and Davis, *Ancient Monuments of the Mississippi Valley*, p. 17.

[160] Ibid, pp. 17-18.

[161] "The Native Americans used the copper from this area for the last 6800 years. The natives mined the copper from the bedrock as well as from glacial deposits. The entire peninsula from Keweenaw Point to the Ontonagon River area contain ancient mining pits. The deposits on Isle Royale were also mined by natives (a conservative estimate is that there were at least 1089 pits on the island)." Collector's Corner, Mineralogical Society of America, http://bit.ly/Moroni144.

[162] One "analysis of 115 geographic features English-speaking colonists called a 'neck of land'" concluded that the Book of Mormon narrow neck of land would be a peninsula rather than an isthmus because 113 of the 115 features studied were peninsulas. "Necks of Land," Book of Mormon Resources, http://bit.ly/Moroni145. Of course, if the narrow neck here was a water feature, it would not be a peninsula.

[163] For a thorough overview of LDS teachings, see Robert E. Parsons, "Hagoth and the Polynesians," in *The Book of Mormon: Alma, the Testimony of the Word*, ed. Monte S. Nyman and Charles D. Tate Jr., (Religious Studies Center, BYU 1992), 249-62, online at http://bit.ly/Moroni146. Genetic data suggests the Polynesians came from Southeast Asia and Taiwan. See K. R. Howe, "Ideas of Maori Origins," The Encyclopedia of New Zealand, available online at http://bit.ly/Moroni147.

[164] Parsons, op cit.

[165] Parsons, opcit.

Chapter 17 – Helaman

Helaman 1

THE FIRST CHAPTER OF HELAMAN SUMMARIZES AN INVASION of Nephite territory by Coriantumr, a descendant of Zarahemla who had dissented from among the Nephites (Helaman 1:15). In about 52 B.C., Tubaloth, the king of the Lamanites, appointed Coriantumr as the leader of the Lamanite armies and "did cause that they should march down to the land of Zarahemla to battle against the Nephites" (Helaman 1:17).

The term *march* deserves comment. Does verse 17 necessarily mean Coriantumr and his arm walked in step all the way to Zarahemla?

That seems unlikely, no matter how great the distance. (The text does not say where Coriantumr's "march" originated, but other travelers from Lamanite territory to Zarahemla took between 20 and 40 days—an exceptionally long march for men traveling by foot in full armor, all while carrying a full complement of weapons.)

The normal connotation of the term, as explained in the Oxford English Dictionary (OED), means "to walk in a military manner with regular and measured tread."[166] However, the text does not imply that Lamanite armies were characterized by military discipline. To the contrary, they are often indecisive, fearful, and easy to scatter.

March can also mean "to approach or enter (a city; etc.) in an organized procession" as a military incursion, or more generally, "to go, proceed." Calvary riders can be said to "march" even though they are riding horses, so long as they are advancing as a body or military formation.

These definitions suggest the term *march* may not be limited to walking; it has a broader application than we might think initially. Its meaning depends on the context and circumstances.

Jonathan Neville

OED also includes a definition based on context: "To travel, esp. by canoe or dog-sledge... 'To march' is the Canadian term for travelling, and is as frequently, if not oftener, applied to express the progress of a canoe or boat as of a pedestrian." Also, "'To march' for instance, generally, is applied to any progression—including canoe or boat travel."

With these alternatives, it is plausible that when Coriantumr "marched" at the head of his army, he was actually leading them from a ship or canoe. The scripture explains why the Nephites didn't resist: "because of so much contention and so much difficulty in the government that they [the Nephites] had not kept sufficient guards in the land of Zarahemla" (Helaman 1:18). Another factor: Coriantumr's "march was with such exceedingly great speed that there was no time for the Nephites to gather their armies" (Helaman 1:19). An approach by water explains how Coriantumr arrived so fast. It is implausible that his army could have moved with that rate of speed after being afoot for 20 or more days.

The assault on the city also suggests an entrance from the water, as no wall is mentioned until after then Lamanites entered the city. "Coriantumr did cut down the watch by the entrance of the city and did march forth with his whole army into the city and they did slay every one who did oppose them insomuch that they did take possession of the whole city" (Helaman 1:20). Once they reached the shore, the men would be advancing on foot. The chief judge, Pacumeni, "did flee before Coriantumr, even to the walls of the city" where Coriantumr "did smite him against the wall, insomuch that he died" (Helaman 1:21).

With this easy success, Coriantumr decided to take the city of Bountiful.

And now he did not tarry in the land of Zarahemla, but he did march forth with a large army, even towards the city of Bountiful; for it was his determination to go forth and cut his way through with the sword, that he might obtain the north parts of the land.
And, supposing that their greatest strength was in the center of the land, therefore he did march forth, giving them no time to assemble themselves together save it were in small bodies; and in this manner they did fall upon them and cut them down to the earth. (Helaman 1:24-25).

Whether they were marching on foot or by water conveyance, they made rapid progress. The Lamanites "were marching through the most capital parts of the land, slaying the people with great slaughter, both men, women, and children, taking possession of many cities and of many strongholds" (Helaman 1:27). Because most ancient cities (and known archaeological sites) were along rivers, it would make sense for Coriantumr to use rivers as much as possible.

Some commentators have proposed that the lands of the Nephites were confined to a relatively small area, but here we have Coriantumr seizing "many cities" and "many strongholds" between Zarahemla and Bountiful. On my proposed map, the distance between the two cities is about 470 miles, but Moronihah intercepted them before they reached the land Bountiful. Coriantumr may have advanced only around 300 miles. (By comparison, Sherman's march to the sea during the Civil War, which involved 62,000 men, covered 300 miles.)

The cities and strongholds had to be less than 30 miles apart for him to capture "many" along the way. Consequently, the proposed distances are consistent with the text.

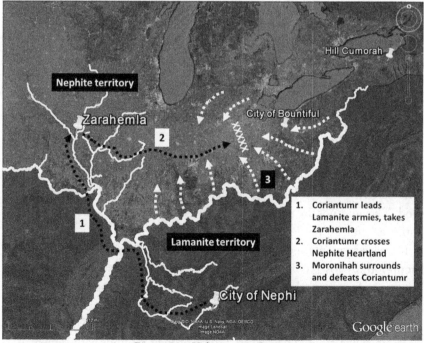

Figure 58 - Helaman 2 - Coriantumr

Helaman 3

Because of contention and dissensions, "an exceedingly great many" left the land of Zarahemla "and went forth unto the land northward to inherit the land" (Helaman 3:2). Typically, the text uses the vague term "northward" which means nearer to the north than the east and west, but not due north. Of course, this is a relative term; Zarahemla was already in the land northward. Alma 22 defines Zarahemla as the land northward. So these people were going northward from Zarahemla.

The text uses interesting language to describe their trip.

> And they did travel to an exceedingly great distance, insomuch that they came to large bodies of water and many rivers. (Helaman 3:3)

Notice they did not *travel* an exceedingly great distance; they traveled *to* an exceedingly great distance. The term exceedingly means "in a degree beyond what is usual."[167] The text is saying only that these people went to an area—a distance—where most people didn't go. They did not travel so far as to cut off communication with Zarahemla, however. They shipped timber because it was scarce in the land northward. (In Nauvoo, the saints sent workers north to Wisconsin to procure lumber, which they shipped down the river for use in Nauvoo—an interesting reversal of the account in the Book of Mormon.)

An important detail is that the people who went northward did build houses of cement because of the lack of lumber. This was unusual enough to be noted in the text, which suggests that most of the Nephites built with wood. They did not use stone or cement in Zarahemla or in the land southward, at least not for buildings.

The earliest mention of cement connected to the Nephites was the in the descriptions by Joseph Smith and Oliver Cowdery of the stone box that Moroni made to store the plates. Moroni kept the stones together with cement, which also kept the box waterproof.

There is also evidence of cement among the Hopewell and later North American civilizations. They covered some of their mounds with cement.

They reinforced their post walls with cement, a technique on display at Cahokia. Cement was well known to the ancient North Americans.

Another verse offers a geographical clue. The people "did suffer whatsoever tree should spring up upon the face of the land that it should grow up" (Helaman 3:9). This sounds like an ecological problem of slow growth. Is that problem more likely in far northern latitude, where growing seasons are short, or in a tropical latitude (Central America) where plants grow year round?

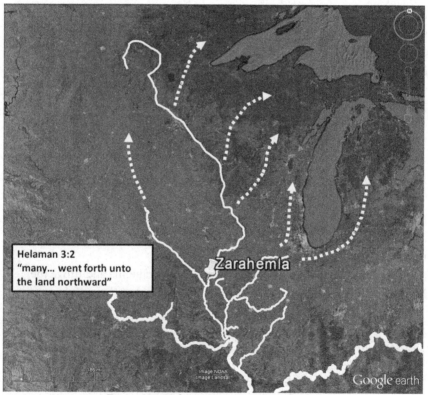

Figure 59 - Helaman 3:2 many went northward

The people who went north thought the lack of trees was due to the "many inhabitants who had before inherited the land" (Helaman 3:5). Presumably they were referring to the Jaredites here. They called the land desolate not because the land itself was desolate (except for lack of timber), but because of the destruction of the previous inhabitants.

Jonathan Neville

This is a useful insight into the meaning of *desolation*. The word means "anguished misery or loneliness" and "a state of complete destruction." Like the term *bountiful*, it is used both as an adjective and a proper noun. In a similar way, Joseph Smith referred to the land near Zelph's mound as *land of desolation* because of the people who had died there.[168]

Mormon mentions that the people who went north kept many records. Apparently he had access to them because he describes them as "particular and very large." He also comments that "a hundredth part of the proceedings of this people... their shipping and building of ships... cannot be contained in this work... there are many books and many records of every kind, and they have been kept chiefly by the Nephites" (Helaman 3:14). This passage explains why the text does not explicitly talk about ships and river traffic—Mormon didn't have the time and space to do so. It also explains why writing vanished among the people when the Nephites were destroyed; i.e., it was the Nephites, not the Lamanites, who kept written records.

Helaman 4

In 38 B.C., there were more dissensions in the church. Rebels were "driven out of the land and they did go unto the king of the Lamanites" (Helaman 4:2). Two years later, more dissenters went up to the Lamanites and "they succeeded with those others in stirring them up to anger against the Nephites" (Helaman 4:4).

This time, the Lamanites seized the land of Zarahemla and drove the Nephites and the armies of Moronihah into the land of Bountiful.

Verse 7 has caused a lot of confusion.

> 7 And there they did fortify against the Lamanites, from the west sea, even unto the east; it being a day's journey for a Nephite, on the line which they had fortified and stationed their armies to defend their north country.

For decades, scholars have interpreted this verse to mean it was a day's journey for a Nephite from the west seat to the east sea.[169] I agree that an *east sea* is implied in the verse, but I disagree that the day's journey is between the seas because I propose an entirely different setting than has been previously identified.

200

Book of Mormon scholars have offered a wide range of opinion about how far "a day's journey for a Nephite" might be. On the high end, one commentator suggests a day and a half's journey (Alma 22:32) might be as much as 118 miles,[170] which would make a day's journey around /8 miles. In modern times, the record for running 100 miles is 12 hours,[171] but would that be feasible for a Nephite? On the low end, another commentator says a day's journey would be about 15 kilometers or 9.3 miles.[172] Since the average human walking speed (all ages, male and female) is about 3.1 miles per hour, 9.3 miles/day seems unreasonably low, even over rough terrain. An average-sized man (a Nephite) can walk 4.5 to 5 miles an hour,[173] but over a long distance, maybe 4 miles/hour is more realistic. In a day (12 hours), that means a distance of 48 miles or so would be reasonable.[174]

What does it mean to say the Nephites fortified "from the west sea even unto the east sea" in this context? The phrase "even unto" is usually equivalent to "all the way to" or "to the extent of." For example, "my joy is carried away, even unto boasting" (Alma 26:35) and "I will confirm all my words even unto the ends of the earth" (Mormon 9:25).

So in this case, Mormon is saying that although the Nephites lost more than half of their territory to the Lamanites, they fortified the land Bountiful from the west sea (Lake Michigan), all the way to the east sea (Lake Ontario). But how would they do that?

The text emphasizes that the Nephites still held the land Bountiful, which meant they still held the north part of the narrow strip of wilderness—the Ohio River—that formed the border with the land of Nephi to the south. They needed to fortify their holdings from there to the west sea (Lake Michigan), which they could do along a river, such as the Scioto River, and then on up northwest to the sea. So now they are fortified from the west sea, down to the narrow strip of wilderness, and all the way up that border until they get to the end of the Allegheny River. From there they have to fortify a line up to the south sea (Lake Erie) because that is the only border not protected by a river. (They are already fortified along the Niagara River from the sea east (Lake Ontario) down to Lake Erie.)

The line they have to fortify is about 45 miles long—the length of a day's journey for a Nephite.

This critical line is what defends their "north country" from attack, meaning the north end of the land Bountiful.

Notice how the verse tells about the fortified line and the day's journey *after* it mentions the east, which is further confirmation of this interpretation. The Nephites were not interested in defending the land Desolation, even though it was north, because they considered the land cursed (3 Nephi 3:24). They kept a defensive position there to prevent Lamanites from entering the cursed land and moving west where they could attack from what is now Michigan and attack the center of the Nephite territory, but that's not the same as defending the north country. Therefore, it was the north part of Bountiful, where their people lived, that they needed to defend. Verse 7 is a perfect description of the Nephites' fortification around the land Bountiful—all the way from the sea west to the sea east.

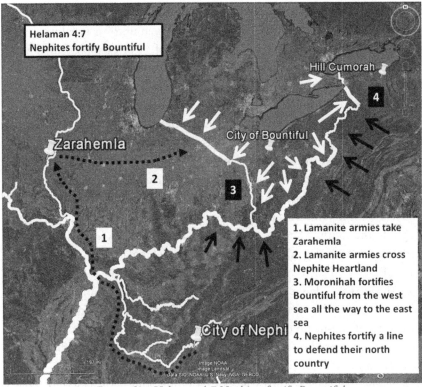

Figure 60 - Helaman 4:7 Nephites fortify Bountiful

Moronihah and the sons of Helaman, Nephi and Lehi, preached many things to the people and persuaded them to repent. As a result, Moronihah was able to lead his armies so they "regained many cities which had fallen into the hands of the Lamanites… they succeeded in regaining even the half of all their possessions" (Helaman 4:9-10). This is shown on the following map that compares the former boundary with a proposed boundary that includes about one half of the former Nephite lands.

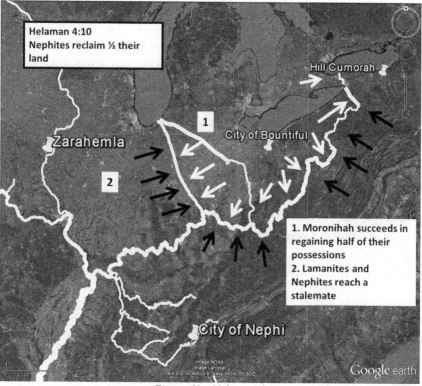

Figure 61 - Helaman 4:10

The Nephites were resigned to this boundary. Because of their wickedness, "they saw that the strength of the Lamanites was as great as their strength, even man for man. And thus had they fallen into this great transgression; yea, thus had they become weak, because of their transgression, in the space of not many years" (Helaman 4:26).

Jonathan Neville

Helaman 5-6

In about 30 B.C., Nephi, the son of Helaman, "had become weary because of their iniquity" so he "yielded up the judgment-seat" and went on a mission with his brother Lehi. (Helaman 5:4).

They started by preaching "at the city Bountiful and from thenceforth to the city of Gid and from the city of Gid to the city of Mulek and even from one city to another until they had gone forth among all the people of Nephi who were in the land southward" (Helaman 5:14-16). The term "land southward" is used in a relative sense. The land of Bountiful was southward of the land Desolation, but still north of the narrow strip of wilderness.

From Bountiful, Nephi and Lehi went "into the land of Zarahemla among the Lamanites" where they converted Nephite dissenters as well as Lamanites because they preached "with such great power and authority" (Helaman 5:16, 18). Next they went to the land of Nephi where they were "cast into the same where Ammon and his brethren were cast by the servants of Limhi" (Helaman 5:20-21). The brothers had so much success here that "the more part of the Lamanites were convinced of them because of the greatness of the evidences which they had received" and those who were convinced "did lay down their weapons of war and also their hatred and the tradition of their fathers and it came to pass that they did yield up unto the Nephites the lands of their possession" (Helaman 5: 51-52).

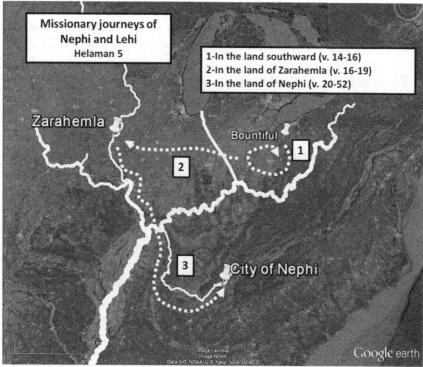

Figure 62 - Missionary Journeys of Nephi and Lehi

The success of Nephi and Lehi led the converted Lamanites to go on missions in the land of Zarahemla and "into the land northward," meaning Bountiful (Helaman 6:4, 6). They followed the reverse of the missionary route Nephi and Lehi had followed.

These conversions produced prosperity.

7. And behold, there was peace in all the land, insomuch that the Nephites did go into whatsoever part of the land they would, whether among the Nephites or the Lamanites.

8 And it came to pass that the Lamanites did also go whithersoever they would, whether it were among the Lamanites or among the Nephites; and thus they did have free intercourse one with another, to buy and to sell, and to get gain, according to their desire.

9 And it came to pass that they became exceedingly rich, both the Lamanites and the Nephites; and they did have an exceeding plenty of gold, and of silver, and of all manner of precious metals, both in the land south and in the land north...

11 And behold, there was all manner of gold in both these lands, and of silver, and of precious ore of every kind; and there were also curious workmen, who did work all kinds of ore and did refine it; and thus they did become rich.

The mention of gold and silver may seem unusual; we don't think of the Midwestern United States as a major source of these metals. However, ancient glaciers left behind gold deposits throughout the Midwest. Even today, two thousand years after the Nephites lived there, gold panning in Ohio is a popular activity.[175] "The nature of glacial gold deposition means that there could be gold literally anywhere within the state [of Ohio]."[176]

In verse 10, perhaps because of the various references to northward and southward, Mormon clarifies which land was north and which was south:

10 Now the land south was called Lehi, and the land north was called Mulek, which was after the son of Zedekiah; for the Lord did bring Mulek into the land north, and Lehi into the land south.

This passage is the only one to identify the land north as Mulek; usually it is called the land of Zarahemla. The verse is a succinct summary of the overall geography; i.e., Mulek's group, led by the Lord, sailed up the Mississippi and founded the city that became known as Zarahemla in Iowa, while Lehi's group, also led by the Lord, landed in Florida.

Another interesting passage is verse 13: "Behold their women did toil and spin, and did make all manner of cloth, of fine-twined linen and cloth of every kind, to clothe their nakedness." Archaeologists have found woven material in Hopewell Indian sites dated to this time period. A museum in Ohio features a mannequin wearing a tunic made from such cloth.

It was during this period that the Gadianton robbers arose. They became successful among the Nephites but the Lamanites destroyed them.

35 And thus we see that the Spirit of the Lord began to withdraw from the Nephites, because of the wickedness and the hardness of their hearts.
36 And thus we see that the Lord began to pour out his Spirit upon the Lamanites, because of their easiness and willingness to believe in his words.

The Gadiantons took over the Nephite government, so that the Nephites were "ripening for an everlasting destruction" (Helaman 6:40).

Helaman 7-16

Nephi, who had been rejected in the "land northward" relative to Zarahemla, returned to the land of Zarahemla, "the land of his nativity" (Helaman 7:1-3).

One of the few headings contained in the printers' manuscript designates the material now in Chapters 7-16 as

> The Prophecy of Nephi, the Son of Helaman—God threatens the people of Nephi that he will visit them in his anger, to their utter destruction except they repent of their wickedness. God smiteth the people of Nephi with pestilence; they repent and turn unto him. Samuel, a Lamanite, prophesies unto the Nephites.

The main geographical information provided in this section of Helaman is in chapter 11. Nephi had asked the Lord to bring a famine to motivate the people to repent. When they did repent, he asked that the famine be lifted. Verse 17 reports

> And it came to pass that in the seventy and sixth year the Lord did turn away his anger from the people, and caused that rain should fall upon the earth, insomuch that it did bring forth her fruit in the season of her fruit. And it came to pass that it did bring forth her grain in the season of her grain.

This is an important verse because it explains that fruit and grains were produced seasonally, and in different seasons. It suggests that there were no year-round crops as are common in tropical areas.

The conclusion of the drought brought more prosperity.

> And thus it did come to pass that the people of Nephi began to prosper again in the land, and began to build up their waste places, and began to multiply and spread, even until they did cover the whole face of the land, both on the northward and on the southward, from the sea west to the sea east (Helaman 11:20).

Jonathan Neville

At this point, the people were united under one government. There was no border; in fact, "the more part of the people, both the Nephites and the Lamanites, did belong to the church" (Helaman 11:21). When Mormon referred to "the whole face of the land both on the northward and on the southward," he seems to mean the entire area of both Zarahemla and Nephi. The people occupied the land "from the sea west to the sea east." In this context, where he is describing the "whole face of the land," the sea west would be the lower Mississippi, while the sea east would be the Atlantic Ocean.

The period of peace did not last long. In the 80th year of the reign of the judges, Nephite dissenters "stirred up to anger" some of the "real descendants of the Lamanites" and began a war (Helaman 11:24). They reinstated the Gadianton robbers:

And they did commit murder and plunder; and then they would retreat back into the mountains, and into the wilderness and secret places, hiding themselves that they could not be discovered, receiving daily an addition to their numbers, inasmuch as there were dissenters that went forth unto them. (Helaman 11:25)

This is the first mention of mountains in the promised land and it requires some attention.

Mountains in the Book of Mormon

In the Old World, Nephi refers to mountains from his own experience as well as in quotations from Isaiah. In the promised land, however, no mountains are mentioned until the Book of Helaman (apart from Jacob's vague reference[177] and the Isaiah quotations in Abinadi's confrontation[178]).

During all the travels between the land of Nephi and the land of Zarahemla, during the missionary journeys of the sons of Mosiah and the sons of Helaman (Lehi and Nephi), during all the wars described in Alma and Helaman—no one mentions mountains.

There are hills, however. The destruction in 3 Nephi created "hills and valleys" (3 Nephi 9:8). Ammon and his brethren taught people "upon their hills" (Alma 26:29).

Several hills are named.

- the hill "north of the land Shilom" (Mosiah 7:5, 16, 11:13)
- the hill Manti (Alma 1:15)
- the hill Amnihu (Alma 2:15-17),
- the hill Onidah (Alma 32:4),
- the hill Riplah (Alma 43:31-35)
- the hill Ehraim (Ether 7:9)
- the hill Comnor (Ether 14:28)
- the hill Ramah (Ether 15:11)
- the hill Shim (Mormon 1:3; 4:23)
- the hill Cumorah (Mormon 6:2, 6, 11)

The text also implies changes in elevation by describing places as being *up* or *down* in relation to one another. Riverbeds necessarily change in elevation for the water to flow.

But no mountains.

Until we get to Helaman.

The absence of mountains suggests that when we're searching for the setting of the Book of Mormon, we would look not for terrain dominated by tall, steep mountains, but instead for a place characterized by hills and rivers and valleys, with ample flat areas suitable for growing crops.

But what about the mountains mentioned in Helaman (as well as in 3 Nephi)?

In all cases, the mountains are mentioned in connection with the Gadianton robbers.

- The robbers "commit murder and plunder; and then they would retreat back into the mountains... hiding themselves" (Helaman 11:25).
- The people were "obliged to return...out of the mountains" because "of those robbers who infested the mountains" (Helaman 11:31).
- The robbers "dwelt upon the mountains" (3 Nephi 1:27).
- The robbers were driven by the Nephites "into the mountains" (3 Nephi 2:17).
- The people wanted to "go up upon the mountains... that we may fall upon the robbers and destroy them" (3 Nephi 3:20).
- The robbers "began to come down and to sally forth from the hills and out of the mountains" (3 Nephi 4:1).

What kind of mountains do these verses describe?

These mountains are habitable; the robbers dwell "upon" them in hiding places. Yet they are in close in proximity to the Nephite communities. The robbers can "sally forth" out of them, a term that means a sudden rushing out, as from a hiding place.

Nephite and Lamanite communities were located along rivers, with nearby fields of crops. Therefore these mountains would have to be in proximity to rivers, yet also in an area that supports extensive agriculture.

The 1828 Webster's Dictionary gives this definition of mountain:

> MOUNTAIN, noun [Latin adjective, montanus.] A large mass of earth and rock, rising above the common level of the earth or adjacent land, but of no definite altitude. We apply mountain to the largest eminences on the globe; but sometimes the word is used for a large hill. In general, mountain denotes an elevation higher and larger than a hill; as the Altaic mountains in Asia, the Alps in Switzerland, the Andes in South America, the Allegheny mountains in Virginia, the Catskill in New York, the White mountains in New Hampshire, and the Green mountains in Vermont. The word is applied to a single elevation, or to an extended range.[179] (emphasis added)

The description in the text implies something more like "large hills" than "the largest eminences on the globe."

A verse in the Doctrine and Covenants supports this interpretation. "Is there not room enough on the mountains of Adam-ondi-Ahman, and on the plains of Olaha Shinehah..." (D&C 117:8).[180]

Adam-ondi-Ahman is located in Daviess County, northern Missouri. The "mountains" there are about 270 feet in elevation, only about 50 feet higher than the river bed. If the elevations there are "mountains," then the areas along the Mississippi and Ohio Rivers would certainly qualify as "mountains." The land adjacent to these rivers includes elevations even higher than those in Adam-ondi-Ahman.

At Keokik, Iowa, the water level now is around 480 feet, with nearby elevations at around 650 feet. Twenty miles south of St. Louis, the river bed is around 400 feet, with elevations on both sides that reach 750-800 feet. Modern communications towers are found at the peaks, such as Buck Knob that is less than 2,000 feet from the current path of the river.

These mountains contain caves and steep ridges that would make good hiding places. In fact, river pirates took advantage of such hiding places along the Mississippi and Ohio Rivers as late as 1830. The efforts to find and eradicate these river pirates is comparable to the efforts of the Nephites and Lamanites to send armies into the mountains to destroy the Gadianton robbers.

> And it came to pass that it was expedient that there should be a stop put to this work of destruction; therefore they sent an army of strong men into the wilderness and upon the mountains to search out this band of robbers, and to destroy them (Helaman 11:28).

The descriptions of mountains in the Book of Mormon are consistent with the terrain throughout the proposed setting in Georgia, Tennessee, Illinois, Missouri, Iowa, Indiana, Ohio, and New York.

Helaman 13-15

This section of the text bears the heading "The prophecy of Samuel, the Lamanite, to the Nephites." Helaman 13:1 explains the context:

> And now it came to pass in the eighty and sixth year, the Nephites did still remain in wickedness, yea, in great wickedness, while the Lamanites did observe strictly to keep the commandments of God, according to the law of Moses.

Throughout the Book of Mormon, the law of Moses was an important part of the culture. Obedience of the law was a key indicator of the righteousness of the people, as this passage shows. Presumably the Lamanites began living the law of Moses as part of their conversion by Nephi and Lehi. (See Helaman 15:5, where Samuel emphasizes this point).

In about 6 B.C., "Samuel, a Lamanite, came into the land of Zarahemla and began to preach unto the people" (Helaman 13:2). He preached "many days" but was rejected. He was going to return home but the Lord told him to "return again" and preach. When the people would not let him into the city—Samuel identifies it as "this great city of Zarahemla"—he "got upon the wall thereof" (Helaman 13:4, 12).

What kind of a wall could a man "get upon" the way the scripture describes Samuel's action? Certainly not the wall depicted in the iconic painting by Arnold Friberg.[181]

Although the painting depicts an undoubtedly dramatic scene, it is nothing remotely comparable to what the text describes. Arnold Friberg specifically set his artwork in Central America, and many if not most LDS have been raised with this understanding of the setting for the Book of Mormon. Overcoming these long-held mental images is one of the challenges of changing the paradigm from Central America to North America.

What would be a more accurate image? The text speaks of "throwing up banks of earth… and also building

Figure 63 - Samuel the Lamanite

walls of stone to encircle them about, round about their cities and the borders of their lands" (Alma 48:8). They built breastworks of timbers; "they had encircled the city of Bountiful round about with a strong wall of timbers and earth to an exceeding height" (Alma 53:4). These are good descriptions of Hopewell sites. They built mostly with earth and timber, but sometimes they built walls of stone by piling stones. Perhaps the actual wall Samuel "got upon" was more like the one shown in this painting,[182] although more likely topped with timber.

The likelihood that Samuel stood on a typical Hopewell wall is attested later in the account. After Samuel had prophesied, many Nephites became angry.

"But as many as there were who did not believe in the words of Samuel were angry with him; and they cast stones at him upon the wall,

Figure 64 - Authentic walls

212

and also many shot arrows at him as he stood upon the wall; but the Spirit of the Lord was with him, insomuch that they could not hit him with their stones neither with their arrows" (Helaman 16:2). The inability of the Nephites to hit Samuel had to be quite miraculous, because "when they saw that they could not hit him, there were many more who did believe on his words, insomuch that they went away unto Nephi to be baptized" (Helaman 16:2).

Had Samuel been standing on a wall such as the one in the Friberg painting, it would have been a miracle for the people to hit him, not to miss him.

Furthermore,

> when they saw that they could not hit him with their stones and their arrows, they cried unto their captains, saying: Take this fellow and bind him, for behold he hath a devil; and because of the power of the devil which is in him we cannot hit him with our stones and our arrows; therefore take him and bind him, and away with him. And as they went forth to lay their hands on him, behold, he did cast himself down from the wall, and did flee out of their lands, yea, even unto his own country, and began to preach and to prophesy among his own people (Helaman 16:6-7).

Samuel had to be close enough that the people could seize him and bind him. And the wall had to be low enough that he could "cast himself down" from it. This entire description suggests the kind of wall built by Hopewell Indians, and not a high wall made of carved blocks of stone.

When Samuel gets upon the wall, he introduces himself and declares an alarming prophecy:

> Behold, I, Samuel, a Lamanite, do speak the words of the Lord which he doth put into my heart; and behold he hath put it into my heart to say unto this people that the sword of justice hangeth over this people; and **four hundred years** pass not away save the sword of justice falleth upon this people… **And four hundred years** shall not pass away before I will cause that they shall be smitten; yea, I will visit them with the sword and with famine and with pestilence. (Helaman 13:5, 9), emphasis added.

What is the significance of the four hundred years?[183] Genesis chapter 15 provides a Hebrew background.

213

13 And he said unto Abram, Know of a surety that thy seed shall be a stranger in a land that is not theirs, and shall serve them; and **they shall afflict them four hundred years;**
14 And also that nation, whom they shall serve, will I judge: and afterward shall they come out with great substance.

The Nephites to whom Samuel was preaching would recognize the symbolic significance of his prophecy. There are several references in the Book of Mormon to the children of Israel being in bondage and being freed. Ancient Israel was afflicted for four hundred years before the nation that subjected them would be judged; now the sword of justice would fall on the Nephite nation in four hundred years.

Samuel's prophecy, particularly in the context of the law of Moses referenced just a few verses earlier, demonstrates the Book of Mormon is a Hebrew text and should be interpreted with that in mind.

Samuel tells the people of Zarahemla that, "if it were not for the righteous who are in this great city, behold, I would cause that fire should come down out of heaven and destroy it" (Helaman 13:13). Later we see that the city of Zarahemla was burned (3 Nephi 9:3).

He names the city of Gideon, and then says "wo be unto all the cities which are in the land round about, which are possessed by the Nephites" (Helaman 13:16). Because Zarahemla and Gideon are on opposite sides of the River Sidon, Samuel's prophecy suggests the cities destroyed in 3 Nephi are along that river.

Samuel condemns the people for having their hearts set on their riches, so the judgment that takes place in 3 Nephi is appropriate. These cities are buried in the earth and the water, and covered with earth, and burned— completely destroying the material wealth that the people valued over living the gospel.

I will address the actual destruction in the chapter on 3 Nephi, but it's important to note that Samuel's prophecy is not necessarily limited to the immediate vicinity of Zarahemla. For example, Samuel prophesied that "there shall be many mountains laid low, like unto a valley, and there shall be many places which are now called valleys which shall become mountains, whose height is great" (Helaman 14:23). Yet when the destruction is described in 3 Nephi, only one mountain is mentioned, and it is formed when "the earth was carried up upon the city of Moronihah that in the place of the city there became a great mountain" (3 Nephi 8:10). This suggests fulfillment of Samuel's prophecy in other parts of the world; even in the case of the mountain on Moronihah, a "great mountain" is not the same as a mountain "whose height is great."

Prophecy about the Lamanites

After noting the righteousness of the Lamanites, Samuel makes an important prophecy, recorded in chapter 15:

> 11 Yea, even if they should dwindle in unbelief the Lord shall prolong their days, until the time shall come which hath been spoken of by our fathers, and also by the prophet Zenos, and many other prophets, concerning the restoration of our brethren, the Lamanites, again to the knowledge of the truth—
> 12 Yea, I say unto you, that in the latter times the promises of the Lord have been extended to our brethren, the Lamanites; and notwithstanding the many afflictions which they shall have, and notwithstanding **they shall be driven to and fro upon the face of the earth, and be hunted, and shall be smitten and scattered abroad, having no place for refuge**, the Lord shall be merciful unto them.
> 13 And this is according to the prophecy, that they shall again be brought to the true knowledge, which is the knowledge of their Redeemer, and their great and true shepherd, and be numbered among his sheep. (emphasis added)

Samuel here gives important keys to identifying the Lamanites in the latter days. We should be looking for a people who were "driven to and fro upon the face of the earth." They will have been "hunted, and smitten and scattered abroad, having no place for refuge." This is an accurate description of the fate of the American Indians, as is well known in history.[184] The Lord sent Oliver Cowdery, Parley P. Pratt and others to the Lamanites—Indian tribes—in New York, Ohio, Missouri and Kansas.

Although Indians had been "to and fro" ever since the Europeans arrived, the Indian Removal Act—enacted in 1830 after the Book of Mormon was translated—gave President Andrew Jackson authority to negotiate removal treaties with Indian tribes who lived east of the Mississippi. Before becoming President, Jackson had waged war against the Indians, including the Creek nation that lost 22 million acres of land in Georgia and Alabama. By 1837, most of the southeastern tribes had been removed from their homeland, "smitten and scattered abroad," with no place for a refuge other than government-operated reservations that were, in many cases, difficult places to live and without resources. The legacy of this treatment continues today, with many Indian nations suffering from high levels of poverty, substance abuse, and poor health.

NOTES:

---

[166] "march, v.2" OED: Oxford English Dictionary, the definitive record of the English language, definition 1 and 4.

[167] "exceedingly" in Webster's Dictionary 1828, online at http://bit.ly/Moroni92.

[168] Levi Hanckock's journal quotes Joseph Smith as saying, ""This is what I told you and now I want to tell you that you may know what I meant; this land was called the land of desolation and Onendagus was the king and a good man was he." I infer from this that any land where many people died is a land of desolation, not that Illinois was the specific "land of Desolation" mentioned in Mormon 2.

[169] John Sorenson claims this passage is referring to a line from the west sea eastward to impassable mountains. He thinks Alma 22:32, a day and a half's journey, is the distance between the two seas on his narrow neck. Mormon's Codex, p. 122.

[170] Sorenson, *Mormon's Codex*, p. 123.

[171] http://bit.ly/Moroni93.

[172] See the detailed analysis at http://bit.ly/Moroni94. That analysis uses backward reasoning, however; it assumes a Mesoamerican setting with identified spots, and then sees what the text says about how long it takes to travel those distances. Since people in our day walk an average of 3.1 miles/hour, it's difficult to justify 9 miles as an all day journey for someone in the ancient world accustomed to walking by foot.

[173] See, e.g., http://bit.ly/Moroni95.

[174] It's possible a "line" is actually a river, as discussed previously, which would let the hypothetical Nephite travel a longer distance, but nothing in this verse suggests a river. This line is fortified and stationed with armies. That sounds more like a fortified wall or barricade.

[175] Allison Ward, "Ohio Gold Panning Brings People from All Over," Washington Times, September 7, 2014, online at http://bit.ly/Moroni96.

[176] "Gold in Ohio," http://bit.ly/Moroni97.

[177] Jacob 4:6 "Wherefore, we search the prophets, and we have many revelations and the spirit of prophecy; and having all these witnesses we obtain a hope, and our faith becometh unshaken, insomuch that we truly can command in the name of Jesus and the very trees obey us, or the mountains, or the waves of the sea." No further explanation is given. It's not even clear whether Jacob actually commanded the trees, mountains or waves of the sea or just cited these as examples of what they could do if they wanted, given the power of their faith. In a similar way, Nephi, son of Helaman, was given power that "if ye shall say unto this mountain, Be thou cast down and become smooth, it shall be done" (Helaman 10:9), but there is no account of him actually exercising this power. Helaman 12 cites moving mountains as within the power of the Lord, again with no specific example. Samuel the Lamanite prophesied about mountains (Helaman 14:23) but there is no account of the fulfillment of that prophecy except for the city of Moronihah which was buried with earth that became a mountain (3 Nephi (8:10).

[178] Mosiah 12:21, "How beautiful upon the mountains are the feet of him that bringeth good tidings; that publisheth peace; that bringeth good tidings of good; that publisheth salvation; that saith unto Zion, Thy God reigneth," and Mosiah 15:18, "And behold, I say

unto you, this is not all. For O how beautiful upon the mountains are the feet of him that bringeth good tidings, that is the founder of peace, yea, even the Lord, who has redeemed his people; yea, him who has granted salvation unto his people."

[179] http://bit.ly/Moroni98.

[180] Elder Bruce R. McConkie commented on this passage: "There is a great valley there in which the righteous will assemble; and where there are valleys, the surrounding elevations are called mountains." Bruce R. McConkie, *The Millennial Messiah: The Second Coming of the Son of Man* (Deseret Book Co., 1982), p. 578-588. Some LDS scholars dispute this interpretation. The website fairmormon.org makes this comment: "However, this verse raises more questions than it answers—there are no mountains of note in Missouri. So, was the geography more expansive than Joseph or the early saints presumed?" http://bit.ly/Moroni99. In my view, whoever wrote this comment at fairmormon is creating his/her own requirement for the text. The verse, as written, is perfectly fine; there are mountains at Adam-ondi-Ahman, according to the ordinary use of the English language.

[181] See http://bit.ly/Moroni100. This painting has appeared as an illustration in the official Book of Mormon, as well as in primary, Sunday School, and other Church publications including the *Ensign*, *New Era*, the *Liahona*, and the *Friend*. It would be safe to say that most, if not every, Latter-day Saint has formed a mental image of Samuel the Lamanite—and the city of Zarahemla—based on this painting.

[182] "American Indian Life in the Early Woodland Period," Ohio History Connection, http://bit.ly/Moroni101.

[183] Proponents of a Mesoamerican theory claim the 400 year prophecy should be viewed in the context of a Mayan culture the text never mentions. For example, in *Mormon's Codex*, Sorenson writes, "An intriguing possibility of a detailed Mesoamerican correspondence with the Book of Mormon arises in connection with the prophecy of Samuel. He had announced that "four hundred years pass not away save the sword of justice falleth upon this people" the Nephites (Helaman 13:5, 9). (Here he nearly echoes Alma in Alma 45:10...) Another cycle in the numeration of some [Mayan] groups was 400 years. The 400-year prophecies by Alma and Samuel would be on a potentially correct calendrical target, even though so far we lack documentation form secular sources that prophecies occurred for a like period." In my view, this is an illusory correspondence that is much better explained by the passage in Genesis, as are the other references to 400 years (Alma 45:10, Mormon 8:6, and Moroni 10:1).

[184] By contrast, Mayan peoples in Central America generally occupy their ancestral homes.

Chapter 18 – 3 Nephi

3 Nephi 1-3

3 NEPHI OPENS WITH NEPHI, THE SON OF HELAMAN, GIVING HIS SON, also named Nephi, charge of the plates. It was about 1 A.D. and "the prophecies of the prophets began to be fulfilled more fully" (3 Nephi 1:4). The sign of the Savior's birth—a day and a night and a day without darkness—arrived. Most of the people were converted and lived in peace.

The Gadianton robbers were still in the mountains and secret places, though. They began attracting dissenters from among the Nephites, as well as Lamanite children. The "wickedness of the rising generation" led to greater wickedness throughout society. The people of Nephi, including the Lamanites who united with them, fought the robbers, but the robbers "did gain many advantages over them" (3 Nephi 2:18).

The text is not specific about where these battles took place. The record suggests they were widespread, probably in the river communities.

Around 16 A.D., the leader of the Gadiantons, Giddianhi, sent an epistle to the chief governor of the land, Lachoneus, demanding that the Nephites give up their lands and subject themselves to the Gadiantons.

In response, Lachoneus

> sent a proclamation among all the people, that they should gather together their women, and their children, their flocks and their herds, and all their substance, save it were their land, unto one place.
> And he caused that fortifications should be built round about them, and the strength thereof should be exceedingly great. And he caused that armies, both of the Nephites and of the Lamanites, or of all them who were numbered among the Nephites, should be placed as guards round about to watch them, and to guard them from the robbers day and night. (3 Nephi 3:13-14).

The people didn't want to leave their homes. They wanted to go upon the mountains and into the wilderness to destroy the robbers in their own lands. However, Gidgiddoni, the chief captain of the armies—also a prophet and the chief judge—said they would lose such an attack. Instead, they'd have to gather as Lachoneus had said and let the robbers come to them.

The people took everything they had and "did march forth by the thousands and by the tens of thousands" to the "place which had been appointed… and the land which was appointed was the land of Zarahemla, and the land which was between the land of Zarahemla and the land Bountiful, yea, to the line which was between the land Bountiful and the land Desolation (3 Nephi 3:22-23).

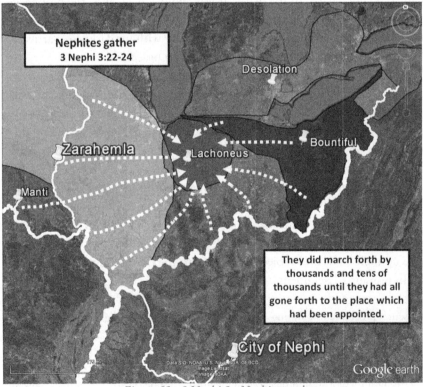

Figure 65 - 3 Nephi 3 - Nephites gather

Nephites were living west of Zarahemla, such as in Manti. To them, gathering to Zarahemla would require leaving their homes to go east, along with the people living in the city of Zarahemla and those living in all the cities along the River Sidon. People living in the land Bountiful would have to gather westward.

It's an interesting observation that the designated land went "to the line which was between the land Bountiful and the land Desolation." It makes sense for Lachoneus to use this as a border; he wouldn't want to be subject to attack from the north, and that land (Desolation) was considered cursed. Presumably not even the Gadianton robbers would go up there. Plus, it would be even further from their food source.

Here again, Mormon uses the terms *southward* and *northward* in a relative sense; the gathering place is *southward* of the line which was between the land Bountiful and the land Desolation; the land *northward* was north of that line (3 Nephi 3:24).

This is the fifth and final time the text uses the term "line" in connection with a boundary. Like the other uses, this one is context-specific. It is the only line that "was between the land Bountiful and the land Desolation" (3 Nephi 3:23). This distinguishes it from the "line between the Nephites and the Lamanites" (Alma 50:11), the "line of the possessions of the Lamanites" (Alma 50:13), and the "line Bountiful and the land Desolation from the east to the west sea," (Alma 22:32) which was the same as the "line which they had fortified and stationed their armies to defend their north country" (Helaman 4:7).

By the time Lachoneus had everyone gather, all the other military lines had been abandoned.

3 Nephi 4-7

The proposed geography explains how the Gadianton robbers responded to the Nephite tactic.

> And it came to pass that in the latter end of the eighteenth year those armies of robbers had prepared for battle, and began to come down and to sally forth from the hills, and out of the mountains, and the wilderness, and their strongholds, and their secret places, and began to take possession of the lands, **both which were in the land south and which were in the land north**, and began to take

possession of all the lands which had been deserted by the Nephites, and the cities which had been left desolate (3 Nephi 4:1), emphasis added.

The *land south* and the *land north* are relative terms, centered on the land where the Nephites had gathered. Because they deserted their cities, the Gadianton robbers could take possession of them, but because the Nephites had taken all their crops and animals and left nothing behind, the Gadiantons had no food. They couldn't plant crops or they would be vulnerable to Nephite attacks.

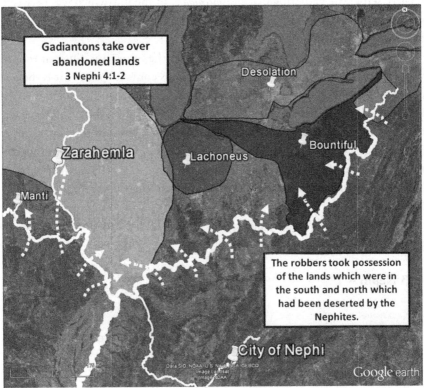

Figure 66 - 3 Nephi 4 - Gadiantons take over

With no alternative, the robbers decided to battle the Nephites.

And it came to pass that they did come up to battle; and it was in the sixth month; and behold, great and terrible was the day that they did come up to battle; and they were girded about after the manner of robbers; and they had a lamb-skin about their loins, and they were dyed in blood, and their heads were shorn, and they had head-plates upon them; and great and terrible was the appearance of the armies of Giddianhi, because of their armor, and because of their being dyed in blood (3 Nephi 4:7).

It's interesting that the robbers had lamb-skin. The Nephites hadn't left their animals, and the robbers were accustomed to living by plunder, so where did the lamb-skin come from? The logical inference is that they had saved lamb skin from previous raids, possibly for clothing in the winter. Of course, this means the Nephites kept lambs in their herds, which is to be expected since they observed the law of Moses.

Although they "had a lamb-skin about their loins," the robbers also wore armor. The text says they came to battle in the sixth month, which the Jewish calendar would put in August or September.

The Nephites fought the robbers with a "great and terrible" slaughter, "insomuch that there never was known so great a slaughter among all the people of Lehi since he left Jerusalem" (3 Nephi 4:11). The Nephites chased the robbers to the borders of the wilderness.

Two years later, the robbers returned to lay siege. That failed, and the robbers started a march "into the furthermost parts of the land northward" (3 Nephi 4:23). This made strategic sense because the robbers had decimated the animal life to the south. However, the Nephites were able to circle the robbers and kill those who did not surrender.

In Chapter 6, the text reports that the Nephites returned to their lands, but it repeats the event in two sequential verses.

1 And now it came to pass that the people of the Nephites **did all return to their own lands** in the twenty and sixth year, every man, with his family, his flocks and his herds, his horses and his cattle, and all things whatsoever did belong unto them.

2 And it came to pass that they had not eaten up all their provisions; therefore they did take with them all that they had not devoured, of all their grain of every kind, and their gold, and their silver, and all their precious things, and they **did return to their own lands** and their possessions, **both on the north and on the south, both on the land northward and on the land southward.**

Jonathan Neville

In the first verse, Mormon lists people and items and says they took everything that belonged to them to their own lands. In the second verse, he details the things that belonged to them and repeats that they returned to their own lands, but he seems to repeat their destination twice.

I think the unusual wording means the people returned to their own lands on the north and on the south on the land northward, and on the north and on the south on the land southward, simply emphasizing they occupied all the territory.

Mormon's frame of reference seems to be his overall geography, invoking the concept from Alma 22 in which Zarahemla is the land northward and Nephi is the land southward. However, there was no mention of the land of Nephi when Lachoneus sent his proclamation to gather. That may have been an oversight which Mormon is correcting here.

The text reports that "there were many cities built anew and there were many old cities repaired. And there were many highways cast up and many roads made which led from city to city, and from land to land, and from place to place" (3 Nephi 6:7-8). From an archaeological perspective, this is an interesting detail. The roads built by the Hopewell Indians were "cast up" in the sense that they were raised and had walls along each side. Roads connected Hopewell cities, just as the text indicates.

In Chapter 7, the people become more wicked, the central government disintegrates, and the people were divided into tribes. The only geographical information of note is in verses 12-13.

12 Therefore, Jacob seeing that their enemies were more numerous than they, he being the king of the band, therefore he commanded his people that they should take their flight into the northernmost part of the land, and there build up unto themselves a kingdom, until they were joined by dissenters, (for he flattered them that there would be many dissenters) and they become sufficiently strong to contend with the tribes of the people; and they did so.
13 And so speedy was their march that it could not be impeded until they had gone forth out of the reach of the people.

The "northernmost part of the land" was the land of Desolation, which the Nephites considered cursed. This may explain what the text means when it says Jacob's band went forth "out of the reach of the people." Surely they could have continued following Jacob and his group, regardless of how fast they traveled. To be "out of the reach" would mean Jacob went somewhere the Nephites could not go; i.e., the cursed land of Desolation.

Wherever it was, Jacob's city, Jacobugath, was "burned with fire" at the time of destruction (3 Nephi 9:9).

3 Nephi 8-10

One of the distinctive elements of the Book of Mormon is the description of the destruction that accompanied the death of the Savior in Israel, half way around the world. It may seem puzzling that the Nephites took the brunt of the destruction, but they had been warned by the prophets and neglected the warnings.

The massive and widespread destruction is one of the most impressive clues about the location of the land of the Nephites. The text reports that, as a consequence of the destruction, the "whole face of the land" changed. Mormon lived centuries *after* the destruction, but he described wars that took place *before* the destruction. He seemed to recognize major landmarks, at least.

What kind of terrain can experience a calamity in which the "whole face of the land" changes, yet it remains recognizable centuries later?

The term "face of the land" suggests the changes affected the face, or surface, of the land but left major features intact. What the text describes is not volcanic action, or a shift in the earth's crust that formed or destroyed huge mountains. Instead, the text describes an earthquake accompanied by a major shift in alluvial lands.

One place in the world where exactly this has occurred is along the Mississippi River.

Chapter 8 describes the destruction in some detail. No specific area is described; the destruction apparently raged throughout the lands of the Nephites, although one region suffered more than another.

Jonathan Neville

Everything started with a storm that contained particular elements: a great and terrible tempest, terrible thunder, and sharp lightnings.

> 5 And it came to pass in the thirty and fourth year, in the first month, on the fourth day of the month, there arose a great storm, such an one as never had been known in all the land.
> 6 And there was also a great and terrible tempest; and there was terrible thunder, insomuch that it did shake the whole earth as if it was about to divide asunder.
> 7 And there were exceedingly sharp lightnings, such as never had been known in all the land.

The text describes these elements as unheard of. People had experienced storms before, as well as thunder and lightning, but never to this extent.

A tempest is a violent wind storm, such as a tornado. The Webster's 1828 dictionary defines it this way:

> An extensive current of wind, rushing with great velocity and violence; a storm of extreme violence. We usually apply the word to a steady wind of long continuance; but **we say also of a tornado, it blew a tempest.** The currents of wind are named, according to their respective degrees of force or rapidity, a breeze, a gale, a storm, a tempest; but gale is also used as synonymous with storm, and storm with tempest. Gust is usually applied to a sudden blast of short duration. A tempest may or may not be attended with rain, snow or hail.[185]

Tornadoes develop from thunderstorms, which are common in the Midwest, throughout the proposed Nephite territory. Thunder and lightning accompany thunderstorms. Satellites report that "Some of the most violent thunderstorms in the world are found in the part of the central United States known as "tornado alley," where storms with large hail, destructive winds and tornadoes strike every year."[186]

The Nephites knew what tempests were. Their scriptures spoke of them, and their prophets had warned them for centuries that great tempests would come (see 2 Nephi 27:2, Helaman 14:23). Of course, some are worse than others. Mormon reports that the people had never seen one as bad as this one.

Three cities are mentioned first.

> 8 And the city of Zarahemla did take fire.

226

9 And the city of Moroni did sink into the depths of the sea, and the inhabitants thereof were drowned.
10 And the earth was carried up upon the city of Moronihah, that in the place of the city there became a great mountain.

Curious why these three were mentioned first, I reached two conclusions.

First, these three disasters represent three of the four basic elements recognized by ancient people:[187] fire, water and earth. The fourth, air, is represented by the tempest that preceded this destruction. The Nephites may have understood the recitation of these specific forms of destruction as a demonstration of the Lord's power over all the elements; i.e., the destruction was complete.

Second, these cities were associated with the source of Nephite power. Zarahemla was the seat of government and the source of their laws. Moroni and Moronihah were the great military leaders who defeated the Lamanites. Destroying these particular cities further demonstrated to the Nephites the futility of trusting in the arm of flesh.

From a practical standpoint, presumably the lightning strikes caused the fire in Zarahemla, although other causes are possible. Because the Nephites (and the Hopewell) built mainly with earth and wood, it's not a surprise that the city would burn.

The city of Moroni (assuming there is only one, a point discussed in the chapter on Alma) was located near the east sea. It sank into the sea, which could be a natural consequence of an earthquake. Another possibility is that this city of Moroni was located along the sea west, where it was flooded and sunk like other cities in that area.

The city of Moronihah is unique. It is the only city described as being covered with earth; "the earth was carried up upon the city." This suggests the action of a great wind storm, or possibly a sand blow, both of which are known to occur in the Midwest along the Mississippi River.

Verses 11 and 12 make an important distinction in geographical terms.

11 And there was a great and terrible destruction in the land southward.
12 But behold, there was a more great and terrible destruction in the land northward; for behold, the whole face of the land was changed, because of the tempest and the whirlwinds, and the thunderings and the lightnings, and the exceedingly great quaking of the whole earth;

13 And the highways were broken up, and the level roads were spoiled, and many smooth places became rough.

14 And many great and notable cities were sunk, and many were burned, and many were shaken till the buildings thereof had fallen to the earth, and the inhabitants thereof were slain, and the places were left desolate.

What accounts for the difference between the land southward and the land northward?

Throughout this passage, Mormon is writing from his global perspective; i.e., he is describing what happened throughout the land of the Nephites. Therefore, the land southward would be the land of Nephi and the land northward would be the land of Zarahemla.

Is there any real-world basis for making this distinction?

Definitely.

According to the North American geography, the original city of Nephi was located near or around Chattanooga, Tennessee, in eastern Tennessee. This area is largely unaffected by the major earthquakes that have struck the Mississippi, Wabash, and Ohio River valleys, where earthquake damage has been severe, such as in the earthquake of 1895.

The U.S. Geological Survey has produced a map showing the relative damage in the two areas.[188]

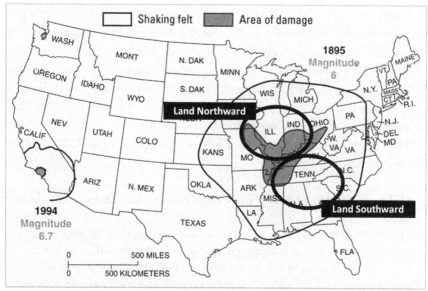

Figure 67 - U.S. Seismic damage

The largest earthquakes known to have struck what is now the continental United States were the New Madrid earthquakes of 1811-1812. New Madrid is located along the Mississippi River, about 170 miles south of St. Louis on the border between Missouri and Tennessee. The earthquakes had a magnitude of around 8.0 and the impact was felt as far away as Washington D.C.

If New Madrid was the site of the earthquake described in 3 Nephi, the damage would have been significant in the land southward (the land of Nephi), but even "more great and terrible in the land northward," meaning the land of Zarahemla. The text matches the findings of modern science.

"The New Madrid Fault is a complex zone of seismically active ancient fractures in bedrock buried several thousand feet beneath river sand and mud."[189] It would not be unusual or surprising to have a massive earthquake along this fault at the time of Christ's crucifixion. "Paleoseismic evidence collected in recent decades indicates that strong "earthquake triplets" similar in magnitude to the 1811-12 temblors have occurred approximately every 500 years along the New Madrid fault and are likely to happen again."[190]

People who survived the 1811-1812 earthquakes described the events in terms comparable to those found in 3 Nephi, such as the appearance of "black sulphurous vapor... completely darkening the atmosphere."[191]

Verse 20 describes the darkness: "And it came to pass that there was thick darkness upon all the face of the land, insomuch that the inhabitants thereof who had not fallen could feel the vapor of darkness." The darkness prevailed for three days and even precluded the creation of fire.

The U.S. Geological Survey describes the geological impact in terms that closely resemble 3 Nephi 8.

Shaking Caused Sand Blows, River Bank Failures, Landslides, and Sunken Land

The earthquakes caused the ground to rise and fall - bending the trees until their branches intertwined and **opening deep cracks in the ground**. Deep seated landslides occurred along the steeper bluffs and hillsides; large areas of land were **uplifted permanently**; and still **larger areas sank and were covered with water** that erupted through fissures or craterlets. Huge waves on the Mississippi River overwhelmed many boats and washed others high onto the shore. High banks caved and collapsed into the river; sand bars and points of islands gave way; **whole islands disappeared**. Surface fault rupturing from these earthquakes has not been detected and was not reported, however. The region most seriously affected was characterized by **raised or sunken lands, fissures, sinks, sand blows**, ... Other areas subsided by as much as 5 meters, ... Lake St. Francis, in eastern Arkansas, which was formed by subsidence during both prehistoric and the 1811-1812 earthquakes, is 64 kilometers long by 1 kilometer wide. Coal and sand were ejected from fissures in the swamp land adjacent to the St. Francis River, and the water level is reported to have risen there by 8 to 9 meters.

Surface Deformation--Evidence for Pre-Historic Earthquakes

The Lake County uplift, about 50 kilometers long and 23 kilometers wide, stands above the surrounding Mississippi River Valley by as much as 10 meters in parts of southwest Kentucky, southeast Missouri, and northwest Tennessee. The uplift apparently resulted from vertical movement along several, ancient, subsurface faults. Most of the uplift occurred during prehistoric earthquakes.[192]

This type of destruction not only can, but has actually changed the face of the whole land, just the way the destruction in 3 Nephi did. Cities found along the river would be sunk and covered over. Rivers would change their courses.

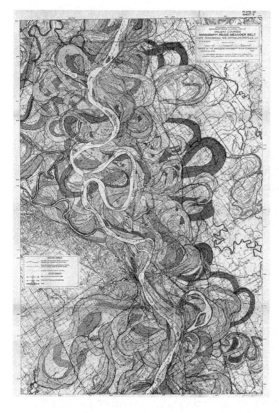

Figure 68 - Mississippi River Courses.

The river continues to change its course even in modern times. Because the river is the boundary between several states, controversies arise still today about where those boundaries should be. For example, the U.S. Supreme Court has issued nine decisions regarding the eastern boundary of Arkansas. In fact, the first capitol of Illinois, a city named Kaskaskia, was located on the Mississippi River. It was a major French colonial town in the 18th century, with a population of about 7,000 people. In 1881, the river flooded the city and the river shifted eastward, forming a new channel. This left capitol of Illinois within the boundaries of Missouri.

In 1993, even with the protection of dams and other flood control measures, the river flooded Kaskaskia again and everyone except for about a dozen residents left.

If, as I propose, most Nephite cities were located along rivers, then the destruction described in 3 Nephi would be expected if a major earthquake struck the faults in the area.

The text indicates that "there were some cities which remained but the damage thereof was exceedingly great" (3 Nephi 8:15). These would perhaps describe cities further from the rivers that felt the impact of the earthquake but not the damage from the water.

Other people were "carried away in the whirlwind" (3 Nephi 8:16), a good description of the tornadoes that strike the Midwest.

In 3 Nephi 9, "there was a voice heard among all the inhabitants of the earth, upon all the face of this land," that told of the destruction of the various cities. Here is the list, grouped by the type of destruction:

- Cities burned: Zarahemla, Jacobugath, Laman, Josh, Gad, Kishkumen
- Cities sunk "in the depths of the sea": Moroni
- Covered with earth: Moronihah
- Cities sunk and "buried in the depths of the earth": Gilgal
- Sunk and "waters have I caused to come up in the stead thereof": Onihah, Mocum, Jerusalem
- Cities "sunk and made hills and valleys in the places thereof, the inhabitants buried up in the depths of the earth": Gadiandi, Gadiomnah, Jacob, Gimgimno

Eight cities were sunk and covered with earth or water. The text does not say these cities fell into crevices made by earthquakes. They were not buried by molten lava. (Nowhere does the text describe or even imply the existence of volcanoes).

Sunken cities are a unique detail that can be demonstrated by a comparable actual experience in the Midwest: the sinking of riverboats.

A famous such case is the Steamboat Arabia. In September 1856, it was traveling up the Missouri River and hit a snag. The hull was punctured and the boat sank quickly—too quickly to salvage the cargo. The boat sunk to the bottom and was never recovered.

In the 1980s, a group of salvagers searched for the Arabia. They were directed to a particular farm where legend had it the boat was buried. With their ground penetrating radar, they detected a large metal object, about the size of the steamboat's smoke stacks.

The site was half a mile away from the river.

They dug with backhoes and found nothing, but the radar still showed the large piece of metal. They dug deeper. They hit the water table and had to pump water around the clock. Still they dug.

They finally found the Arabia—45 feet underground.

Here is a photo of the excavation.[193]

Figure 69 - Steamboat Arabia excavation

Today, you can visit the museum in Kansas City that displays the abundant cargo of the Steamboat Arabia (a visit I highly recommend).[194]

If a steamboat, after only 130 years, can sink 45 feet and end up half a mile away from the river in which it sank, could not a city along the banks of a river also sink and be buried in the depths of the earth, or be covered with water, or hills and valleys?

The answer should be obvious.

There are few places in the world where such a phenomenon is possible, let alone demonstrable. These cities were not sunk in the sea; they were sunk in the earth, alongside a mighty river like the Mississippi.

Because they were sunk 2,100 years ago, they may never be found. The Steamboat Arabia is an exception; many sunken riverboats have never been found.

But the reality of geology in the Midwest, particularly along the rivers, shows that the descriptions of destruction in 3 Nephi are not only plausible but have happened in the real world.

So long as you look in the right place.

3 Nephi 11-30

After the voice explained the destruction to the people, "there were a great multitude gathered together, of the people of Nephi, round about the temple which was in the land Bountiful; and they were marveling and wondering one with another, and were showing one to another the great and marvelous change which had taken place" (3 Nephi 11:1).

The reference to "the" temple in the land Bountiful suggests there was only one temple there. Perhaps it was in the city Bountiful, but perhaps not. Two thousand ad five hundred people gathered (3 Nephi 17:25). They lived in the vicinity of the temple; the Savior later told them "go ye unto your homes and ponder upon the things which I have said" (3 Nephi 17:3).

This tells us that the destruction in Bountiful was not severe enough to destroy the homes of the people, suggesting that the destruction here was not as significant as that along the rivers closer to Zarahemla. The New Madrid earthquakes in 1811 and 1812 were felt as far away as Boston and Washington, D.C., so it stands to reason there would be "great and marvelous change" in the land Bountiful even without damaging homes.

The Savior ascended to heaven after the first day. Word spread quickly, and "an exceedingly great number did labor exceedingly all that night that they might be on the morrow in the place where Jesus should show himself unto the multitude" (3 Nephi 19:3). It is impossible to know how far the word spread, but something on the order of 50 miles would be plausible. People may have come from nearby cities or villages or farms.

At any rate, the crowd on the second day was much larger than the 2,500 who were present on the first day.

On the second day, the disciples baptized "as many as did come unto them" (3 Nephi 26:17). The size of the crowd suggests this was a large number of people, which in turn suggests a large body of water. Because the proposed land of Bountiful borders what now is Lake Ontario, the Savior's appearance at the temple in Bountiful raises the intriguing possibility that the Savior may have appeared in the vicinity of Lake Ontario. Perhaps it was in the same place as the Kirtland temple, where the Lord appeared in 1835 to Joseph Smith and Oliver Cowdery.

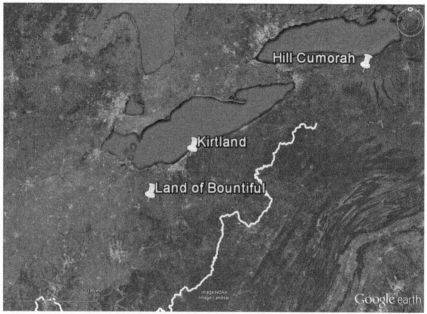

Figure 70 - Kirtland and Bountiful

The rest of 3 Nephi includes the Savior's teachings and prophecies, some of which are discussed in Chapter 29.

Jonathan Neville

NOTES

---

[185] http://bit.ly/Moroni102.

[186] Mike Bettwy, "NASA Satellite Finds the World's Most Intense Thunderstorms," University of Utah Media Advisory, http://bit.ly/Moroni103.

[187] The four elements are commonly associated with the ancient Greeks, beginning in the fifth century B.C., but they are also part of the earliest Indian and Babylonian view of the elements. They are referenced in Genesis and in Jewish thought through Midrashic literature. Josephus related the four elements to the colors of the Temple.

[188] USGS, map at http://bit.ly/Moroni104. For additional maps and detail, see http://bit.ly/Moroni105.

[189] Missouri Department of Public Safety, "Fault Zone," map available at http://bit.ly/Moroni106.

[190] See http://bit.ly/Moroni107.

[191] Michael Braunm account in Ron Street, Documentation for the New Madrid, Missouri, Earthquakes, http://bit.ly/Moroni08. See also the accounts at http://bit.ly/Moroni109.

[192] New Madrid 181101812 Earthquakes, Historic Earthquakes, Earthquake Hazards Program, USGS. http://bit.ly/Moroni110.

[193] Photo from Arabia Steamboat Museum, http://bit.ly/Moroni111.

[194] Information available on the Museum's web site here: http://bit.ly/Moroni112.

Chapter 19 – 4 Nephi

→≫ ≪←

4 NEPHI EXPLAINS THAT ALL THE PEOPLE WHO SURVIVED the destruction, both Nephites and Lamanites, were converted unto the Lord. They "had all things common among them; therefore they were not rich and poor, bond and free, but they were all made free, and partakers of the heavenly gift" (4 Nephi 1:3).

In terms of geography, the chapter provides only brief information.

7 And the Lord did prosper them exceedingly in the land; yea, insomuch that they did build cities again where there had been cities burned.
8 Yea, even that great city Zarahemla did they cause to be built again.
9 But there were many cities which had been sunk, and waters came up in the stead thereof; therefore these cities could not be renewed.

People who were spared, presumably mostly in Bountiful, reclaimed the land of Zarahemla and rebuilt the main city. This suggests that the site itself was important for commerce, as they would have no need for defenses with everyone having been converted. Other burned cities were also rebuilt.

However, cities that had been buried by water could not be rebuilt, presumably because the rivers' courses had changed. The passage doesn't say what happened to cities that were sunk into the earth; maybe they were left alone, or maybe the sites had changed so much they were no longer suitable or attractive for rebuilding.

For a while, the people lived in peace, with no contention. But then "a small part of the people had revolted from the church and taken upon them the name of Lamanites" (4 Nephi 1:20).

In verse 24, "in this two hundred and first year there began to be among them those who were lifted up in pride, such as the wearing of costly apparel, and all manner of fine pearls, and of the fine things of the world." Pearls are found in abundance in Hopewell burial sites, along with other artifacts that the ancient people considered fine. Most apparel in these sites has deteriorated, but occasionally woven cloth, dyed in colorful patterns, has been found.

The pride led to class divisions and "all manner of wickedness" (4 Nephi 1:27), and eventually society broke up into the old tribes: Nephites, Jacobites, Josephites, Zoramites, Lamanites, Lemuelites, and Ishmaelites (4 Nephi 1:36-38). The Gadianton oaths and combinations were revived and "did spread over all the face of the land," (4 Nephi 1:46).

It was at this point that Ammaron, the keeper of the record, "did hide up all the records which were sacred—yea, even all the sacred records which had been handed down from generation to generation, which were sacred" (4 Nephi 1:48).

Chapter 20 – Mormon

Mormon 1

MORMON ABRIDGED THE ENTIRE RECORD OF THE DESCENDANTS of
Lehi. How did he learn so much about his country?

Mormon's book begins with him at age ten. He writes,

> "I began to be learned somewhat after the manner of the learning of my people
> and Ammaron said unto me: I perceive that thou art a sober child, and art quick
> to observe;
> 3 Therefore, when ye are about twenty and four years old I would that ye should
> remember the things that ye have observed concerning this people; and when ye
> are of that age **go to the land Antum,** unto **a hill which shall be called Shim**;
> and there have I deposited unto the Lord all the sacred engravings concerning
> this people.
> 4 And behold, **ye shall take the plates of Nephi unto yourself,** and the
> remainder shall ye leave in the place where they are; and **ye shall engrave on the
> plates of Nephi all the things that ye have observed concerning this people.**
> 5 And I, Mormon, being a descendant of Nephi, (and my father's name was
> Mormon) I remembered the things which Ammaron commanded me. (Mormon
> 1:2-5) emphasis added.

The text gives no information about the location of the "land Antum,"
but it does mention "the hill of Shim" in Ether 9:3. In that verse, Omer
passes by the hill after he is overthrown. The way Moroni (who abridged
Ether) refers to the hill suggests he was familiar with it.

> 3 And the Lord warned Omer in a dream that he should depart out of the land;
> wherefore Omer departed out of the land with his family, and traveled many
> days, and came over and **passed by the hill of Shim, and came over by the
> place where the Nephites were destroyed,** and from thence eastward, and came

to a place which was called Ablom, by the seashore, and there he pitched his tent, and also his sons and his daughters, and all his household, save it were Jared and his family.

Certainly Moroni knew the place where the Nephites were destroyed. According to Oliver Cowdery and Joseph Smith, this was the valley west of the Hill Cumorah in New York, just south of Palmyra. Moroni refers to "the hill of Shim" specifically. Since he had Mormon's record and knew all about the hill Shim and the plates, I infer Moroni identified the hill Omer by name so his readers would make the connection.

In other words, the hill Shim was in western New York, somewhere in proximity to the Hill Cumorah. That would put the land Antum in the general area, which means Ammaron was in that area when he hid the records. Ammaron didn't have to explain to young Mormon where the land Antum was; I infer from this that as a boy, Mormon lived not too far away from Antum.

Later, when he reaches the age of 24, Mormon will do as Ammaron told him (See Mormon 2:17-18), and get the plates of Nephi. Later he will remove all the plates from the hill Shim (Mormon 4:23) to keep them from the Lamanites.

But first, Mormon needs to learn about his country.

The text doesn't say why he did it, but Mormon's father takes his son on a long field trip. I think the father was present when Ammaron told the ten-year-old boy what his calling would be and took it upon himself to educate his son.

6 And it came to pass that I, being eleven years old, was carried by my father into **the land southward, even to the land of Zarahemla.**

Mormon's father waited only about a year before taking his son on the trip. He "carried" the boy, a term that suggests a mode of conveyance. Surely Mormon the father didn't carry his eleven-year-old son in his arms or on his shoulders. I think the most likely conveyance was a boat, like a canoe.

Maybe it was just Mormon and his father, or maybe the entire family went on the journey.

Mormon refers to the land of Zarahemla as "the land southward." What is his frame of reference?

Many times in the text, Mormon refers to Zarahemla as the land northward. For example, he explained that "Now the land south was called Lehi, and the land north was called Mulek, which was after the son of Zedekiah; for the Lord did bring Mulek into the land north, and Lehi into the land south" (Helaman 6:10).

But here, he refers to Zarahemla as "the land southward." Obviously he is writing from a reference point north of Zarahemla.

A look at the map shows how this fits the proposed geography.

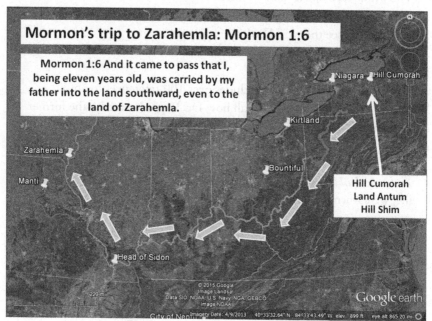

Figure 71 - Mormon's trip to Zarahemla

Starting from the northern area near the land Antum, Mormon and his father would travel south to reach the Allegheny River, then south to join the Ohio River, then south along the Ohio River until it moves more westerly. Only once he reaches the head of Sidon would he turn north.

Mormon wouldn't be looking at Google Earth or a map of the globe to determine the relative latitude of his destination (although, even technically, Zarahemla is south of his starting point). Mormon would refer to the direction they headed; i.e., they went "into the land southward" from the perspective of someone leaving from the Cumorah area.

Later, Mormon will write about how the Lamanites drove the Nephites northward, back to the area of his homeland.

During his field trip, the boy Mormon was amazed at what he saw.

7 The **whole face of the land** had become **covered with buildings**, and the people were as numerous almost, as it were the sand of the sea.

The whole face of the land would be the areas through which Mormon traveled. Imagine what it would be like for a young boy to leave his homeland and "see the world" with his parents.

What does it mean that the "land had become covered with buildings" in this context?

The Book of Mormon text includes over 100 references to "build," "building," and "buildings." Recall how Dr. Roger Kennedy, the former director of the Smithsonian's American History Museum, explained this term.

Build and *building* are also very old words, often used in this text [his book] as they were when the English language was being invented, to denote earthen structures.

About 1150, when the word *build* was first employed in English, it referred to the construction of an earthen grave. Three hundred and fifty years later, an early use of the term to build up was the description of the process by which King Priam of Troy constructed a "big town of bare earth." So when we refer to the earthworks of the Ohio and Mississippi Valleys as buildings no one should be surprised. [195]

All along the Ohio and Mississippi Rivers, young Mormon would have passed by these earthworks and mounds. Most of the hundreds of thousands of sites have long since been destroyed, but many can still be visited today. Along the Ohio River, there are sites such as the one in Moundsville, West Virginia that I discussed in the Mosiah chapter. Other sites include Marietta and Portsmouth, Ohio, the Mann site near Evansville, Indiana, and several in Illinois.

Mormon's father may have taken his son to visit historic sites along tributaries, such as the Scioto and Tennessee Rivers. He could have visited the ancient city of Nephi, the places where the sons of Mosiah taught the gospel to the Lamanites, and Alma's land of Helam. He could have visited the battlefields described in Alma.

The journey would be the perfect preparation for the future prophet and historian who would compile the history of Lehi's descendants.

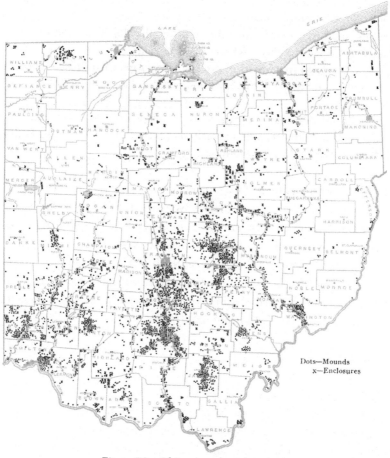

Dots—Mounds
x—Enclosures

Figure 72 - Ohio mounds and enclosures

In the same year that young Mormon was traveling to Zarahemla, a war between the reconstituted Nephites and Lamanites began "in the borders of Zarahemla by the waters of Sidon" (Mormon 1:10). The Nephite army exceeded 30,000 men, and they defeated the Lamanites. There was peace for four years. Presumably Mormon spent these years in Zarahemla, pursuing his education and training.

He writes that he lived in a corrupt society.

> 13 But **wickedness did prevail upon the face of the whole land**, insomuch that the Lord did take away his beloved disciples, and the work of miracles and of healing did cease because of the iniquity of the people.
> 14 And there were no gifts from the Lord, and the Holy Ghost did not come upon any, because of their wickedness and unbelief.
> 15 And I, **being fifteen years of age and being somewhat of a sober mind**, therefore I **was visited of the Lord**, and tasted and knew of the goodness of Jesus.
> 16 And I **did endeavor to preach** unto this people, but my mouth was shut, and I **was forbidden that I should preach** unto them; for behold they had wilfully rebelled against their God (Mormon 1:13-16).

Mormon's parents must have taught him well. He recognized that "sorceries, and witchcrafts, and magics" were the fulfillment of the words of Abinadi and Samuel the Lamanite (Mormon 1:19). He would later include these prophecies verbatim when he abridged the history of the Nephites.

After he had written on the plates of Nephi, Mormon summarized his life experience among his people: "a continual scene of wickedness and abominations has been before mine eyes ever since I have been sufficient to behold the ways of man" (Mormon 2:18).

Mormon 2

Mormon grew not only in wisdom and knowledge but in stature. When he was in his sixteenth year, the Nephites made him the leader of their armies. In 327 A.D., Mormon led the Nephites into battle, but the Lamanites frightened his armies and "they began to retreat towards the north countries" (Mormon 2:3).

The text does not give many specifics about these battles. Mormon had considered Zarahemla the land southward when he left his homeland. Maybe this explains his use of the term "retreat" here; i.e., his armies were withdrawing and returning toward the land he had come from.

He describes the retreat by naming the cities and lands they were driven out of. These places were not named previously in the text, whether because they were built after the Savior visited or because they were among the many unnamed cities and lands that existed prior to the destruction described in 3 Nephi.

The Nephites retreated to the city of Angola, which they fortified, but the Lamanites drove them out of the city through the land of David to the land of Joshua "which was in the borders west by the seashore" (Mormon 2:6). A seashore makes a good place to defend because it prevents the enemy from surrounding you; you can confine the battlefront.

We're not told what frame of reference Mormon is using here, but the seashore appears to be part of the border he refers to. He is saying Joshua is on the western side of the seashore. At this point, Mormon knows he is headed for the area he left as a boy. The land of Joshua was west of that area.

Mormon chose this place by the seashore to gather his people. With his army of 42,000, Mormon withstood the Lamanite army of 44,000 and sent them fleeing. This was in the 330th year.

The battles continued to rage for another 14 years. "I saw thousands of them hewn down in open rebellion against their God, and heaped up as dung upon the face of the land" (Mormon 2:15).

In the 345th year, the retreat resumed. The Lamanites pursued the Nephites all the way to the land of Jashon, another place never before mentioned in the text. At this place, the Nephites stopped their retreat.

Jashon was near the land Antum where Ammaron had deposited the records. Mormon reports that "I had gone according to the word of Ammaron and taken the plates of Nephi and did make a record according to the words of Ammaron" (Mormon 2:17). Ammaron had told Mormon to do this when he was 24 years old. If Mormon had done so, he had retrieved the plates while the Nephites were in the land of Joshua. Perhaps circumstances prevented him from getting the plates until he reached Jashon with his armies.

At any rate, the Nephites were "were driven forth until we had come northward to the land which was called Shem" (Mormon 2:20).

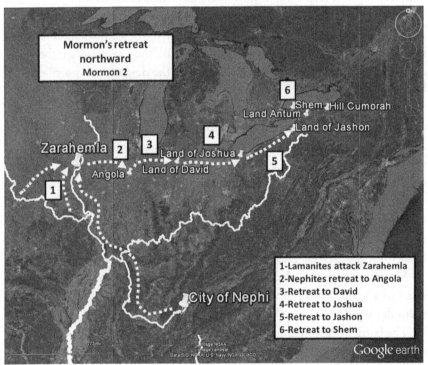

Figure 73 - Mormon's retreat

Shem was not previously mentioned in the text. After such a long retreat, there must have been something unique about Shem for the Nephites to be able to make a stand there. It was an area Mormon was familiar with, having grown up there. That knowledge would give him a strategic advantage over the Lamanites, so it makes sense that he would choose this place to "fortify the city of Shem and… gather in our people as much as it were possible that perhaps we might save them from destruction" (Mormon 2:21).

With his people in a fortified city, Mormon urged them "with great energy, that they would stand boldly before the Lamanites and fight for their wives, and their children, and their house, and their homes" (Mormon 2:23). Perhaps Mormon felt a special attachment to this area because he had grown up nearby. His "great energy" proved successful. "My words did arouse them somewhat to vigor, insomuch that they did not flee from before the Lamanites, but did stand with boldness against them" (Mormon 2:24).

Mormon's army of 30,000 fought the Lamanite army of 50,000. The Lamanites retreated, and the Nephites pursued them. Mormon writes "we had again taken possession of the lands of our inheritance" (Mormon 2:27). Does this mean he had reconquered all the land back to Zarahemla?

That seems unlikely.

Mormon doesn't say how far the Nephites pushed the Lamanites, but he emphasizes that his people did not have the Spirit of the Lord; "therefore we had become weak like unto our brethren" (Mormon 2:26). The retreat from Zarahemla began in the 327th year (Mormon 2:3) and ended at the city of Shem in the 346th year. Mormon's army had declined from 42,000 to 30,000, while the Lamanite army had grown from 44,000 to 50,000. (Presumably these numbers represent recruitment of new troops to replace the dead.)

After twenty years of retreat, from Zarahemla all the way back to his homeland, with a declining Nephite army against a growing Lamanite army, Mormon would be hard pressed to reclaim all the land back to Zarahemla within just a few years. What seems more plausible is that he recovered the land where he had grown up, in the vicinity of Shem, Antum, and Jashon. After all, it was in Shem where he motivated his people to stand and fight for their houses and their homes. The people could hardly fight for their houses all the way back in Zarahemla.

This interpretation of the text is corroborated by the treaty the Nephites made with the Lamanites in the 350th year. Mormon writes that "we made a treaty with the Lamanites and the robbers of Gadianton in which we did get the lands of our inheritance divided" (Mormon 2:28).

The antecedent for the pronoun "we" in this passage is the Nephites. Consequently, the Nephites made a treaty in which the Nephites did get the lands of the Nephites' inheritance divided. They did not get *all* the lands of their inheritance; their inheritance was divided, and the Lamanites gave them only the land northward.

> And the Lamanites did give unto us **the land northward**, yea, **even to the narrow passage which led into the land southward**. And we did give unto the Lamanites **all the land southward** (Mormon 2:29), emphasis added.

What is Mormon's frame of reference here? He is writing from his own homeland, where he grew up. It is the same perspective he had when, as a boy, his father took him "into the land southward, even to the land of Zarahemla" (Mormon 1:6). The Lamanites received *all* the land southward.

This is the only mention in the text of a "narrow passage." It is not a neck or even a pass; it may not be a natural feature at all. A passage is a "road; way; avenue; a place where men or things may pass or be conveyed."[196]

As part of a treaty, it appears to be an agreed-upon route or way—a corridor—through which access between the two lands would be permitted.

The narrow passage specified in this treaty reminds me of the narrow passages, also established by treaty, between West Germany and Berlin during the cold war. One could travel within these passages, but veering outside could mean arrest and imprisonment.

In terms of real world geography, there are numerous valleys, long narrow rises and hills, and other features in western New York that could have served as the narrow passage defined by this treaty. Presumably this narrow passage would give access to the river system that led into the land southward—the very river system Mormon's father took him on when he was eleven years old.

Mormon 3

Mormon apparently didn't think the treaty would hold. He spent the next ten years with the Nephites, "preparing their lands and their arms against the time of battle" (Mormon 3:1). As he anticipated, "the king of the Lamanites sent an epistle unto me which gave unto me to know that they were preparing to come again to battle against us" (Mormon 3:4).

In response to the threat, Mormon had his people gather "at the land Desolation to a city which was in the borders by the narrow pass which led into the land southward" (Mormon 3:5).

This verse contains several interesting features. First, the people were to gather "at the land Desolation." Previously, the land northward was considered cursed (3 Nephi 3:24). Maybe it still was, or maybe the curse was considered lifted, or maybe only part of the land Desolation was cursed. The borders of the land Desolation are never specified, but the term seems to refer both to any land where people were killed, and to the land occupied by the Jaredites as they destroyed themselves. Whatever the origin of the name and the extent of the territory it refers to, the name Desolation seems to be a bad omen.

Mormon doesn't name the city to which the people were to gather. He identifies it only as a city "which was in the borders by the narrow pass which led into the land southward." People presumably knew where this was.

Is the "narrow pass" the same thing as the "narrow passage" from Mormon 2:29? I think not, although I understand the argument that it could be. My rationale depends first on the different terms, which are used on consecutive pages on the printer's manuscript. Oliver Cowdery made no attempt to match the terms, even though both the pass and the passage "lead [sic] into the land Southward" (spelling and capitalization from the printer's manuscript).

The second reason I think they are different is that a "passage" mentioned in connection with the treaty has a connotation of official designation and permission that would be well fortified. It seems unlikely that Mormon would have the people gather to a place so fortified and under observation by the enemy, even if it was only "in the borders" by such a passage.

By contrast, the term "pass" suggests a natural feature—a logical point of invasion. Perhaps the Lamanite king even told Mormon they would invade by the pass. Mormon suggests as much when he writes "there we did place our armies that we might stop the armies of the Lamanites."

Whether he was forewarned by the Lamanite king or he relied on his own prescience, Mormon chose the right place. In the 361st year, "the Lamanites did come down to the city of Desolation to battle against us… we did beat them" (Mormon 3:7).

I note here that "city of Desolation" is not necessarily the name of the city. It could also be a reference to the unnamed city that was in the land of Desolation.

The Lamanites returned in the 362nd year and again the Nephites prevailed. Mormon notes "their dead were cast into the sea." On this

Jonathan Neville

occasion, he doesn't specify that the battle was fought at the city of
Desolation, but we see that the battle was fought near a "sea."

This is a good place to illustrate the challenges and opportunities of
looking for specific archaeological sites. As I explained at the outset, and for
the reasons given, I do not want to associate specific Book of Mormon sites
to known archaeological sites. However, I offer this one as an illustration.

Western New York is the setting for numerous ancient sites. Some were
surveyed by E.G. Squire in 1849. His book, *Aboriginal Monuments of New
York*, includes illustrations of many of the earthworks he found. His
introductory observations include this overview of western New York.

> it has long been known that many evidences of ancient labor and skill are to be
> found in the western parts of New York and Pennsylvania, upon the upper
> tributaries of the Ohio, and along the shores of Lakes Erie and Ontario. Here we
> find a series of ancient earth-works, entrenched hills, and occasional mounds, or
> tumuli, concerning which history is mute, and the origin of which has been
> regarded as involved in impenetrable mystery…. Many are said to exist in
> Chautauque; but the lateness of the season, and the unsuspected number of
> remains elsewhere claiming attention, prevented me from examining them.[197]

Because my proposed geography happens to include parts of Chautauque
County, I consulted another source for information about known ruins in
that area. The following narrative includes references to existing cities that
I've highlighted in **bold** and placed on Figure 74 for reference. (I realize the
passage is long but it includes a lot of detail.)

> The history of any region properly begins with its original inhabitants †. In
> western New York inquiry relative to this subject is beset with difficulty and
> admits of no certain solution. This difficulty arises from the discovery of relics
> indicative of a race inhabiting the country prior to the period of Indian
> occupation.

> In the silent depths of the unbroken wilderness the explorer was often startled at
> the discovery of traces of ancient fortifications, generally circular in form and
> upon whose embankments trees were standing, the concentric circles of which
> denoted the growth of centuries. …

Moroni's America

Careful investigation has demonstrated that these relics are of so great antiquity
that even tradition fails to throw its feeble light upon them. The Iroquois had
traditions relative to them, but so various and contradictory that no real
knowledge is derived from that source. The elaborate character of these relics
indicates that the constructors were a race of greater industry and resource than
the Indians.

Traces of ancient occupancy were discovered in several places upon the territory
now embraced in **Chautauqua county**. Near the crossing of the Erie Railway
and the Frederica and Forestville road, in the town of **Sheridan**, an ancient
fortification, circular in form and inclosing many acres, was visible at an early
day. It was evident that the land there had once been cleared, though it was then
covered with a growth of timber undisputably three hundred years old. Various
useful implements were found and pits were observed at regular intervals. Many
human bones have been discovered there from time to time. A large grave was
opened in the summer of 1870, from which many human skeletons were taken.

Fort Hill, near **Fredonia**, received its name from an ancient intrenchment, in
front of which were discovered traces of a large pit. The most extensive remains
in the county were at the extremity of the cape which extends from the
southwestern side into the lower of the Cassadaga lakes. Here several acres were
enclosed by earthworks and the shores of the lake. It has been claimed that this
apparent fortification was of natural formation; it seems, however, to have been
anciently occupied, for relics of prehistoric civilization were found there in
abundance. There was a large mound near the northern shore of the lake, which
frequent plowing has reduced to four or five feet in height and only three or four
rods in diameter. When settlement began it is said to have been twelve feet high
and to have been surmounted by forest trees which had been growing for
centuries. A large number of human skeletons were exhumed here about 1822.
Near by are still to be seen the remains of what was evidently once a graded
roadway.

At various other places in the vicinity traces of ancient occupancy were formerly
visible. At **Sinclairville** and in its vicinity extensive remains have been found. In
the town of **Gerry**, about a mile south of the village mentioned, was a circular
intrenchment, enclosing several acres. About a hundred and thirty rods northeast
of this was an ancient cemetery, by some called "the Indian burying ground."
Many skeletons, some of them of almost superhuman proportions, have been
disinterred here, and within the intrenchment were found others and numerous
stone implements.

251

Two miles southeast of **Sinclairville**, in **Gerry**, a circular fortification is visible in the woods with large trees growing from its ditch and wall. Upon the high bluff which rises from Mill creek, just west of **Sinclairville**, was formerly an elevated earthwork, circular in form, with a deep excavation in the center. Enclosing six or seven acres of what is now the central portion of the village was an extensive circular earthwork, having a trench without and a gateway opening to a small stream passing along is southern side.

At other points in **Gerry** and in **Stockton**; in **Ellington**, along the hills bordering Clear creek, and at other localities in the county, were early visible vestiges of similar circular enclosures, near which many stone implements and other relics have been plentifully discovered. Two of these old tumuli and the traces of an old roadway are still visible near the eastern shore of **Chautauqua lake**, at Griffith's Point, in **Ellery**. The relics described and other similar ones in other parts if the county prove this region to have been, at a recent period, a favorite abiding place of an unknown race.

There can be little doubt that here were once rudely cultivated fields and ancient and perhaps populous villages, inhabited by a strange and primitive people. Whence they came, how long they remained and what fortunes attended their sojourn here, is unknown, and it would be useless to pursue the subject, aided only by speculative theories.[198]

I pinned each of the mentioned locations on the map to show the proximity to one another. The distance between Ellery and Gerry is about five miles.

At the bottom of the map I show a proposed "city of Desolation" for illustration purposes (the site of Jamestown, New York). It is located in a valley on the shores of the lake (possibly a sea) and is at the south end of a long narrow valley from Stockton to Gerry. The valley continues south of the proposed city of Desolation directly to the Allegheny River, which of course leads to the land southward.

This proposed location would make a good point of attack for the Lamanites coming from the mountains to the south, so it meets that requirement from the text. It is an area known for abundant ancient sites of the type described in the Book of Mormon. It is in the general location where my proposed geography would put it.

But it is only one of many possible sites.

Figure 74 - Chautaugua County, NY

A close-up topographical map shows the lake on one side and the valley on the other.

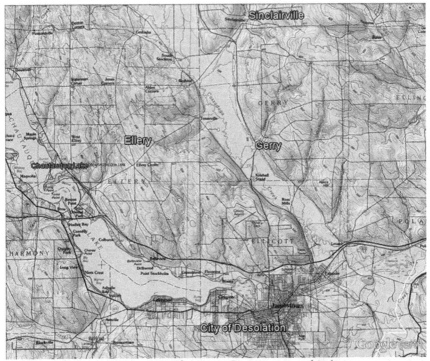

Figure 75 - Chautauga County topographical

The narrative in Mormon 3-6 consists of a series of battles with the Lamanites. When the Lamanites came against the Nephites in the city of Desolation and the Nephites prevailed, the Nephites "began to boast in their own strength" (Mormon 3:9).

In 363, the Nephites went on the attack, out of the land Desolation, but the Lamanites drove them back and took possession of Desolation. The survivors fled to the city Teancum, which was in the borders by the seashore and near Desolation.

In 364, the Lamanites attacked Teancum, but the Nephites prevailed and even retook Desolation.

In 367, the Lamanites came again. They took possession of the city Desolation, as well as Teancum. They took women and children prisoners and offered them up as sacrifices. The Nephites retaliated and drove the Lamanites out of the land again.

In 375, the Lamanites come again with a big army. Mormon writes that "from this time forth did the Nephites gain no power over the Lamanites but began to be swept off by them even as dew before the sun" (Mormon 4:18). The Lamanites took the city Desolation. The Nephites fled to the city Boaz, which they eventually lost to the Lamanites. Then they fled, gathering the inhabitants of towns and villages, down and take Desolation. Nephites flee to Boaz, then flee again from towns and villages, until they reached the city of Jordan, which they held. The Nephites held other cities, but the Lamanites burned all the cities, towns and villages that were not protected.

In 380, the Lamanites came yet again and the Nephites fled. Mormon wrote to the king of the Lamanites, asking if he could gather all the Nephites to the land of Cumorah for a final battle. The king agreed.

In 384, the Nephites were gathered. Mormon writes:

> knowing it to be the last struggle of my people, and having been commanded of the Lord that I should not suffer the records which had been handed down by our fathers, which were sacred, to fall into the hands of the Lamanites, (for the Lamanites would destroy them) therefore I made this record out of the plates of Nephi, and hid up in the hill Cumorah all the records which had been entrusted to me by the hand of the Lord, save it were these few plates which I gave unto my son Moroni (Mormon 6:6).

Then the final battle at Cumorah took place.

Jonathan Neville

NOTES

[195] Roger G. Kennedy, Hidden Cities: The Discovery and Loss of Ancient North American Civilization (The Free Press, New York, 1994), p.vii. (hereafter Hidden Cities)

[196] "Passage," Webster's 1828 Dictionary, http://bit.ly/Moroni113.

[197] E.G. Squier, Aboriginal Monuments of The State of New York, (Smithsonian Institution 1849), reprinted by Hayriver Press (Colfax, Wisconsin 2006), pp. 9-11.

[198] History of Chatautauqua County, New York (F.W. Beers & Col, New York 1881), available online at http://bit.ly/Moroni114.

Chapter 21 – Ether

-->>>> <<<<-

MORONI ABRIDGED THE RECORD OF THE JAREDITES, translated by Mosiah from the 24 gold plates found by Limhi's 43 explorers. Presumably that record was succinct—how much history could 24 plates hold? Yet Moroni abridged even that short record, giving us merely cursory information about geography in the Book of Ether.

One thing we can be sure of: the final battles were at Cumorah, in western New York. Presumably that's the most important point, because that's all Moroni tells us for sure.

However, we can infer a few other things.

The Jaredites left from "the great tower at the time the Lord confounded the language of the people." This was presumably the tower of Babel, located in what is now Iraq, near Bagdad. The group consisted of Jared and his brother and their families, with "some others and their families" (Ether 1:33). The Lord led them "down into the valley which is northward," a valley named Nimrod, from where they would be led "into a land which is choice above all the lands of the earth" (Ether 1:42).

They traveled in the wilderness, "yeah, into that quarter where there never had man been." They built barges to cross many waters, and eventually came "even to that great sea which divideth the lands" (Ether 2:5, 6, 13), where they dwelt in tents for four years.

The description is so vague they could have gone just about anywhere. The phrase "great sea which divideth the lands" has been interpreted to mean the Atlantic Ocean (on the premise that the continents were separated in the days of Peleg and the Atlantic therefore divided the lands) as well as the Pacific Ocean (on the premise that before the continents were separated, only one large sea separated east from west).

If they crossed the Atlantic, the Jaredites could have come up the St. Lawrence Seaway to reach what became the land of Desolation around the Great Lakes.

If they crossed the Pacific, the Jaredites could have landed on the west coast and spread throughout the land until a portion of them reached the Great Lakes area. This is the scenario I find most persuasive, although I think the text and the data are equivocal on this point.

Here is my rationale.

First, the text says when they left the tower they went into "that quarter where there never had man been." At a minimum, that means they avoided populated areas. This would exclude much of the ancient world, particularly along sea coasts, but seems most possible if they traveled across Asia. This is the route Hugh Nibley favored, for example.[199]

Second, the Jaredite barges seemed to have no means of propulsion; "they were driven forth, three hundred and forty and four days upon the water" (Ether 6:11). That is a very long time to cross the Atlantic. Perhaps they followed Lehi's route, leaving from somewhere in the Persian Gulf, circling Africa, and then crossing the Atlantic. However, this does not account for their long journey in the wilderness before they left, building barges and crossing water, avoiding populated areas, etc.

Just as there is actual precedent for Lehi's travel across the Atlantic, there is also precedent for ships drifting across the Pacific. Debris from the tsunami that struck Japan on March 11, 2011, took about a year to reach North American shores. One fishing vessel that broke free from a dock in Japan after the tsunami drifted for about a year before being sunk by the Coast Guard off the coast of Alaska. A blog maintained by the National Oceanic and Atmospheric Administration mentioned this ship as well as others, including an 1872 "Record of Japanese Vessels Driven Upon the North-West Coast of America and its Outlying Island."[200] There is a strong current that flows from Japan east; "for a ship caught in it, the next stop would be the Aleutian Islands, or the American coast between Vancouver and Los Angeles."[201] A 344-day drifting journey from Asia to North America fits the known currents.

Third, the text says they grew in numbers and spread upon the face of the land. There are several studies of demographics that attempt to determine how fast the Jaredites could have multiplied, but the text indicates they were both fertile and healthy. The population of the Jaredites could have multiplied faster than other groups used by comparison in these studies.

13 And it came to pass that they went forth upon the face of the land, and began to till the earth.
16 And the friends of Jared and his brother were in number about twenty and two souls; and they also begat sons and daughters before they came to the promised land, and therefore they began to be many.
18 And it came to pass that they began to spread upon the face of the land, and to multiply and to till the earth; and they did wax strong in the land.

The text suggests the Jaredites spread out. Moroni specifically limited the scope of the record he abridged to the area where he lived.

And now I, Moroni, proceed to give an account of those ancient inhabitants who were destroyed by the hand of the Lord upon the face *of this north country* (Ether 1:1), emphasis added.

Ether himself was the descendant of at least 30 generations of descendants of Jared, and possibly many more. In two places of his genealogy, the record merely says one of Ether's ancestors "was a descendant" of someone. That leaves open the possibility of an extra several generations.

I think the text not only allows but implies that descendants of the Jaredites spread throughout the Americas. Evidence of their influence in Central America, such as among the Olmecs, is consistent with this view.

Fourth, related to the third point, is that the Jaredites presumably had Asian DNA, which is the predominant source of indigenous DNA throughout Latin America. I say presumably because they originated in Asia and crossed Asia before coming to the promised land.

Fifth, migratory patterns show a general migration from the west coast throughout the Americas. Indian legends are consistent with this. One tribe in British Columbia claims their ancestors came from the west in "tight barges" each of which contained a pearl that gave light."[202] One Haida artist has created sculptures of the "first Men" squeezing out from clam shells.[203]

Figure 76 - First Men

Certainly much more work needs to be done on the origin of the Jaredites and the distribution of their population in the promised land. There are many unknowns, but there is a potential for further clarification as more information becomes available. Updating Brother Nibley's work would be a productive project, for example.

Moroni used Ether's account of the Jaredites to teach lessons and give warnings to his readers, particularly the future occupants of his homeland—the Jaredite and Nephite promised land, today called America. All three groups occupy the promised land. All three are under the covenant to keep the commandments, which brings the promised blessings.

Most of the Book of Ether refers to place names with little geographical information. Moroni put five pins in the map, however—just enough for us to make no mistake about where the promised land is.

Pin 1 goes on the plains. Ether 13 and 14 describe battles taking place "upon the plains" generally, with the "plains of Agosh" and the "plains of Heshlon" being named. These references compare with the Nephite battles "upon the plains" generally (Alma 52:20), with the "plains of Nephihah" being named (Alma 62:18). When Joseph Smith told Emma he was crossing the "plains of the Nephites," could he also have been referring to the plains of the Jaredites?

The greatest concentration of Adena sites, dating to Jaredite time periods, is in the plains of Ohio and along the Ohio River up to West Virginia, Pennsylvania, and New York. These are the same areas where Hopewell (Nephite time era) sites are found.

Pin 2 is the land Desolation. Ether 7:6 says, "Now the land of Moron, where the king dwelt, was near the land which is called Desolation by the

Nephites." Of course, "near the land" is fairly vague on its own, and we have few specifics on the exact location of the land the Nephites called Desolation, but at least we know it is around the Great Lakes, in the "north country" where Moroni lived when he wrote this record.

Pin 3 is the New Jerusalem. Moroni explains that "Ether saw the days of Christ, and he spake concerning a New Jerusalem upon this land" (Ether 13:4). From latter-day revelation, we know this New Jerusalem will be built in Jackson County, Missouri. This means Moroni considered Missouri to be part of "this land."

People have debated the meaning and scope of the term "this land," arguing it can mean anything from a designated spot within sight to the entire North American continent, or even all of North and South America. In my view, the example Moroni provides (presumably taken from Ether) explains the meaning of the term.

> 6 And that a New Jerusalem should be built up upon **this land**, unto the remnant of the seed of Joseph, for which things there has been a type.
> 7 For as Joseph brought his father down into the land of Egypt, even so he died there; wherefore, the Lord brought a remnant of the seed of Joseph out of the land of Jerusalem, that he might be merciful unto the seed of Joseph that they should perish not, even as he was merciful unto the father of Joseph that he should perish not.
> 8 Wherefore, the remnant of the house of Joseph shall be built upon **this land**; and it shall be a land of their inheritance; and they shall build up a holy city unto the Lord, like unto the Jerusalem of old; and they shall no more be confounded, until the end come when the earth shall pass away.

If the example of Joseph in Egypt was a type, then the remnant of Joseph would have to also occupy the very land that was to be the site of the New Jerusalem. Soon after the Church was organized, the Lord sent Oliver Cowdery, Parley P. Pratt and others on a mission to the Lamanites—the remnant of Joseph—in New York, Ohio, and Missouri. This was before the Lord revealed where the future New Jerusalem would be located.

Jonathan Neville

To argue that "this land" refers to all of North and South America renders the term meaningless, in my opinion. For Moroni and Ether, "this land" meant the land where the remnant of the house of Joseph would live, and that means the places where the Lord sent missionaries to the Lamanites, from New York to Missouri.

Pin 4 is the land of Zarahemla. Moroni describes a strange occurrence: poisonous serpents came forth upon the land as a result of a dearth (drought).

> And there came forth poisonous serpents also upon the face of the land, and did poison many people. And it came to pass that their flocks began to flee before the poisonous serpents, towards the land southward, which was called by the Nephites Zarahemla (Ether 9:13)

Recall that Moroni was writing about the people who lived in "*this* north country," implying he was living in the north country while he was engraving the plates. (Oliver Cowdery said the book was *written and hidden* near Joseph's home in Palmyra, which corroborates what Moroni wrote.)

Because the terms "land southward" and "land northward" are relative terms, the key is always to understand the frame of reference. From Moroni's perspective, writing in the north country, Zarahemla would be southward. (Of course, Zarahemla is also the land northward in relation to the land of Nephi, which was south of the narrow strip of wilderness.)

This passage also deserves mention because it's the *only place* in the Book of Mormon that mentions a "narrow neck of land."

> Ether 10: 19 And it came to pass that Lib also did that which was good in the sight of the Lord. And in the days of Lib the poisonous serpents were destroyed. Wherefore they did go into the land southward, to hunt food for the people of the land, for the land was covered with animals of the forest. And Lib also himself became a great hunter.
> **20 And they built a great city by the narrow neck of land by the place where the sea divides the land.**

21 And they did preserve the land southward for a wilderness, to get game. And the whole face of the land northward was covered with inhabitants.

This one passage has been the source of endless debate about Book of Mormon geography and is the premise for the mistaken hourglass shape commonly depicted on maps. The great Jaredite city was between the land northward (sometimes referred to as Desolation) and the land southward (which Ether 9 called Zarahemla, which included Bountiful).

The Jaredites built a "great city" at this location. The definition of city is a place with a market, which makes sense in this context because the hunters went into the land southward to get game, which they then sold to people in the land northward.

What is a "narrow neck of land" in this context? We looked at the definitions in Chapter 6. The 1828 Webster's Dictionary gives two definitions, both of which could apply.

2. A long narrow tract of land projecting from the main body, or a narrow tract connecting two larger tracts; as the neck of land between Boston and Roxbury.[204]

There is nothing unique about a narrow neck of land; a glance at the map of Lake Erie, for example, shows several necks of land protruding into the water. Of course, the land forms at the time of the Jaredites could have been much different than they are today, but ruins in this area dating to Jaredite time frames largely track the existing shape of the Great Lakes. A modern map therefore is probably close to what the Jaredites knew, except the water levels are lower now.

The map below shows three possible "necks of land" connecting the land north of Lake Erie with the land south of Lake Erie. Two are on either side of Detroit, while the other is north and west of Buffalo. All three border on seas that "divide the land," and the land of Zarahemla is south of all three. However, the Niagara neck by Buffalo divides the land more distinctly than the ones near Detroit. It looks like the point of a knife, piercing the land mass.

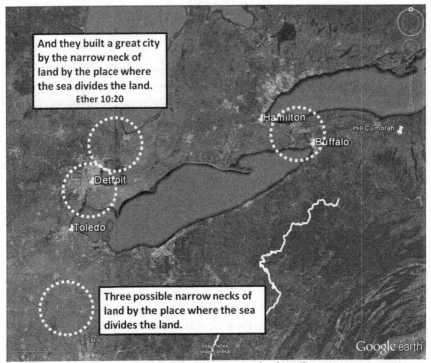

And they built a great city by the narrow neck of land by the place where the sea divides the land.
Ether 10:20

Three possible narrow necks of land by the place where the sea divides the land.

Figure 77 - Narrow Neck of Land

The origin of the name *Niagara* is obscure, but it may come from the Mohawk language and refers to "the portage or neck of land between lakes Erie and Ontario."[205] Obviously, this is a nice fit with the geography here.

The scripture says "the whole face of the land northward was covered with inhabitants." In reference to Buffalo (the proposed site of the great city), the land northward was the Niagara peninsula and further north and west of there. This is consistent with the archaeological record; the Niagara Peninsula has a very long history of native occupation, dating back thousands of years, and rich archaeological sites have been unearthed at Fort Erie, Grimsby, Thorold and St. Davids."[206]

Regardless of where this ancient Jaredite city was actually built, there is no basis in the text for treating this relatively obscure verse—almost a throwaway line about a Jaredite marketplace—as the pivotal piece in the Book of Mormon geography puzzle.

Pin 5 is Cumorah. Moroni writes:

> And it came to pass that the army of Coriantumr did pitch their tents by the hill Ramah; and it was that same hill where my father Mormon did hide up the records unto the Lord, which were sacred (Ether 15:11).

Ramah is the same as the Nephite Cumorah, which is the same as Joseph Smith's Cumorah in western New York. Oliver Cowdery made this explicit in his Letter VII. In Ether 9:3, the text says

> 3 And the Lord warned Omer in a dream that he should depart out of the land; wherefore Omer departed out of the land with his family, and traveled many days, and came over and passed by the hill of Shim, and came over by the place where the Nephites were destroyed, and from thence eastward, and came to a place which was called Ablom, by the seashore, and there he pitched his tent.

This verse reinforces what we know about the hill of Shim from Mormon's account; i.e., that it was in proximity to Cumorah. Ammaron hid the records there (4 Nephi 1:48). Mormon took the plates of Nephi from the hill and continued the record (Mormon 1:2-4; 2:17-19). Later, fearing the Lamanites might discover them, Mormon removed all the records from Shim and put them in Cumorah (Mormon 4:23; 6:6).

The verse also informs us that there was a place called Ablom by the seashore east of Cumorah. This could have been along the eastern portion of Lake Ontario (the sea east) or even all the way to the Atlantic Ocean. I think the Atlantic is an unlikely choice because the text says he traveled "many days" *before* passing Shim and Cumorah, not afterward.

These five pins give us the information we need to know the most important point of the Book of Ether: *the Jaredite promised land was the same as the Nephite promised land, which is the same as today's promised land: Moroni's America.*

Jonathan Neville

NOTES

[199] Hugh Nibley, Chapter 3, "Jared on the Steppes," *Lehi in the Desert; The World of the Jaredites; There Were Jaredites*, Deseret Book/FARMS, 1988, available through the Maxwell Institute at http://bit.ly/Moroni142.

[200] See http://bit.ly/Moroni115.

[201] "The Shogun's reluctant ambassadors," http://bit.ly/Moroni116.

[202] Personal account related to me, including notes of the interview, in 2015.

[203] Bill Reid, "The Raven and the First Men," Collection of the UBC Museum of Anthropology, Vancouver, Canada. MOA #Nb1.481, 689/1. Photo by Linda Stanfield.

[204] "Neck," 1828 Webster's Dictionary, http://bit.ly/Moroni117.

[205] Alun Hughes, "On the Meaning of 'Niagara'," *Newsletter of the Historical Society of St. Catharines*, June 2010, p. 9. Online at http://bit.ly/Moroni118.

[206] Ibid, p. 8.

Chapter 22 – Moroni

MORONI FOCUSES ON THE GEOGRAPHY OF THE SOUL.

He writes nothing about the lands of the Nephites. He includes an epistle from his father that references sites not otherwise mentioned in the text: the tower and land of Sherrizah and the abominations of the Nephites in Moriantum. Both locations symbolize the darkest recesses of the human soul, and the end of the epistle contrasts that darkness to the light of Christ.

Sherrizah had a tower, presumably a fortress but possibly a steep ridge or hill, from which the Lamanites took prisoners, men, women and children. They killed the men and fed their flesh to their wives and children (Moroni 9:7-8). The Lamanites left some widows and daughters behind in Sherrizah but took all the food, so "many old women do faint by the way and die." Mormon was unable to rescue them because the Lamanite armies were "betwixt Sherrizah and me" (Moroni 9:16-17).

Moriantum was another Nephite land, but here, it was the Nephites who were depraved. They took Lamanite daughters prisoner, raped them, tortured them to death, and then ate their flesh (Moroni 9:9-10).

Mormon concludes his epistle by looking away from the darkness of the souls of his people and turning to Christ:

> 25 My son, be faithful in Christ; and may not the things which I have written grieve thee, to weigh thee down unto death; but may Christ lift thee up, and may his sufferings and death, and the showing his body unto our fathers, and his mercy and long-suffering, and the hope of his glory and of eternal life, rest in your mind forever.
> 26 And may the grace of God the Father, whose throne is high in the heavens, and our Lord Jesus Christ, who sitteth on the right hand of his power, until all things shall become subject unto him, be, and abide with you forever. Amen.

Moroni's writings also display the geography of his own soul.

Even when he is pursued by the Lamanites, those fierce warriors who will kill him because he will not deny the Christ, Moroni risks his life to "write a few more things that perhaps they may be of worth unto my brethren, the Lamanites, in some future day, according to the will of the Lord" (Moroni 1:4).

In his final chapter, Moroni writes about how each individual can navigate through the geography of his or her own life. He shows that the power of the Holy Ghost lets each person know "the truth of all things" (Moroni 10:5), including the record of the Nephites. He explains how spiritual gifts guide us through the challenges of life, avoiding or overcoming obstacles we encounter.

The one place where Moroni writes about borders is metaphorically, in speaking of the establishment of Zion.

> 31 And awake, and arise from the dust, O Jerusalem; yea, and put on thy beautiful garments, O daughter of Zion; and strengthen thy stakes and enlarge thy borders forever, that thou mayest no more be confounded, that the covenants of the Eternal Father which he hath made unto thee, O house of Israel, may be fulfilled.

This seems to be Moroni's hope not only for the promised land—for America—but for every land and nation and people who embrace the covenants.

Section 3 – Additional Detail

Chapter 23 – Evidence, Proof, and Historicity

PEOPLE OFTEN ASK ME, "HOW MUCH EVIDENCE DOES IT TAKE to prove something?" My answer: "It depends on the individual and what he or she *wants* to believe."

When I was a prosecutor, preparing a case for trial involved assembling and presenting evidence to prove elements of a crime beyond a reasonable doubt. In civil cases, the burden of proof is a preponderance of the evidence, meaning more likely than not. There are statutes and rules and court decisions about the fine points of these formal standards of proof.

But no such rules apply to our individual lives.

A person who *wants* to believe something will be convinced by little, or no, evidence. A person who *doesn't want* to believe something may not be convinced by any amount of evidence. But most people, in most aspects of their lives, do tend to want to know the truth, even if it is "hard" because it contradicts what they've been taught or what they've believed before.

I wrote this book to offer evidence about the historical authenticity—the *historicity*—of the Book of Mormon.

In my view, the Mesoamerican theory has eroded faith in the Book of Mormon among those who look objectively at the evidence and arguments. The "evidence" usually cited to support Mesoamerica as the setting for the Book of Mormon narrative is illusory. Proponents find similarities between Mesoamerican culture and the culture described in the text of the Book of Mormon, but such similarities occur in many human cultures. Worse, they contradict the plain meaning of the text, which describes a Hebrew culture, not a Mayan one.

These similarities or "correspondences" are often dressed up in sophisticated rhetoric, but they boil down to this:

1. Nephi planted seeds and harvested them.
2. The Mayans planted seeds and harvested them.
Therefore, Nephi was a Mayan.

I realize no Mesoamerican proponents have made that specific argument, but the correspondences you read about—John Sorenson alone had 140 such correspondences in his book, *Mormon's Codex*—follow that logic.

Meanwhile, the Mesoamerican proponents distort the text so it will fit their theory. *Mormon's Codex* and many other publications and web pages that support the Mesoamerican theory claim the textual term "north" doesn't really mean north. They substitute Mayan animals and plants for those mentioned in the text. They also insist Joseph Smith was merely speculating about where the Book of Mormon took place.

If you're wondering where the Mesoamerican theory originated, Chapter 29 addresses that.

Any standard of proof is subjective. Proof is whatever is sufficient to satisfy an individual about the truth or falsity of a given proposition. Because of different backgrounds, priorities, and values, some people require more proof of a given proposition than others. This subjectivity explains why we use juries in courts of law and peer reviews in science. In both cases, we assume that if evidence persuades a group, it is more likely to be accurate. Convince enough people—members of a jury, qualified scientists—and the law and public opinion will generally go along with the conclusion.

Yet human judgments are fallible. History is replete with examples of a "consensus" being wrong. Einstein famously challenged the consensus of his day with his own theory of relativity. The germ theory revolutionized medicine. Technology in all its forms has challenged prior consensus and dramatically changed the way people live and think.

Along the way, every challenge to the consensus faced opposition. Individuals with strong convictions used evidence and rational arguments to persuade others, but it is almost always a gradual process. What may be considered as "fact" in one time and place may be shown to be error in another time and place. New knowledge supersedes old, but old knowledge may be sustained when seen from a different perspective. Even where people agree on a set of facts (which itself can be a challenge), they differ regarding the interpretation and importance of those facts.

Religious leaders face similar obstacles. Moses presented a tremendous challenge, not only to the Egyptians but to the Israelite slaves who had grown accustomed to their status. Many prophets and religious leaders have been killed for what they preached. Jesus was crucified. Stephen was stoned. Many of the original apostles were killed.

When it comes to personal convictions, the views of a majority are irrelevant. Belief in God is an individual choice, not the product of a vote. In the same way, one's acceptance or rejection of the Book of Mormon is highly personal, and may be the product of objective reasoning based on facts, spiritual insights based on personal experience, or a combination of the two.

In my view, even spiritual choices are improved with consideration of the best available evidence.

This book is the second in a three-part series.

The Lost City of Zarahemla: from Iowa to Guatemala and Back Again investigates LDS Church history—specifically the *Times and Seasons* in 1842—and proposes that the Mesoamerican theory of Book of Mormon geography originated not with Joseph Smith but with a man whom the Prophet described as having a "rotten heart." Joseph prophesied that the man would "injure the Church as much as he could." The evidence of the fulfillment of that prophecy is abundant; as described in *Lost City*, many people have lost faith in the Book of Mormon—or refused to even read it—because of the absence of corroborating evidence in Mesoamerica, the proposition that some terms in the Book of Mormon were not properly translated, and the assertion by Mesoamerican advocates that Joseph Smith didn't know much about the Book of Mormon and merely speculated about the geography, culture, and legacy of its peoples. *Lost City* also sets out the accurate history behind D&C 125, the revelation that revealed the name of a city to be built across the Mississippi River from Nauvoo and thereby raised an inference that ancient Zarahemla was in fact located in Iowa.

The third in the series, *Mormon's History: Back to the Beginning*, examines the historical context of the Book of Mormon. Early claims that Joseph Smith copied from another source are refuted, but more importantly, the unique and prescient elements of the Book of Mormon are placed in their historical context. The Book of Mormon revealed things about the history of North America that no one at the time knew or could have known. That book also looks at the history of Book of Mormon geography, including an extensive review of the literature, much of it published by affiliates of Brigham Young University: FARMS and the Neal A. Maxwell Institute for Religious Studies.

This book—*Moroni's America: The North American Setting for the Book of Mormon*, examines the setting for the Book of Mormon in detail.

This series of books responds to the modern demand for facts and evidence. As an empiricist myself, I seek physical confirmation of historical and scientific claims. In my opinion, Joseph Smith himself was an empiricist. He described Moroni's visits with specific details about his appearance and apparel. He dug the plates out of the hill Cumorah, lugged them around, and protected them. But he never used them for the actual translation.

Told he would be an instrument in the hands of God, Joseph knew he was responsible to translate the plates. First, he copied some of the figures and sent Martin Harris to find someone who could translate them. Only after Harris returned, unsuccessful, did Joseph realize he—Joseph—would have to translate them. He had no way to learn the language written on the plates. His tutor, Moroni, had provided him the necessary context. He informed Joseph about Lehi and his descendants, showing him their origin, progress, civilization, laws, governments, and their history of righteousness and iniquity. But in the economy of heaven, would it make sense for Moroni to teach Joseph a complex language he would use only once in his lifetime? How accurate a translation could Joseph have made even with such training? Translation is subjective; even professional, experienced translators never produce identical versions of a given text.

No, the only practical means for accurately translating an ancient religious text written in an unknown language was through the gift of tongues. As an empiricist, Joseph would understand this. The only solution was to use a seer stone, blocking out ambient light with a hat so he could see the words that appeared on the stone. Then why the plates?

I think he needed them as physical, tangible proof that the ancient record he was "translating" actually existed. It was one thing to have Moroni—a long-deceased ancient inhabitant of the land where Joseph lived—appear to him. It was one thing for a voice to speak to his mind or even for words to appear on a stone. But it was something else entirely to pry open an ancient stone box and find gold (or tumbaga) plates, a breastplate, a sword, and other artifacts. That the plates contained writing no one could read—a proposition confirmed by Dr. Charles Anthon—was confirmation, too, of their authenticity. Had they been written in legible Hebrew, they could have been dismissed like the many other artifacts containing forms of Hebrew found in North America.

Anything short of such tangible, physical evidence could have left Joseph with an excuse to walk away from the project when opposition grew. He had plenty of reasons to rationalize it away, to succumb to the wishes of his peers and agree that the whole project was, in fact, a hallucination.

But the plates prevented that.

Joseph knew the plates were real. There was no denying that. The three witnesses, the eight witnesses, and the many other people who saw the plates confirmed what Joseph knew: he had an actual, ancient record.

And now, in 2015, we have the same kind of physical evidence.

Physical evidence is no substitute for spiritual connection and knowledge. As an empiricist, I recognize that a spiritual witness far exceeds any material witness in terms of impact on one's mind and soul. Who would deny that the feeling of love is more powerful than a textbook knowledge of biochemistry? Another way to express this is that the things of God are made known by the Spirit of God.

And yet, physical evidence is an important component of any spiritual conviction. At the most fundamental level, no one could believe in the Bible if the Bible didn't exist. Of course, the fact someone believes something does not make it real (let alone true), but the existence of the Bible—something one can touch and feel and read—provides the necessary premise for belief.

Jesus performed miracles to give the people something physical to believe while they developed their spirituality. He knew most people cannot accept mere words; there must be evidence. Indeed, isn't that why Christ became mortal in the first place?

No oyster can produce a pearl unless there is a grain of sand to build upon. So, too, faith builds upon some initial physical reality, whether that's a book, an experience, a physical sensation—or a set of metal plates.

Since 1830, the existence of the Book of Mormon itself was sufficient for millions of people to accept it as a revelation from God. There were no viable explanations for its existence other than pure serendipity (itself a miracle) and Joseph Smith's own explanation. Claims that Joseph copied it, collaborated with others, or even wrote it himself have all been advanced and exposed as highly implausible, at best. And yet, for most people, any shred of possibility that Joseph Smith composed the book is sufficient to reject it. Such rejection is far more palatable than the alternative of acceptance and all that entails. Accepting the divine authenticity of the Book of Mormon requires first, acceptance of metaphysical reality—that God exists and intervenes in human affairs—and second, acceptance that whatever one had believed that contradicted Joseph's explanation was incorrect.

Those are difficult propositions, no doubt, in any age of the world.

But now, in 2015, the mere existence of the Book of Mormon is hardly persuasive. There are over 150 million copies of the book in existence but only around 7.5 million people who actually believe its claims (assuming an activity rate of 50% among nominal Mormons, which might be high). Pure faith has become less and less prevalent in light of scientific advances that have explained so many things that were once the province of faith alone.

Which is what makes the Book of Mormon all the more convincing.

Critics have long focused on the inconsistency between Book of Mormon claims the Mesoamerican setting that has long prevailed in the Church. To their credit, they were largely correct. I propose that the Book of Mormon events did not occur in Mesoamerica (or anywhere south of Texas). My conclusion that the Mesoamerican theory was initiated by an overzealous

Mormon missionary whose efforts succeeded for over 170 years may reflect on the work of LDS scholars (who, by and large, sought to vindicate what they thought were Joseph Smith's teachings), but can have no bearing on the Book of Mormon itself.

Only now, in 2015, can we see the Book of Mormon for what it has always been: a complex history of the Native American Indians who inhabited what was, in 1830-1842, the United States of America. Only now, with the benefit of modern archaeology, geology, and other tools can we understand what the Book of Mormon was saying about its time, place, and people.

The timing could not have been better. As I write, we live in a society and world that largely rejects any claims that are not supported by solid evidence. Rightly so. Science has exposed hundreds of false ideas and beliefs. But it has verified others. That science would establish the historicity of the Book of Mormon is an outcome that would have been unimaginable only a few years ago. But now that it has happened, detractors are put to the test.

I'll repeat the question I posed at the beginning: "How much evidence does it take to prove something?"

Only time will tell, and each individual must decide for herself or himself.

Jonathan Neville

Chapter 24 – The River Sidon

-→≫ ≪←-

I BRIEFLY ADDRESSED THE RIVER SIDON IN CHAPTER 5, but the topic comes up so frequently that more analysis is warranted.

In *The Lost City of Zarahemla*, I discussed the origin of the name and its relevance to Book of Mormon geography. I concluded that the Nephites inherited the name from the Mulekites, who in turn were influenced by the Phoenicians who presumably brought them to America. The name Sidon recognizes the river for its properties as a source of food, and also for its utility as a border, the same way the ancient city of Sidon was used to mark a border in the Old Testament. I proposed that references to the river Sidon in the Book of Mormon amount to references to the river *border*, particularly in connection with the narrow strip of wilderness.

I also pointed out that the phrase "head of Sidon" cannot mean the source, but instead means the confluence of rivers. Figure 78 illustrates where the Mississippi joins the Missouri and Ohio Rivers. The Illinois River joins just north of the Missouri River. Somewhere in that area, or perhaps the entire section from the Missouri to the Ohio River, is the head of Sidon.

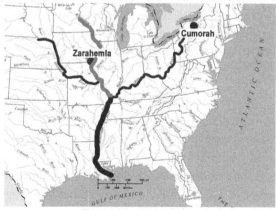

Figure 78 - River Sidon

Jonathan Neville

Flowing North or South?

A common objection to the North American setting relies on the theory
that the River Sidon flows north like the major rivers in Central America.
Because the Mississippi flows south, goes the argument, North America
cannot be the setting.[207]

To address this issue, I refer to an analysis by one of the most thoughtful
and careful advocates of the Mesoamerican theory.[208] He summarizes the
history of the issue and identifies his proposed location in Mesoamerica.

> The northerly flow of the Sidon has been well-understood by Book of Mormon
> students for over a century. In his notes to the 1879 edition of the Book of
> Mormon, Orson Pratt said the river flowed northward, an observation that
> persisted in the indices to the 1920 edition prepared under the direction of James
> E. Talmage and the 1980 edition prepared under the direction of Bruce R.
> McConkie. In his magnum opus published in 1899 (*A Complete Concordance of
> the Book of Mormon*), George Reynolds correlated the Sidon with the north-
> flowing Magdalena in modern Colombia. In his 1917 work *Geography of Mexico
> and Central America from 2234 BC to 421 AD* Louis Edward Hills correlated the
> Sidon with the north-flowing Usumacinta. The New World Archaeological
> Foundation's first season of field work in 1953 was near Huimanguillo, Tabasco
> west of the north-flowing Grijalva. Daniel H. Ludlow's internal reconstruction
> of Book of Mormon geography, distributed throughout the Church Educational
> System for decades, shows the Sidon flowing north to the sea. John E. Clark's
> article "Book of Mormon Geography" in the 1992 semi-official *Encyclopedia of
> Mormonism* includes the north-flowing Sidon as one of the few tenets of Book of
> Mormon geography unambiguously attested in the text. We established
> previously that the Usumacinta River is the viable candidate for The Book of
> Mormon's river Sidon… As we would expect, the Usumacinta flows generally
> from south to north.

Despite that impressive history, the most recent editions of the Book of
Mormon *deleted* the description of Sidon as a north-flowing river. The text
simply does not say that the river flows north.

The argument for a north-flowing Sidon is well presented in the
following seven answers to the initial question.[209] I offer my own analysis
(designated JNx) after the answers provided by the original author.

Q. How do we know the river Sidon flowed south to north?

A1. Near the land of Zarahemla, the hill Amnihu Alma 2:15, 17 and the valley of Gideon Alma 6:7 were both east of the river Sidon. Near the city of Zarahemla, the river Sidon had a west bank Alma 2:34. These data points all imply a general north/south orientation for the river in that part of its course.

JN1: I agree.

A2. Beyond (south of) the land of Manti, a south wilderness Alma 16:6, 7 lay east of the river Sidon. This implies a general north/south orientation for the river in that part of its course.

JN2: I agree, except for the parenthetical (south of). The text doesn't say *south of* Manti, it says *beyond* Manti. Beyond the land of Manti can be on the east side of the river, with the wilderness still designated as south in relation to Zarahemla and other sites to the north.

A3. Upstream from (south of) the land of Manti Alma 43:32, Captain Moroni placed part of the Nephite army west of the river Sidon Alma 43:27 and another part east of the river Sidon Alma 43:53. These data points imply a general north/south orientation for the river in that part of its course.

JN3: The first part of this answer—*upstream from*—simply assumes the conclusion. The text never says which way the river is flowing. Moroni concealed part of his army in the valley that was on the west of the river Sidon and part into the valley on the east "and so down into the borders of the land Manti." The text doesn't say whether Moroni started out north or south of Manti, but Manti was on or near the border. It wouldn't make sense to have Moroni crossing the border into Lamanite territory and fortifying northward; instead, he would be fortifying the Nephite side of the border, from the north toward the south. That he went "down into the borders" shows the river flowed from the north to the south.

A4. One verse in the text has been interpreted to mean that the river Sidon flowed from east to west in part of its course. Alma 22:27 is ambiguous. It could mean that the river Sidon flowed from east to west at that point. Given the repetitive nature of Mormon's phrasing, though, it is more likely that all the east to west references in Alma 22:27-29 refer to the narrow strip of wilderness that separated Nephite lands on the north from Lamanite lands on the south. The text mentions several geographic entities or human activities either east or west of the river Sidon. The text never mentions entities or activities directly north or south of the Sidon. All of these data points reinforce the notion that the Sidon flowed in a general north/south direction over most of its length.

JN4: I agree with this, and add that my chiastic analysis explains it in more detail. Nothing here speaks to the direction of flow, however.

A5. The land of Manti was south of the land of Zarahemla Alma 17:1. The land of Manti was also near the head of the river Sidon Alma 43:22. From the head of the river Sidon, one went down in elevation to Zarahemla Alma 56:25. These data points indicate that the river Sidon flowed generally northward from Manti to Zarahemla.

JN5: I agree with the first two sentences, but the third one is not what the text says, and the fourth is a faulty inference. Alma 56:25 says the Lamanites had a choice to "march down against the city of Zarahemla" or they could "cross the head of Sidon." It doesn't say they were *at* the head of Sidon. Instead, in 56:29, it says the Lamanites, who had decided neither to march against Zarahemla nor to cross the head of Sidon, "began to sally forth," a concept that is repeated in 3 Nephi 4:1 when the Gadianton robbers began to "sally forth" out of the mountains and hills. The text indicates that the Lamanites in Alma 56 were in a highland area, from which they could *either* march against Zarahemla *or* cross the head of Sidon. The area around the head of Sidon in Missouri and Illinois has many high areas that the river flows through—from the north to the south— even though the elevations are higher in the south than in the north. It's the elevation of the riverbed that determines flow, not the elevation of the surrounding areas, as I'll show below.

A6. The greater land of Nephi was south of the greater land of Zarahemla Alma 50:7. An east/west dividing line separating the two lands ran by the head of the river Sidon Alma 50:11. To go from Zarahemla to Nephi, one went up in elevation Alma 2:24. Therefore, the river Sidon which bordered the land of Zarahemla Alma 2:15 flowed generally from south to north.

JN6: The error here is easy to see. The argument would make sense if all terrain followed the river, meaning it drops in elevation along with the flow of the river. However, that is true only of the riverbed itself, not the surrounding area. In Egypt, the Nile flows north through some wide valleys at low elevation before cutting through higher elevation mountains to the north. Similarly, the Rhine River flows through a low elevation through central Germany before carving its way through the mountains between Bingen and Koblenz. In the U.S., the Mississippi River flows south, but on its way south it passes by higher elevations in Missouri on the west and in Tennessee and Alabama on the east. The banks of the Mississippi south of St. Louis rise over 650 feet above sea level. Montrose, Iowa—260 miles *north* of Arcadia—is at 531 feet. So even though the river is flowing south, it is flowing through terrain that is higher in elevation.

The other major error here is that the text never says the *River Sidon* leads up to the land of Nephi. While I agree people had to travel upstream—and south—to get to the land of Nephi, it wasn't along the River Sidon that they did so. The text says only that the River Sidon flowed next to Zarahemla, not next to the city of Nephi. So how did people travel upstream to get to Nephi? They would travel from the head of Sidon up the Ohio River to the Tennessee River, and then up that river to Nephi. The Tennessee River flows north from the land of Nephi.

A7. The Mulekites made landfall in the land northward Alma 22:30, then founded their capital, Zarahemla, in the land southward Mormon 1:6 along the Sidon Mormon 1:10. As the Mulekites traveled south from the seacoast they went up in elevation Alma 22:31. This means the Sidon flowed downhill toward the north.

JN7: This is a common misunderstanding, based on an erroneous conflation of two different accounts that referred to two entirely different events. I explain this in more detail in the chapter on Omni, but for now I note that the account in Alma 22:30-31 was not referring to the people of Zarahemla who came from Jerusalem, but to the 43 scouts—people of Zarahemla—sent by King Limhi to find Zarahemla (Mosiah 8 and 22). This becomes evident when the text is carefully examined.

Mormon correctly described the land of Zarahemla as southward from where he was at the time. Throughout the text, the phrase "the land southward" is not a proper noun but a relative designation. Mormon's use of the term in Mormon 1:6 does not equate to the land southward as defined in Alma 22.

Zarahemla *was* located along the river Sidon. However, the conclusion that the river flowed south does not follow. Even if someone traveled south and went up in elevation, a river in that area could still flow north or south. It is the elevation in *the river bed* that matters, not the elevation of surrounding terrain, as I've shown in the examples from Egypt, Germany, and North America.

Jonathan Neville

Conclusion.

The text describes the River Sidon as having a north/south orientation, but it does not specify the direction of flow. One must infer direction of flow from other information about proximate locations, but these show the river flowing south, not north—just like the Mississippi River. Passages in the text that refer to going "up" to the land of Nephi and "down" to the land of Zarahemla are explained by the Tennessee River, which did flow down—northward—through the Land of Nephi to the land of Zarahemla.

So the notion that there is a north-flowing river is correct, but it's not the Sidon River. Translated into the modern world, the Sidon is the Mississippi, and the river flowing up and south to the land of Nephi is the Tennessee River.

NOTES

[207] There are some small rivers in North America that flow north, which is the basis for some proposed geographies in limited areas such as western New York, but these models have other problems. Besides, a north-flowing river contradicts the text.

[208] The discussion of the River Sidon in this section is a response to a blog entry titled "River Sidon South to North," dated November 8, 2011, by Kirk Magleby. It is located online here: http://bit.ly/Moroni125. Brother Magleby is one of the founders of FARMS and is an outstanding scholar of the Book of Mormon. His posts on his blog are thoughtful and detailed. I think his focus on Mesoamerica has affected his interpretations of the text, but his analysis of the various issues is superb.

[209] Ibid. The original answers are designated by A1, A2, etc.

Chapter 25 – Chiasmus and the Book of Mormon

CHIASMUS IS A HEBREW LITERARY FORM FIRST NOTICED in The Book of Mormon by John W. Welch in 1967 when he was a young missionary in Germany.[210] Numerous books and articles have been written on the topic, including Dr. Donald Parry's *Poetic Parallelisms in* The Book of Mormon[211], which seeks to reformat the complete text wherever there are parallel structures.

"Chiasmus is an inverted parallelism, a presentation of a series of words or thoughts followed by a second presentation of a series of words or thoughts, but in reverse order."[212] It is commonly presented by using capital letters to denote each line and its correspondent. Here is the example from Mosiah 2:56 that I showed in Chapter 3.

> A And it came to pass that when they came up to the <u>temple</u>,
>> B they pitched their tents round about,
>>> C every man according to his <u>family</u>,
>>>> D consisting of his wife, and his <u>sons</u>, and his <u>daughters</u>,
>>>> D and their <u>sons</u>, and their <u>daughters</u>, from the eldest down to the youngest,
>>> C every <u>family</u> being separate one from another.
>> B And they pitched their tents round about
> A the <u>temple</u> (chiasmus)[213]

Throughout this chapter I will follow the same nomenclature Parry uses (ABCD/DCBA), except I will annotate parallel lines with superscripts to make analysis of each line easier and clearer.

Welch describes the benefits of chiasmus:

Jonathan Neville

The repeating of key words in the two halves underlines the importance of the concepts they present. Furthermore, the main idea of the passage is placed at the turning point where the second half begins, which emphasizes it. The repeating form also enhances clarity and speeds memorizing. Readers (or listeners) gain a pleasing sense of completeness as the passage returns at the end to the idea that began it. Identifying the presence of chiasmus in a composition can reveal many complex and subtle features of the text.[214]

Dr. Parry has identified hundreds of chiastic and other parallel structures in The Book of Mormon. I looked at Alma 22 in Parry's excellent book. There are some parallel structures identified in the early parts of Alma 22, but none after verse 17. I met with Dr. Parry on 14 January 2015 to discuss my findings. He agreed that verses 27-34 have chiastic elements that he had not seen before. Pending his further review, in this article I present my own ideas. In doing so, I'm cognizant of Welch's observation regarding the technical requirements for identifying chiastic structures.

> Even if the example is not a very good one, a personally discovered chiasm tends to become a treasured piece of knowledge that the reader will continue to enjoy even if the example is not clear enough to convince anyone else that the passage should be called chiastic.[215]

My objective here is not to convince anyone that the parallel structures in Alma 22 should be used as evidence of the ancient origins of the text. I assume readers have accepted its ancient origins; if not, many other sources can be consulted on that issue, including the ones I cite here. Instead, my objective is to use these structures to better understand what the author, Mormon, was trying to communicate.

My analysis includes an assessment of Royal Skousen's work on the textual variants of The Book of Mormon as applied to these verses. I also disregard punctuation because, as Skousen notes, "The original manuscript basically had no punctuation except for some dashes in the book summaries. The scribes for the printer's manuscript occasionally supplied some punctuation as they copied the text."[216] Ancient languages such as Hebrew and Greek did not use punctuation, and I infer that because the original manuscript lacked punctuation, the ancient Nephite language also did not use punctuation.

Parallel structures in an ancient text can help clarify meaning similar to the way modern punctuation does in a modern text. Of course, modern punctuation placement can dramatically alter the meaning of a text. Ignoring parallel structures in an ancient text, or incorrectly arranging the structure,[217] could also dramatically alter the meaning. In my view, ignoring the parallel structures in Alma 22 has led to confusion in interpreting the text.

Parallel Structures and Technical Rules

Chiasmus is one of several types of parallel structures, including simple and extended synonymous, simple, repeated, and extended alternate, synthetic parallelism, graduation parallelism, detailing, working out, and contrasting ideas.[218] Repetition or reiteration of words and phrases is a subcategory of parallelism. Each occurrence of the repeated expression "takes on a certain coloration from the surrounding material and from its position in the series."[219]

The utility and even the validity of chiasmus is a topic of debate. Critics argue that chiasmus may be more the product of modern analysis than anything an ancient author intended. It is possible to find chiasmus in instruction manuals and Dr. Seuss books.[220] Chiasms may be proposed for a variety of reasons unrelated to the original author's intent.

> Welch's discovery [of chiasmus in The Book of Mormon] opened a Pandora's box of chiasms that have been identified in various works—it seems that in some Mormon circles chiasms are sought 'everywhere.' Some chiasms are used in an attempt to uncover hidden meanings, while others are treated as evidence of particular points of view in debates about Book of Mormon origins.[221]

Edwards and Edwards have developed an "admissibility test" based on mathematics to assess the intentionality of a proposed chiasm.[222] Welch has defined fifteen criteria useful to measure the strength or weakness of a proposed chiastic pattern.[223]

Here is the proposed chiastic structure for verse 27. Following normal convention, each line is lettered and chiastic terms are underlined. For clarity purposes, the repeated first word is bolded.

Jonathan Neville

And it came to pass that the king sent a proclamation throughout all the land
A amongst all his <u>people</u> who were in all his land who were in all the regions round about
  B **which** was <u>bordering</u> even to the sea on the <u>east</u> and on the <u>west</u> and
    C **which** was divided from the <u>land of Zarahemla</u> by a narrow strip of wilderness
      D a **which** ran from the <u>sea east</u>
        b even to the <u>sea west</u>
     D¹ a and round about on the <u>borders</u> of the seashore
        b and the <u>borders</u> of the wilderness
    C¹ **which** was on the north by the <u>land of Zarahemla</u>
  B¹ through the <u>borders</u> of Manti by the head of the river Sidon running from the <u>east</u> towards the <u>west</u>
A¹ —and thus were the <u>Lamanites</u> and the <u>Nephites</u> divided.

There are seven chiastic or parallel terms (*people, bordering, east, west, land of Zarahemla, sea east/sea west,* and *borders*) that occur only in their corresponding lines, and there is only one chiastic term that appears outside its corresponding line (*wilderness* in line C), giving this structure a low P score under the Edwards test, which is strong evidence of intentionality. But there are three important caveats: (i) the comparison of <u>his</u> <u>people</u> with <u>Lamanites</u>, (ii) the repetition of the word **which**, and (iii) the crux of the chiasm, which is a dual couplet that repeats the chiastic terms sequentially in groups of two instead of repeating them in inverse order.

1. COMPARISON OF <u>PEOPLE</u> WITH <u>LAMANITES</u>. The verse begins with the king sending a proclamation throughout all the land, but Mormon quickly notes it wasn't really all the land; the proclamation only went to the king's people who were in the king's land. Mormon takes this opportunity to outline the basic geographical distinction between the Lamanite king's lands and the lands of the Nephites, knowing this will become important later in his narrative. Inherent in the geography is the distinction between the king's people and the Nephites, or the Lamanites and the Nephites. Hence, *his people* is parallel to *Lamanites,* even though the words are not identical. Mormon makes a similar correlation between these terms in Helaman 11:21:

"the more part of the <u>people</u>, both the <u>Nephites and the Lamanites</u>, did belong to the church."

2. REPETITION OF THE WORD WHICH. The technical term for this usage is *like sentence beginnings*.[224] As a competing parallel structure, this repetition argues against the chiastic structure. However, Mormon needed to use the term to make it clear that each line refers back to the king's land that he was describing. Each phrase beginning with **which** provides more detailed understanding of the boundaries of the king's *land*, not the preceding phrase. The chiastic structure assists with this interpretation.

This is Parry's structure:

A   Behold <u>we will give</u> up
    B   The <u>land of Jershon</u>
       C   Which is <u>on the east</u> by the sea which joins the <u>land Bountiful</u>
       C¹   Which is <u>on the south</u> of the <u>land Bountiful</u>
    B¹   And this <u>land Jershon</u> is the land
A¹   Which <u>we will give</u> unto our brethren for an inheritance.[225]

Parry's interpretation of this verse balances the chiasmus (with respect to the term Bountiful) and places both Jershon and Bountiful on the sea, with Jershon south of Bountiful.

I propose a different structure for this verse. I think Mormon uses **which** as a serial modifier of an initial term in Alma 27:22 (ironically the inverse of Alma 22:27), not twice but each time it is used. I also note that in the printer's manuscript, *bountiful* is not capitalized in this passage. I propose that is not a mistake, but that in this case, *bountiful* is being used as an adjective, as I explain in the chapter on Alma.

  A Behold <u>we will give</u> up
    B The <u>land of Jershon</u>
      C <u>Which</u> is <u>on the east</u> by the sea
      C¹ <u>Which</u> joins the land bountiful
      C² <u>Which</u> is <u>on the south</u> of the land bountiful
    B¹ And this <u>land Jershon</u> is the land
  A¹ Which <u>we will give</u> unto our brethren for an inheritance.[226]

Jonathan Neville

This interpretation would break out *which joins the land bountiful* as a separate line, giving three distinct descriptions of Jershon: it is on the east by the sea, it joins the land bountiful (which presumably means it is adjacent to bountiful) and it is on the south of bountiful—but bountiful is not necessarily on the sea.

Regardless of which structure one applies to Alma 27:22, this is another example of Mormon using at least three **which** clauses to refer back to the original land being described. It is important to note that the use of **which** as a *like sentence beginning* does not undo the chiasm.

Referring back to Alma 22:27, what impact does the absence of a **which** beginning in line B^1 have?

The **which** beginnings do not destroy the chiasm, but neither are they essential to it. In this context, **which** is not even a chiastic term. Its presence is immaterial to the chiastic structure. It exists solely to explain to what precedent each line refers (in this case, the king's land). The absence of **which** at the beginning of line B^1 informs the reader that line B^1 modifies the preceding line. It describes the northern border with Zarahemla.

3. CRUX OF THE CHIASM. The crux or centerpiece of this chiasm is a dual couplet that repeats the chiastic terms sequentially in groups of two lines instead of repeating them in inverse order. Is this a unique or random structure? And does its inclusion at the crux of the chiasm impair or destroy the structure?

Parry describes a *simple alternate* as four lines placed in an AB/AB pattern.[227] In some cases, the AB/AB pattern contains elements that form an AA/BB pattern. For clarity purposes, I refer to the latter pattern as a *dual couplet*. Sometimes these are embedded inside a longer chiasm, and sometimes they are found at the crux or centerpiece of a chiasm.

A good example of a chiasm with an embedded couplet that is both a *dual couplet* and a *simple alternate* is Alma 36, one of the best-known chiasms in The Book of Mormon. This one is found in verse 26, embedded in section G of the chiasm:

a And have <u>tasted</u>
  b As I have <u>tasted</u>

a And have <u>seen</u> eye to eye
  b As I have <u>seen</u>

This passage repeats the chiastic terms *tasted* and *seen* in sequential lines instead of in reverse order. Parry designates this as an ab/ab structure, part of an *extended alternate* that continues in section F[228], yet the terms he underlines are in an aa/bb structure.

A similar structure occurs in 3 Nephi 27:8, this time at the crux of an important chiasm. Christ uses a structure Parry designates as *simple alternate* ab/ab, but He repeats chiastic terms sequentially instead of in reverse order—an aa/bb structure as well as an ab/ab structure.

  C
    a For if a church be called in <u>Moses' name</u>
      b then it be <u>Moses' church</u>
  C
    a or if it be called in the <u>name of a man</u>
      b then it be the <u>church of a man</u>[229]

Samuel the Lamanite also embeds a *simple alternate* at the crux of his chiasmus in Helaman 13:7.[230]

These examples show that Alma 22:27 is not unique in having a non-chiastic parallel structure at the crux of even a prominent chiasm, but what about Mormon as an author? Are there other examples of him combining parallel forms within a chiasmus that suggest the chiasm in this verse was intentional?

In Words of Mormon 1:3-11, Mormon writes a chiasmus with an embedded *repeated alternate* (verse 4).[231] In Mosiah 26:1-3, he places a *simple alternate* at the crux of a chiasmus.[232] In Alma 13:6-10, Mormon uses an *extended alternate and progression* at the crux of his chiasmus.[233] He uses both a simple alternate and a repeated alternate at the crux of his chiasmus in Alma 30:4-12.[234]

Combined with the examples from other authors, these samples of Mormon's writing demonstrate his familiarity with chiastic and other parallel structures. Alma 22:27 does appear to be an intentional chiasm.

Because Welch's fifteen criteria[235] contribute to understanding verse 27 and, in my view, support the validity of the chiastic structure, I apply them here.

1. OBJECTIVITY. The chiastic elements are objectively observable in the text, as I showed by underlining the parallel terms. The discussion above shows how these elements are used specifically to create the chiastic form.

2. PURPOSE. Mormon describes the boundaries of the king's land knowing he cannot refer to names familiar to his future readers. He also seeks to establish a framework for presenting the war maneuvers and strategies to come. How does chiasmus help with this? Possibly it's simply a function of how he thinks; i.e., he has read (and copied) so many chiasms that he organizes his thoughts in a chiastic structure. He goes from specifics to the overall picture and back to specifics, all in an attempt to convey geographical boundaries that his readers will be unfamiliar with.

3. BOUNDARIES. Mormon establishes clear boundaries for his discussion of geography. Verse 27 begins and ends with a declaration about the division between the people. Mormon's overall description of geography ends at verse 35, when he declares, "And now I, after having said this, return again to the account . . ."

4. COMPETITION WITH OTHER FORMS. By using *which* at the start of most of his lines in verse 27, Mormon does combine other forms of parallel structure, which could argue against a pure chiasm. But as explained above, *which* is neither an impediment to chiastic structure nor necessary for it.

5. LENGTH. Mormon introduces seven words or concepts in one order and then repeats them in the opposite order.

6. DENSITY. With only 111 words, verse 27 is compact.

7. DOMINANCE. The chiastic terms in the passage focus on Mormon's objective of describing the extent of the king's land. The construction relies on no insubstantial words.

8. MAVERICKS. There are no key elements in the system that appear extraneously outside the proposed structure, apart from one use of *wilderness*.

9. REDUPLICATION. There is reduplication in the passage; the terms sea, east, west, borders, seashore and wilderness appear in the couplets at the crux as well as in the parallel lines. This does not appear random, however,

because the dual couplets at the crux describe the overall boundaries of the land that the rest of the passage defines more specifically.

10. CENTRALITY. There is a well-defined centerpiece in verse 27, consisting of a dual couplet that defines the extent of the king's land. The dual couplet gives the east, west, north and south boundaries, as well as the general shape of the territory. The lines leading to it, and the parallel lines leading away from it, offer details about these boundaries.

11. BALANCE. The proposed chiasm is balanced in terms of lines and elements.

12. CLIMAX. The concept at the center is the main point of the passage; i.e., the extent of the king's land.

13. RETURN. The beginning and end create a strong sense of return and completion. The passage begins by referring to the king's people and ends with "thus were the Lamanites and Nephites divided."

14. COMPATIBILITY. The return is consistent with the overall style of Mormon as an author. As discussed above, Mormon uses the same parallel terms (people being parallel to Nephites and Lamanites) in Helaman 11:21, and in several other passages, Mormon combines different parallel elements in chiasms as he has here.

15. AESTHETICS. Like most of Mormon's parallel writings, this passage is not as fluid as chiasms written by the authors he quotes, such as Nephi and Alma. That helps to establish his unique writing style.

This application of Welch's criteria suggests that the structure in verse 27 satisfies most criteria of a legitimate, intentional chiasmus.

Alma 22:27-34 contains several forms of parallelism, including repetition. I propose that verse 27 is a chiasmus that includes repetition and fulfills the poetic purpose of detailing and working out, while verses 28-34 have variations of other forms of parallelism that achieve similar poetic purposes.

According to Parry, a detailing pattern "features an introductory phrase of sentence, followed by one or more subsequent lines that 'detail' what was said in line one . . . additional lines are presented for the purpose of adding details to the first line. Detailing frequently answers one of the questions— who, which, where, why, what, or how?"[236]

Jonathan Neville

The chiasmus in verse 27 answers the questions of which and where raised by the introductory clause; i.e., which land was the king's, and where was it?

A related poetic pattern is "working out," which "is a figure where two or more lines deliberate or explain what was first said in line one."[237]

Parry offers Helaman 1:31 as an example of working out:[238]

And now, behold, the Lamanites could not retreat either way
neither on the north,
nor on the south,
nor on the east,
nor on the west,
for they were surrounded on every hand by the Nephites.

The introductory phrase in verse 27 of Alma 22 starts with a declaration that the king spoke to his people who were in *his land*, in all the regions round about. The subsequent lines give detail about what his land consisted of.

Another parallel structure Parry describes is "repetition," which is "a subcategory of the poetic forms called parallelism."[239] "Like sentence beginnings" is a significant type of repetition. Parry offers Mormon 9:26 as an example:

And now behold,
<u>Who</u> can stand against the works of the Lord?
<u>Who</u> can deny his saying?
<u>Who</u> will rise up against the almighty power of the Lord?
<u>Who</u> will despise the works of the Lord?
<u>Who</u> will despise the children of Christ? (Mormon 9:26)

Another example is Alma 37:3. In this case Alma uses *which* in what Parry identifies as *like sentence beginnings* to modify the plates of brass:

Which contain these engravings
Which have the records of the holy scriptures upon them
Which have the genealogy of our forefathers[240]

Helaman 7:10 is another example that repeats the word *which* but the structure changes the way the term is used.

> And behold, now it came to pass that it was upon a <u>tower</u>,
>   <u>which</u> was in the <u>garden</u> of Nephi,
>   <u>which</u> was by the <u>highway</u>
>   <u>which</u> led to the chief market,
>   <u>which</u> was in the city of Zarahemla;
> therefore, Nephi had bowed himself upon the <u>tower</u>
>   <u>which</u> was in his <u>garden</u>,
>   <u>which</u> tower was also near unto the garden gate
>   by which led the <u>highway.</u> (Helaman 7:10)

This example is not a chiasmus; it does not repeat the words or concepts in reverse order. In this example, each *which* modifies the clause that precedes it.

Parry describes the first four lines of Helaman 7:10 as *like sentence beginnings* but does not identify a pattern in the lines beginning with *therefore*.[241] I infer that he does so because the pattern is not perfect—it only repeats the word *which* two times, and does not satisfy the technical elements of a specific parallel structure. From an analytical and academic perspective, this is a critical check on exuberance. Searching for parallel structures raises a risk of finding supposed parallels that do not meet the technical requirements; i.e., a reader may "stretch" the definitions of chiasmus too far, thereby diluting the concept.

However, I propose that the entire verse is a repetition that serves the objective of detailing. I categorize this structure as an *extended alternate*, which, according to Parry, differs from a simple and repeated alternate "in that additional alternating lines are present in extended alternate."[242] In other words, the lines repeat themselves in ABC/ABC pattern—but not exactly in this case. *Tower* and *garden* are parallel, but in the second stanza Mormon inserts the *garden gate* before repeating *highway*, and leaves out the market and reference to the city of Zarahemla.

Mormon as Author

Jonathan Neville

Despite the technical inadequacy of Helaman 7:10, I propose there are reasons to look at imperfect, broken, and mixed parallel structures in Mormon's writing. As I assess the parallel structures in Alma 22, I keep in mind that Mormon was a military man. He thinks in terms of borders and defense and offense, setting the stage for the war chapters he will spend a lot of time on. He's not a poet. His parallel structures are not as expertly designed as some of those he quotes, originally written by Nephi or King Benjamin or Alma, all of whom the text implies had training in the language.

In fact, in my view, this disparity in the quality of parallel structures is additional evidence of multiple authors (and of a complexity far beyond what Joseph Smith or any of his contemporaries were capable of writing on their own).[243] For example, in Helaman 7, we have a definite chiasmus in verses 6-9, but that is a quotation from Nephi. Verse 10 breaks away from Nephi's exclamation (And behold, now it came to pass) and Mormon writes this imperfect parallel structure. Helaman 10 is another good example of a chiastic quotation from Nephi. Helaman 6 is a chiastic chronicle of an entire year, presumably quoted by Mormon.

One more example of Mormon's style is found in Moroni 7:6-9, as structured by Parry.[244]

A   For behold, God hath said <u>a man being evil</u> cannot do that which is good
    B   for if <u>he offereth a gift, or prayeth</u> unto God,
       C   except he shall <u>do it with real intent</u>
          D   it <u>profiteth him nothing</u>.
          For behold, it is not counted unto him for righteousness.
A   For behold, if a <u>man being evil</u>
    B   <u>giveth a gift</u>,
       C   he <u>doeth it grudgingly</u>
          D   wherefore <u>it is counted unto him the same as if he had retained the gift</u>; wherefore he is counted evil before God.
A   And likewise also is it <u>counted evil unto a man</u>,
    B   if he shall <u>pray</u>
       C   and not <u>with real intent</u> of heart;
          D   yea, and it <u>profiteth him nothing</u>, for God receiveth none such.
          (Extended alternate)

This is a sermon by Mormon that Moroni added once he took over the record. Presumably it is from a document prepared by Mormon. As such, we might expect the sermon to be more formal than the historical narrative Mormon writes. And yet, the parallel structures even here are imperfect.

Parry describes verses 6-9 as an "extended alternate"[245] but the parallel lines are somewhat jumbled. Line b in verse 6 has two elements repeated, repeated separately in line b of verses 8 and 9. Lines d of verses 6 and 9 use *profited* but verse 8 doesn't. The last line of the first two verses is not repeated in the third verse. This is not to criticize Mormon but to show how he tends to use parallel structure.

Although he was no expert, certainly Mormon was familiar with parallel structures; that is evident from his selections of chiastic material for his compilation. In my lay opinion, Mormon's own efforts are more a natural product of a way of thinking than a product of formal training.

Welch comments on Mormon specifically:

> Mormon seems to have been relatively careful to quote entire texts—such as King Benjamin's speech, Alma's blessing to Helaman, and the annual report for the sixty-fourth year of the reign of the judges—as he incorporated those records into his own account. Mormon was often careful to identify when he was quoting from underlying sources as opposed to paraphrasing them. That his paraphrases tend to feature very little in the way of chiasmus also shows that the style of the abridger was different from the style of the underlying texts brought into the final record by direct quotation.[246]

Verses 27-34 in Alma 22 are unquestionably Mormon's own words. At the conclusion of the passage, in verse 35, he writes "And now I, after having said this, return again to the account of Ammon and Aaron, Omner and Himni, and their brethren." In my view, he provides this overview of geography not just to explain to whom the king's proclamation went, but to prepare the reader for the upcoming war chapters. The reader has no reason to care about the delineation of the borders with respect to the king's proclamation per se, but these borders are essential to understanding the different fronts in the wars, the movement of men and supplies, etc. that Mormon knows he will cover in future chapters. Alma 22 thus establishes a map, or at least an overall framework, for understanding Mormon's war material.

Mormon also knew he could not name a future landmark—say, New York City (or Guatemala City)—as a reference point or touchstone. He could only write in general terms, using bodies of water and wilderness to give an overall lay of the land. It is logical to expect Mormon to use the parallel structure to help orient the reader and explain the geographic challenges his people faced, especially in time of war.

Most of Mormon's own writings lack parallel structures, but he does use some in connection with geography in Alma 22, Helaman 6:10, 3 Nephi 1:27-28 (which is an example of working out or explaining a concept similar to Alma 22), 3 Nephi 6:2, and Mormon 3:7-8.

In assessing parallel structures in the next chapter, I ignore the verses as they are currently laid out in the text of The Book of Mormon. The text was divided into chapters and verses in 1879 by Orson Pratt, on assignment from John Taylor. This made it much easier to refer to particular passages, but does not reflect the original manuscript's structure—or the parallel structure.

Nevertheless, in some cases, the verses do coincide with the parallel structure, as in verses 27 and 28. In other cases, my assessment of the parallel structure leads me to consider portions of verses separately or combine portions of two adjoining verses.

Notes

[210] John W. Welch, "Chiasmus in The Book of Mormon," *BYU Studies* 10/1 (1969): 69-84.

[211] Donald W. Parry, *Poetic Parallelisms in* The Book of Mormon (Neal A. Maxwell Institute for Religious Scholarship, BYU, Provo, Utah, 2007). The book, cited herein as Parry, is available here: http://bit.ly/Moroni126.

[212] Parry, p. xvi.

[213] Parry, p. 160.

[214] John W. Welch, "A Masterpiece: Alma 36," in *Rediscovering* The Book of Mormon: *Insights you may have missed before* (Deseret Book Company, Salt Lake City, Utah, 1991, edited by John L. Sorenson and Melvin J. Thorne), p. 114.

[215] John W. Welch, "What Does Chiasmus in The Book of Mormon Prove?", found in Book of Mormon *Authorship Revisited: The Evidence for Ancient Origins,* (Foundation for Ancient Research and Mormon Studies, Provo, Utah, 1997, edited by Noel B. Reynolds): 202, herein cited as Welch, *Chiasmus.*

[216] Royal Skousen, *The Printer's Manuscript of* The Book of Mormon: *Typographical Facsimile of the Entire Text in Two Parts, Part One* (Foundation for Ancient Research and Mormon Studies, Brigham Young University, Provo, Utah 2001): 15.

[217] An example of what I consider an incorrect framing of Alma 22 is offered by F. Richard Hauck, Ph.D., "Recent Book of Mormon Research in Central America: Coming to Grips with Geography," *Meridian Magazine,* March 19, 2013, http://bit.ly/Moroni127. Dr. Hauck reaches conclusions similar to mine but with major differences attributable to his different structure, to inferences he draws from other verses, and to his insertion of a requirement for a mountainous terrain that is not in the text.

[218] For explanations and examples of these, see Parry, pp. xvi-xxxiv.

[219] Alter, *Art of Biblical Poetry,* 64, cited in Parry, xxxv.

[220] Boyd F. Edwards and W. Farrell Edwards, "When Are Chiasms Admissible as Evidence?" BYU Studies, Vol. 49, No. 4 (2010): 134.

[221] Ibid, 133.

[222] Ibid.

[223] John W. Welch, "Criteria for Identifying and Evaluating the Presence of Chiasmus," *Journal of Book of Mormon Studies* 4/2 (1995), referred to herein as Welch, "Criteria." Available online at http://bit.ly/Moroni128.

[224] Parry, xxxv.

[225] Parry, 296.

[226] Parry, 296. Parry includes my line D with his line C. His interpretation balances the chiasmus but changes the meaning; i.e., he would have the sea join the land Bountiful, making Jershon on the east by the sea and on the south of Bountiful. My interpretation describes Jershon as running from the east by the sea along the border of Bountiful to the area south of Bountiful.

[227] Parry, xxi.

[228] Parry, 321.

[229] Parry, 489-90.
[230] Parry, 423.
[231] Parry, 156.
[232] Parry, 211-2.
[233] Parry, 259-60.
[234] Parry, 300-1.
[235] Welch, "Criteria," p.
[236] Parry, xxxiii.
[237] Ibid.
[238] Parry, p. xxxiii-xxxiv.
[239] Parry, p. xxxiv.
[240] Parry, 322.
[241] Parry, 409.
[242] Parry, p. xxiii.
[243] Welch, *Chiasmus*, 207-213.
[244] Parry, 553-4.
[245] Parry, p. 426.
[246] Ibid, pp. 212-3.

Chapter 26 – A Chiastic Book of Mormon Geography

THIS CHAPTER OUTLINES AND ANALYZES the parallel structures in Alma 22 to create an overall abstract model of Book of Mormon geography. It shows that the text describes the setting proposed in previous chapters.

Alma 22:27—a Chiastic Overview of Book of Mormon Geography

And it came to pass that the king sent a proclamation throughout all the land
A   amongst all his <u>people</u> who were in all his land who were in all the regions round about
     B   **which** was <u>bordering</u> even to the sea on the <u>east</u> and on the <u>west</u> and
         C   **which** was divided from the <u>land of Zarahemla</u> by a narrow strip of wilderness
             D   a   **which** ran from the <u>sea east</u>
                  b   even to the <u>sea west</u>
             D¹   a   and round about on the <u>borders</u> of the seashore
                  b   and the <u>borders</u> of the wilderness
         C¹   **which** was on the north by the <u>land of Zarahemla</u>
     B¹   through the <u>borders</u> of Manti by the head of the river Sidon running from the <u>east</u> towards the <u>west</u>
A¹   —and thus were the <u>Lamanites</u> and the <u>Nephites</u> divided.

Analysis

The first fifteen words in the verse explain the main action; i.e., the king sent a proclamation throughout all the land. But it wasn't really *all* the land; it was only to *his* people in *his* land. Mormon realizes his readers need more clarification (if not necessarily now, they will in a few more chapters when he describes the wars), so he takes this opportunity to explain how the land was divided between the two main groups.

Lines A and A¹ both address the concept that there the king's people (Lamanites) were separate from others (Nephites). Note that Mormon uses the same parallel terms (<u>people</u> being parallel to <u>Nephites</u> and <u>Lamanites</u>) in Helaman 11:21 ("the more part of the people, both the Nephites and the Lamanites").

Lines B, C, D, and their counterparts describe what land was subject to the king. When read as an ordinary paragraph, this verse has led to a variety of interpretations. When read in chiastic format, it becomes clearer.

The chiastic structure with the repeating first term leads me to conclude that each line beginning with *which* is a description of the king's land—not a modification of the preceding line. This structure differs from the repeated parallel structure of Helaman 7:10, discussed above. In that case, the *which* clauses modified the preceding line. In this case the *which* clauses relate back to the main objective of the stanza—to describe the extent of the king's land.

This is evident in the grammar of Line B. The line begins with *which was,* a singular verb. If this line modified the preceding line (regions round about) the verb would have been plural.

(I realize other reasonable conclusions could be drawn, and I expect others will offer additional insight. I've worked out a few other alternatives but the one I describe here seems the most consistent with the structure Mormon created and is also the most internally consistent not only in Alma 22 but in the subsequent war chapters of Alma and the geographical references in Helaman.)

Lines B and B¹ refer to the east/west orientation of the Lamanite land. B explains that the land was bordering even to—in other words, extended as far as—*the sea on the east* and *on the west.* The omission of the term *sea* before *on the west* leaves the phrase somewhat ambiguous. The text could have said "the sea on the east and *the sea* on the west." Alternatively, it could have said "the *seas* on the east and on the west." The ambiguity can be resolved by inferring either that there was a sea on the west, or that if there was a sea, the border did not coincide with it; i.e., the border may have extended beyond or fallen short of any sea west. Or maybe it was just undefined—somewhere out west.

Although B¹ lacks the word *which*, it has elements parallel to B. I interpret it as a continuation of C¹. The king's land bordered the land of Zarahemla on the north, then bordered Manti, beginning at the head of Sidon, from east to west. The sequence of the northern border, from east to west, goes like this: Zarahemla, head of Sidon, Manti.

Lines C and C¹ explain the division between the king's land and the land of Zarahemla. The border consisted of a narrow strip of wilderness. The parallel structure helps us understand that C¹ explains that the border with Zarahemla—the narrow strip of wilderness—was on the north of the king's land "through the borders of Manti by the head of the river Sidon."

Lines D and D¹ are couplets. This is the "turning point" of the chiasmus, the most important point. These four lines describe the overall shape and dimensions of the king's land—the Lamanite territory. D describes the east/west boundary, while D¹ describes the north/south boundary. You start at the sea east and go to the sea west, then "round about" on the borders of the seashore (coming back to the sea east) and continuing round about on the borders of the wilderness back to the sea west.

Graphically, it looks like this:

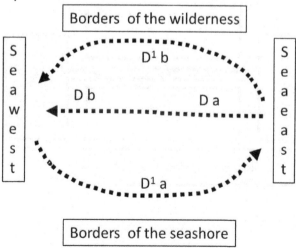

Figure 79 - Chiastic Diagram of Alma 22

We understand the "borders of the seashore" are on the south because we're also told that the north part of the king's land was the wilderness bordering on the land of Zarahemla.

Mormon could have simply described the king's land with D and D¹ but the lines ABC and C¹B¹A¹ offer additional detail and clarity.

An obvious question arises about the sea west, which is mentioned in Db but not in B. This supports the interpretation that the sea was omitted in B because it was implied.

An additional comment about directions is important. Some commentators, to rationalize a Mesoamerican setting, hypothesize that the Nephites did not use cardinal directions as we know them today. I find no justification in the text for that interpretation. Therefore, for purposes of this analysis, I assume the text describes cardinal directions, as we know them today; i.e., the sun rises in the east and sets in the west.

Accordingly, my understanding of verse 27 produces this general geography:

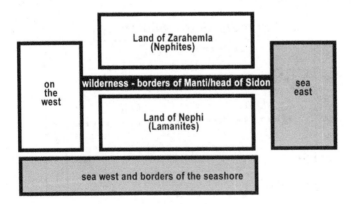

Alma 22:28

Now, the more idle part of the Lamanites lived in the wilderness and dwelt in tents

- A   and they were spread through the wilderness <u>on the west in</u> the <u>land of Nephi</u>
  - C   [yea, and also <u>on the west of the land of Zarahemla</u>]
- B   in the <u>borders by the seashore</u>
- A¹   and <u>on the west in the land of Nephi</u> in the place of their fathers' first inheritance
  - B¹   and thus <u>bordering</u> along <u>by the seashore</u>.

Analysis

This verse explains where the idle Lamanites live, what the term *wilderness* means, and where it is found in relation to the overall geography. *Wilderness* normally means a place where there are no cities or permanent dwellings. People live in tents, apparently because they are "idle," meaning they do not work hard or at least do not have a sophisticated social structure.

This is a parallel structure that I understand as a simple alternate (AB/AB), with an opposite (the C line) inserted as a sort of parenthetical to A. "More than one hundred examples of simple alternate forms can be found in The Book of Mormon,"[247] so this would be a common structure but for the problematic B line. Had Mormon included a second B line here, this would have been an extended alternate. (An extended alternate has more than the two repeated lines of a simple alternate, such as ABC/ABC.)

Line B could be interpreted several ways, but as an opposite (Zarahemla instead of Nephi), its insertion here suggests it operates as a parenthetical clarification, so I put it in brackets. Mormon has already told us that Zarahemla is north of Nephi, and that the Lamanite territory was bordering on the west. Line B appears to be a clarification; i.e., line B tells us there is land west of Zarahemla that is not part of the land of Nephi—sort of a no-man's land, or an unclaimed wilderness where idle Lamanites live in tents.

A and A¹ match, as do B and B¹. C does not have a match. (Structurally, the phrase *in the place of their fathers' first inheritance* might be C¹ except his has no linguistic correlation to B.) The *first inheritance* clause informs us that

Jonathan Neville

there are east and west sides of the land of Nephi, and that Lehi landed on the west side.

Lines A/A¹ and B/B¹ repeat the point that the idle Lamanites live on the west *in* the land of Nephi (*within* Lamanite territory) and along the borders by the seashore, but setting off C this way suggests that those living on the west of the land of Zarahemla do not live by the borders of the seashore. In other words, those idle Lamanites living in the wilderness west of Zarahemla do not live by a seashore. The "sea west" does not extend north or west far enough to form a western border near Zarahemla.

Verse 27 explained that the Lamanite territory "was bordering even to the sea on the east and on the west." Verse 28 seems to clarify that all of the west does not border on a sea; only those areas that are in the land of Nephi border on the sea.

This verse leads me to modify my schematic.

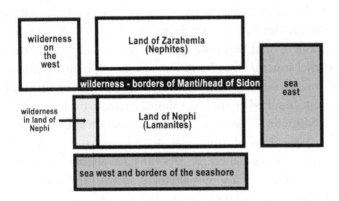

Alma 22:29a

And also there were many Lamanites on the east by the seashore whither the Nephites had driven them.

Analysis

In this sentence, Mormon makes a clear break from the seashore he referred to in the preceding stanza. Now he's talking about a seashore on the east inside the land of Nephi. He makes no distinction between Nephi and

306

Zarahemla on the east, implying the Lamanites occupy the east all the way north to the top of Zarahemla. The east side lacks a "no-man's land;" all those Lamanites on the east are by the seashore. This means the narrow strip of wilderness does not extend all the way to the east coast.

With this information, I modify the diagram again.

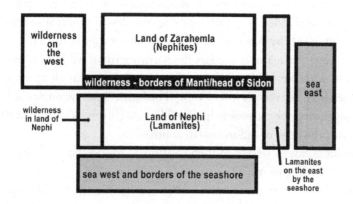

Alma 22:29b

And thus the Nephites were nearly surrounded by the Lamanites;

A   nevertheless the Nephites had taken possession of all the <u>northern</u> parts of the land
    B   bordering on the <u>wilderness</u>
        C   at the head of the river Sidon
        C¹   from the east to the west
    B¹   round about on the <u>wilderness</u> side
A¹   on the <u>north</u>, even until they came to the land which they called Bountiful

Analysis

Here, Mormon makes several important observations. First, he's now going to explain the Nephite territory. The Nephites are nearly surrounded. From what he's explained so far, we have Lamanites on the south, on the east, and at least sparsely populating the wilderness west of Zarahemla where there is no sea. This leaves only the north—which is exactly what Mormon says the Nephites have possessed in A and A^1.

Second, Mormon previously explained that the border between Zarahemla and Nephi was on the north of Nephi, making the border also on the south of Zarahemla. We can infer that *bordering on the wilderness* means the narrow strip of wilderness south of Zarahemla because he ties it back to the head of the river Sidon. C and C^1 pick up the description from verse 27 (the borders of Manti by the head of the river Sidon running from the east towards the west). So again, it appears the narrow strip of wilderness runs east and west, with the *head of Sidon* being a significant point along the border somewhere between east and west. The border goes through the head of Sidon, suggesting the narrow strip of wilderness (east/west) is a river that intersects with the head of Sidon (north/south).

The border is east to west, and then continues "round about on the wilderness side on the north."

As we saw from the previous verses, Mormon mentions no wilderness on the east. There was a narrow strip of wilderness along the east-west border, leading to the wilderness on the west of Zarahemla.

Here, Mormon directs us along the border from east to west, passing through or by the head of Sidon, and then "round about" on the wilderness (or west side) on the north, until we reach Bountiful. He's describing a loop; i.e., start in the east, follow the boundary west, circle north until we reach Bountiful. This implies Bountiful extends the rest of the way back to the east where we started; otherwise, the description of the border leaves a gap.

The diagram now focuses on the land of Zarahemla.

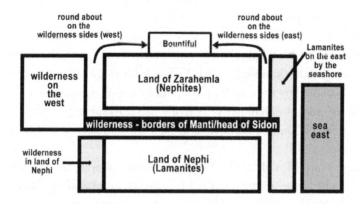

Alma 22:30

A   And <u>it bordered</u> upon the <u>land</u>

    B   <u>which</u> they called Desolation,

A¹   <u>it being</u> so far northward that <u>it came</u> into the <u>land</u>

    B¹   <u>which</u> had been peopled and [had] been destroyed, of whose bones we have spoken,

    B²   <u>which</u> was discovered by the people of Zarahemla

A²   <u>it being</u> the place of their first landing and they came from there up into the south wilderness.

Analysis

This structure helps clarify this otherwise confusing and controversial passage. The entire passage is a parenthetical explanation of Bountiful, a digression from the overall map Mormon is describing. By using *it* to refer to Bountiful and *which* to refer to Desolation, the structure clarifies which attributes apply to which areas. It resembles a simple alternate, AB/AB, with an added B². Also, I inserted [had] as Skousen did in his critical text. This is a small detail that plays a significant role.[248]

The passage tells us three things about the land Bountiful: 1) it bordered upon the land Desolation; 2) it was so far northward that it came into the land Desolation (the territories overlapped); and 3) it was the place of the first landing of the people of Zarahemla (Limhi's 43 explorers).

Actually, the explorers found *both* Bountiful and Desolation, since the two areas overlapped. Mormon is writing hundreds of years in the future, looking back with his knowledge that the Nephites would occupy the land previously occupied by the Jaredites. But when Limhi's 43 explorers discovered the area, no Nephites were living there. Relative to the land of Nephi from which Limhi's explorers left, the land Bountiful was "far northward."

We know from Mosiah 21:25-27 that the explorers were looking for Zarahemla, which they understood to be a large city on the river Sidon. Naturally their first landing would be at a large city on the river. This turned out to be a place that "had been people and had been destroyed." Thinking it was Zarahemla that had been destroyed, they found the plates of Ether and saw no reason to explore further, so they left from there and returned to the south wilderness (Mosiah 21:26 explains they arrived the borders of the land not many days before Ammon came).

Alma 22:31

Thus [a summary]

A   the land on the northward was called Desolation and
A¹   the land on the southward was called Bountiful,
     B   it being the wilderness which [was] filled with all manner of wild animals of every kind, a part of which had come from the land northward for food.

Analysis

The parallel structure here contrasts the land Desolation from the land Bountiful, but the northward/southward designation is *only relative to one another.* From the previous passage, we know the lands overlap. (The Jaredite lands were not defined by the Ohio River; the land they occupied included both of the lands designated by the Nephites as Desolation and Bountiful.)

Verse 31 explains that Desolation was northward and Bountiful southward, but *both* are within the *land* northward; i.e., within the greater land of Zarahemla. This clarifies a key point in Book of Mormon geography; i.e., in the overall picture, the land northward, controlled by the Nephites, is Zarahemla, and the land southward, controlled by the Lamanites, is the land of Nephi. Desolation and Bountiful are distinct areas, possibly similar to provinces, within greater Zarahemla.

(Note 1: the parenthetical about wild animals merely explains the origin of the name Bountiful. Note 2: I inserted [was] as Skousen does in the critical text. The current edition of the Book of Mormon has *is* here, contrary to the printer's manuscript.)

Another way to restate the meaning of this passage: both Desolation and Bountiful are in territory controlled by the Nephites becaue "the Nephites had taken possession of all the northern parts of the land bordering on the wilderness" (Alma 22:29). But relative to a particular point within Nephite territory, Desolation was northward and Bountiful was southward.

What is the particular point Mormon is using as a reference here?

He tells us in the next sentence.

Alma 22:32a

And now it was only the distance of a day and a half's journey for a Nephite on the line Bountiful and the land Desolation from the east to the west sea.

Analysis

This passage has caused tremendous confusion. It lacks parallel structure so there is no help from reformatting it. We have part of the original manuscript for this passage and it reads exactly like the printers manuscript,[249] so there is no help from those manuscripts, either.

Nevertheless, Skousen asserts that "the extant reading for Alma 22:32 is quite unacceptable [so] the critical text will assume that some phrase was accidentally omitted in O as Oliver Cowdery took down Joseph Smith's dictation."[250] Skousen suggests[251] adding the phrase *between the land* between *line* and *Bountiful* so the verse reads "on the line between the land Bountiful and the land Desolation." One reason is 3 Nephi 3:23, which refers to "the

line which was between the land Bountiful and the land Desolation."
Skousen's suggestion is understandable but I disagree with it. (The reference
in 3 Nephi involves a different location, but that's not my main reason.)

I think the passage here is correct as is, although this may not be apparent
at first.

Essentially, Mormon is describing two segments of the unnamed
Nephite's journey. Part of it is along the line Bountiful, and part is on the
land Desolation from the east to the west sea.

This is not the only passage that refers to a *line* and a *Nephite's journey*.
Helaman 4:7 explains: "it being a day's journey for a Nephite on the line
which they had fortified and stationed their armies to defend their north
country."

I think Mormon is referring to the same line in both verses.

In other words, it was a day's journey for a Nephite on the line (both the
line Bountiful and the line they fortified to defend their north country). It
was a half day's journey to go from the east to the west sea in the land
Desolation.

The *combined* journey took a day and a half.

The verse is correct.

It was this standard "journey for a Nephite" that was Mormon's reference
point when he wrote "the land on the northward was called Desolation and
the land on the southward was called Bountiful." Relative to this area,
Desolation is northward and Bountiful is southward.

How far does "a Nephite" journey in a day?

A day consists of 12 hours, on average. The average human walking speed
is about 3.1 miles/hour, but an average man walks 4-5 miles/hour.
Presumably "a Nephite" would walk at least 4 miles/hour. According to the
text, the line Bountiful is one day's journey—48 miles—and the land
Desolation takes one half of a day—24 miles. (If the Nephite journeys over
Desolation by water, presumably he can go a little faster).

The particular area I propose for the "journey for a Nephite" is the
Niagara peninsula in New York. The area fits Mormon's description almost
exactly. The line Bountiful—from the Allegheny River to Lake Ontario—is
about 48 miles. One day's journey for a Nephite. The land Desolation, from
the east to the west sea, is about 22-26 miles by land. A half day's journey for

a Nephite. Combined, they are a day and a half's journey, exactly as the scripture says.

(There is also a waterway across Niagara, which is about 30 miles long because of curves. Presumably a Nephite could travel a little faster by water than by walking.)

Figure 80 shows the location of these features.

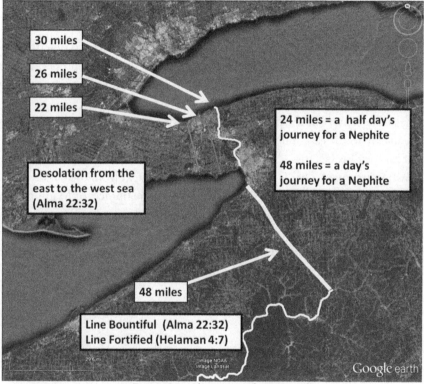

30 miles

26 miles

22 miles

24 miles = a half day's journey for a Nephite

48 miles = a day's journey for a Nephite

Desolation from the east to the west sea (Alma 22:32)

48 miles

Line Bountiful (Alma 22:32)
Line Fortified (Helaman 4:7)

Figure 80 - Alma 22:32 diagrammed

The passage, as it is written, fits the geography.

Skousen also recommends that the phrase *from the east* be left unchanged, relying on the other conjunctive occurrences that combine sea with east and west, "with the understanding that the word *sea* is purposely ellipted."[252] In other words, the original text omitted the word *sea*, whether to save space or because it was clearly implied; i.e., it should read "the land Desolation from the east *sea* to the west sea."

While it is possible *east* in this passage could refer to a well-known landmark in the east, it makes more sense that an east sea is implied, so I agree with Skousen on this point.

This brings up the problem of *seas*.

There has been considerable confusion about the various seas described in the text for two reasons. One, people have assumed these were proper nouns instead of generalized directional designations. Two, people have not taken into consideration the context of each particular passage.

In the context of the passage in verse 32, Mormon is referring specifically to the east and west sea that are part of the Nephite's "day and a half journey" as he crosses Desolation from the east sea to the west sea, as shown in the map. That is an entirely different context from the context of the narrow strip of wilderness that flows through the borders of Manti by the head of the river Sidon. And it is an entirely different context from when Mormon mentions to the sea west in Helaman 4:7, referring to the fortified western border of Bountiful.

The importance of context is portrayed in Figure 81:

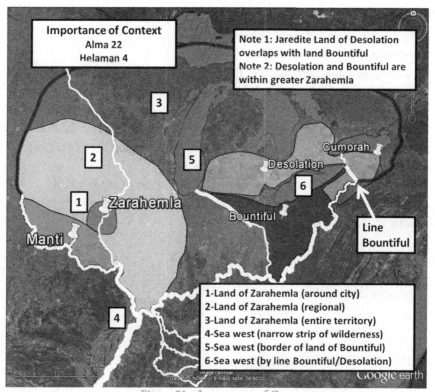

Figure 81 - Importance of Context

The "land of Zarahemla" can have at least three meanings, based on context. It can be the area immediately around the city of Zarahemla, the regional area along the River Sidon (the original territory when Mosiah first entered the land), and the entire Nephite territory. Bountiful and Desolation both fit within the greater land of Zarahemla, but they are quite a distance away from the regional land of Zarahemla. Context is key. When considering the meaning of lands northward and lands southward, the same principle applies. Context is key.

Context is also essential to understand references to the seas, including the sea west. Literally, all the term means is a sea west of the speaker's (or author's) frame of reference. Certainly it would have been easier had the Nephites given these seas names, but once we understand the designations are relative, the geography becomes clear.

Jonathan Neville

Critics may complain that a context-based interpretation is too easy, or too subjective, but I disagree. One still must read the text carefully and compare it to a real world setting.

The more important question is, what did the authors intend?

The fact that the Nephites didn't use proper nouns when referring to the various seas indicates that they relied on context themselves. Perhaps they had an aversion to naming bodies of water. Nephi didn't name the ocean they crossed. The Sidon River and the waters of Mormon are named, but other bodies of water remain generic in the text.

What sense does it make to insist that the authors of the Book of Mormon intended proper nouns for these seas when they explicitly used generic terms instead?

Alma 22:32b

and thus [a summary]

A   the land of Nephi
   B   and the land of Zarahemla
      C   were nearly surrounded by water,
      C¹   there being a small neck of land between
   B¹   the land northward
A¹   and the land southward.

Analysis

This chiastic structure reminds us that the land northward was the land of Zarahemla and the land southward was the land of Nephi. Both were nearly surrounded by water, with a small neck of land between them.

The text does not say these lands were nearly surrounded by *seas*. It uses the term *water*, which includes any body of water. To a military general such as Mormon, water in whatever form creates particular challenges and opportunities, so it is not surprising that he would make this observation.

If the land of Nephi and the land of Zarahemla are each surrounded by water (except for the small neck of land), then the border *between* them must be water. This confirms my conclusion that the *narrow strip of wilderness* consists of major rivers.

Relating the Book of Mormon geography to modern references, the land of Nephi is surrounded by seas on the east, south, and west (the Atlantic, Gulf of Mexico, and lower Mississippi, respectively). The land of Zarahemla is surrounded by rivers and the Great Lakes.

The only area between Nephi and Zarahemla that was not a water boundary was the small neck *of land* at the line Bountiful. This was a strategic area because, left undefended, the Lamanites would have access directly into Nephite territory. Consequently, this neck of land was well fortified and measured (a day's journey for a Nephite).

Alma 22:33a

And it came to pass that the Nephites had inhabited the land Bountiful even from the east unto the west sea.

Analysis

It's not clear why Mormon included this sentence. We infer from what he has already written that the Nephites inhabited this land. What does he mean by "And it came to pass" and "had inhabited" the land?

I think he is looking back, from centuries in the future, at the day when the Nephites were "driven even into the land of Bountiful and there they did fortify against the Lamanites from the west sea even unto the east" (Helaman 4:7). There is parallelism here, albeit separated by considerable distance.

Even from the east unto the west sea (Alma 22:33)
From the west sea even unto the east (Helaman 4:7)

These are also the two passages that refer to the "journey for a Nephite" in connection with the line and the small neck of land. In Mormon's day, the Nephites lost this land. The line Bountiful was obliterated on the way to Cumorah. Perhaps he is expressing nostalgia here, remembering the days when the Nephites still occupied the land of Bountiful.

Jonathan Neville

Alma 22:33b-34a

and thus [a summary]

the Nephites in their wisdom with their guards and their armies

A   had hemmed in
    B   the <u>Lamanites</u> on the south,
        C that thereby they should have <u>no more possession</u> on the <u>north</u>
        C^1 that they might not overrun the land <u>northward</u>.
    B^1 Therefore the <u>Lamanites</u>
        C^2 could have no more <u>possessions</u>
A^1 only in the land of Nephi and the wilderness round about.

Analysis

There are parallel elements here, but they are too disjointed to constitute a formal parallel structure. Still, Mormon emphasizes the main points through repetition, and his structure offers an insight into his opinion of the situation. For example, the line I designate as A^1 could actually be a C^3, since it is a contrast to C^1. But I placed it as A^1 because I think it relates back to A.

In A, Mormon writes that the Nephites had *hemmed in* the Lamanites by limiting their possessions to the land of Nephi and the wilderness round about (A^1). In other words, the Nephites have managed to get themselves surrounded!

This passage is ironic in tone. How does one "hem in" an enemy when one is surrounded? Normally, the person *surrounded* is the one who is hemmed in. When Mormon writes that the Nephites got themselves into this precarious position *in their wisdom*, I think he is actually adding to the irony. As he will explain in the war chapters, the Nephites' strategic position was not all that effective, after all.

Of course, it is possible Mormon actually thinks it was wisdom for the Nephites to "hem in" the Lamanites on the south and in the wilderness round about. Maybe, given the numerical superiority of the Lamanites, they had no alternatives. Maybe this was the best they could do under the circumstances. If so, then the structure would change my line A^1 to C^3, as mentioned above. This is an example of how structure can change meaning or at least nuance.

Regardless of any intended irony, the parallel structure suggests Mormon has two separate concerns. The Nephites want to prevent the Lamanites from having possession of any territory on the north, meaning the land of Zarahemla, but they are also concerned about the Lamanites overrunning the land northward, meaning the land of Desolation. Is Mormon implying there was some way for the Lamanites to overrun Desolation even if they had no possessions in the north? I think so, and the war chapters explain how this happened.

Alma 22:34b

Now this was wisdom in the Nephites—as the Lamanites were an enemy to them, they would not suffer their afflictions on every hand, and also that they might have a country whither they might flee, according to their desires.

Analysis

Here, Mormon does find wisdom in the Nephite strategy, at least to the extent that they had a defended border and a defined territory. Separately, the Nephites retained the land northward as a place for a strategic retreat in case retreat became necessary because of a breakdown of their border defenses. Again, Mormon is setting the stage for the war chapters.

Conclusion

Alma 22:27-34 provides the longest comprehensive description of Book of Mormon geography in the text. As published, The Book of Mormon does not reveal the hundreds of parallel structures it contains. Readers must consult resources such as Parry's book or Welch's articles to see the structures. Reformatting passages that contain such structures adds meaning and insight into the intent of the various authors of the Book of Mormon, as well as the intent of Mormon, the overall editor.

In the case of Alma 22:27-34, the parallel structures provide an entirely new abstract geography of Book of Mormon events that suggests a predominantly east/west orientation of the Nephite territory. By contrast, traditional models focus on a north/south orientation, separated by a narrow neck of land—the hourglass shape I discussed in Chapter 3.

I offer this chiastic analysis as a tool to help understand the text. I think it makes a big difference to structure the text this way, instead of relying on punctuation inserted by the original printer.

It has been surprising to discover this level of complexity in the text. Surely Joseph Smith and Oliver Cowdery could not have known about this; in fact, I think they could not understand how the text describes the geography they had learned by revelation and experience.

It is even more astonishing that the parallel structure describes a real-world geography in North America that aligns with everything Joseph and Oliver actually said and wrote on the topic.

NOTES

---

[247] Parry, p. xxi.

[248] Skousen, p. 2066. Previously I explained how the restoration of [had] makes it more obvious that Mormon is quoting from the Mosiah account of Limhi's explorers.

[249] Skousen notes there is a crossed out *w* before *bountiful*. He suggests Oliver started to write *which*, caught his error, erased the w he had written, and then skipped *between the land*. I don't know why Oliver wrote the w, but the passage wouldn't make sense with *between the land*. It's better as is.

[250] Skousen, p. 2068.

[251] Skousen, p. 2070.

[252] Skousen, p. 2070.

Chapter 27 – Summary of Book of Mormon Geography Theories

—≫ ≪—

THE CHURCH OF JESUS CHRIST OF LATTER-DAY SAINTS has no formal position on Book of Mormon geography, which leaves the question of geography open to interpretation.[253] The search for Book of Mormon locations has been underway for over a hundred years. While the search has led to dozens of theories, that doesn't mean the truth will never be known.

Church leaders have emphasized that the geography question is not as important as the doctrines, a proposition with which I think all believers agree. But they have also indicated that the truth, someday, would be discovered.

In 1903, President Joseph F. Smith reportedly "expressed the idea that the question of the situation of the city [of Zarahemla] was one of interest certainly, but **if it could not be located** the matter was not of vital importance, and if there were differences of opinion on the question it would not affect the salvation of the people."[254]

In 1929, Anthony W. Ivins of the First Presidency said, "There is a great deal of talk about the geography of the Book of Mormon. Where was the land of Zarahemla? Where was the City of Zarahemla? and other geographic matters. It does not make any difference to us. There has never been anything yet set forth that definitely settles that question. So the Church says **we are just waiting until we discover the truth**."[255]

In 1929, James E. Talmage said, "**I encourage and recommend all possible investigation, comparison and research in this matter.** The more thinkers, investigators, workers we have in the field the better; but our brethren who devote themselves to that kind of research should remember that they must **speak with caution and not declare as demonstrated truths points that are not really proved**."[256]

In 1947, John A Widtsoe wrote a forward to Thomas S. Ferguson's book, *Cumorah—Where?* that included this statement: "out of the studies of faithful Latter-day Saints **may yet come a unity of opinion** concerning Book of Mormon geography."[257]

Latter day scriptures anticipate a day when more knowledge shall be revealed. An article in the New Era[258] answered the question, "What is the 'sealed portion' of the Book of Mormon and will we ever know what's in it?"

When Moroni was finishing the Book of Mormon record, he was commanded to seal up some of the plates, and Joseph Smith was later commanded not to translate them. This sealed portion contains the complete record of the vision of the brother of Jared (see Ether 4:4–5). This vision included "all things from the foundation of the world unto the end thereof" (2 Nephi 27:10–11; see also Ether 3:25). So basically the Lord revealed to the brother of Jared the history of mankind, and the sealed portion of the plates was Moroni's translated copy of it.

Few people have seen the sealed record—for instance, the Nephites in the land Bountiful at the Savior's coming (see Ether 4:1–2) and Moroni (see Ether 12:24). The Lord said the sealed portion would be revealed to the world "in mine own due time" (Ether 3:27). He also said it would "not go forth unto the Gentiles until the day that they shall repent of their iniquity, and become clean before the Lord" (Ether 4:6; see also 2 Nephi 27:8).

According to Joseph Smith's associates who saw the golden plates, anywhere from half to two-thirds of all the plates were in the sealed portion (see Kirk B. Henrichsen, "What Did the Golden Plates Look Like?" New Era, July 2007, 31).

D&C 121:28 refers to "a time to come in the which nothing shall be withheld." The 9th Article of Faith affirms that "We believe all that God has revealed, all that He does now reveal, and we believe that He will yet reveal many great and important things pertaining to the Kingdom of God."

From these and other references, we conclude it's not a question of whether we'll ever know the location of Book of Mormon events, but when.

Moroni's America

In the meantime, we can work to build consensus based on all the available evidence. The first step in doing that is to *consider* all the available evidence. The next step is to seek to integrate and harmonize it all.

The following table illustrates how the two most prominent models of Book of Mormon geography reconcile the extrinsic evidence.

Authorities	Mesoamerica	Heartland
Relies on BoM text for abstract map of geography	Yes	Yes
Fits BoM text to real-world geography	Yes	Yes
Accepts entire text literally		
- Cardinal directions (N,S,E,W)	No	Yes
- Animals and plants	No	Yes
- Surrounded by water	No	Yes
- Four seas	No	Yes
- 3 Nephi change face of land	No	Yes
- Law of Moses	No	Yes
Relies on *Times and Seasons* articles about Stephens	Yes	No
Accepts D&C on Lamanites	No	Yes
Accepts D&C on Cumorah	No	Yes
Accepts D&C on Zarahemla	No	Yes
Accepts Oliver Cowdery on Cumorah in New York	No	Yes
Accepts David Whitmer on Cumorah in New York	No	Yes
Accepts Joseph Smith on Cumorah in New York	No	Yes
Accepts Joseph Smith on mounds in Midwest as evidence of BoM people	No	Yes
Accepts Joseph Smith in Wentworth letter that Lamanites are Indians living in "this country" meaning United States	No	Yes
Accepts archaeology	Yes	Yes
Accepts DNA evidence	No	Yes
Promised land is Mexico/Guatemala	Yes	No
Promised land is US/Canada	No	Yes

Jonathan Neville

Some may quibble with my characterizations, but as I've explained, I believed in the Mesoamerican theory for 40 years. I know it pretty well.

In my view, the various Mesoamerican models do not and *cannot* lead to a consensus because they fail to reconcile so much extrinsic yet relevant, authoritative and credible evidence. Other models, such as the ones based in Baja Mexico, South America, and limited areas of New York, Pennsylvania, and other locations, also fail to reconcile most of the extrinsic evidence.

What I've sought to present in this book is a model that does harmonize all this evidence with the text, as well as with the relevant geology, geography, archaeology, and anthropology, is the Heartland model.

Roger Terry, Senior Associate Editor, BYU Studies, once wrote, "Obviously, if one of the models answered all the questions presented by the scriptural text, there would be consensus on where the Book of Mormon history actually occurred."

Like me, most believers in the Book of Mormon agree with Brother Terry. We wish that consensus already existed, but at least now it's in sight.

NOTES

[253] Anyone who peruses the Church's web page, manuals, magazines, and officially approved art might conclude that the Church's policy, in practical terms, is actually to not take an official position on *where in Mesoamerica* the Book of Mormon events took place. Building a replica Mayan temple on the Hill Cumorah in New York each year for the Hill Cumorah Pageant is a prime example of the confusion that currently exists among believers. There are examples of true neutrality, though. The video presentation titled "Scriptures Legacy" appears to portray Christ visiting the Nephites in a North American setting. But other parts of the film depict Book of Mormon events in Mayan-looking buildings and cities.

[254] Deseret News, 25 May 1903, online at fairmormon.org http://bit.ly/Moroni140.

[255] Anthony W. Ivins, Conference Report (April 1929), 16. http://bit.ly/Moroni140.

[256] James E. Talmage, Conference Report (April 1929), 44, http://bit.ly/Moroni140.

[257] Cited by Sorenson in *Mormon's Map*, p. 7, http://bit.ly/Moroni140.

[258] *New Era*, October 2011, http://bit.ly/Moroni141.

Chapter 28 – Mesoamerica as Hinterlands

—≫≫ ≪≪—

FOR DECADES, LDS SCHOLARS HAVE LABORED TO ESTABLISH and defend a Mesoamerican setting for the Book of Mormon because they believed they were vindicating what Joseph Smith wrote (or approved) in three articles published in the *Times and Seasons* on 15 September and 1 October 1842. The discovery that it was someone other than Joseph Smith, Wilford Woodruff, or John Taylor who wrote the articles,[259] led to the further discovery that Benjamin Winchester wrote the articles linking the Book of Mormon to Central America, and that William Smith edited and published them.[260] These discoveries raise serious questions about the original premise for both hemispheric and Mesoamerican theories of Book of Mormon geography. Although now discredited, these *Times and Seasons* articles have influenced generations of Latter-day Saints—members, scholars, and leaders[261]—and have been frequently cited by those who advocate a Mesoamerican setting.

In response to the Winchester saga, some proponents of the Mesoamerican setting now claim the *Times and Seasons* articles are ancillary, or even irrelevant, to Book of Mormon geography. This article accepts that premise for the sake of argument and examines Mesoamerican geography on the merits, without the implied imprimatur of Joseph Smith's authorship— or editorial approval—of the *Times and Seasons* articles. As John Sorenson wrote, "If we are to progress in this task, we must chop away and burn the conceptual underbrush that has afflicted the effort in the past. We must stop asking, as so many do, what have the Brethren said about this in the past?"[262]

A separate reason for taking another look at the Mesoamerican theory stems from a 2014 article by Mark Alan Wright. Wright proposes that the "best available evidence for the Book of Mormon continues to support a limited Mesoamerican model," with North America being the "hinterlands."[263] The hinterlands approach seeks to account for various statements by Joseph Smith and his associates (including other articles Winchester wrote for the *Times and Seasons*) that suggest a North American setting for the Book of Mormon. Wright's hinterlands argument goes like this. The Book of Mormon text covers less than one percent of Nephite history; the other ninety-nine percent could have included people and places well outside the scope of the text. In addition, Alma 63 describes northward migration of people who are never heard from again. Therefore, Joseph Smith's references to Nephites in North America involved those migrants, not the inhabitants of Zarahemla, Bountiful, etc.

One example of Wright's analysis involves the phrase "plains of the Nephites" that Joseph Smith claimed he crossed during Zion's camp. Here's Wright's explanation:

Likewise, the "plains of the Nephites" are never mentioned in the Book of Mormon. To be sure, there are "plains" mentioned between the cities Bountiful and Mulek in Alma 52:20, and we read of the "plains of Nephihah" in Alma 62:18, but the general term "plains of the Nephites" is absent from the Book of Mormon. Because there are multiple plains attested to in the text, the general phrase "plains of the Nephites" is too vague to be of any use in pinpointing it geographically. Even among the Jaredites we read of the "plains of Heshlon" (Ether 13:28) and the "plains of Agosh" (Ether 14:15), but significantly, never just "the plains of the Jaredites." Plains in the text of the Book of Mormon are always attached to a specific city. Those in Joseph's letter to Emma are not.[264]

Wright overlooks two obvious points. First, Joseph could have been referring to *all* of the plains of mentioned in the Book of Mormon. After all, he had traversed Ohio, Indiana, and Illinois—a distance of over 650 miles, most of it consisting of plains—by the time he wrote the letter to Emma. Why would he feel compelled to cite specific names from the text, especially when one of the plains Wright himself refers to was not named? Second, Joseph's mother related how Joseph described the Nephites as if he had lived among them. He could have been aware of additional Nephite plains not specifically named in the Book of Mormon. If so, and if he knew he had just crossed them, one would expect him to describe them as *plains*, plural, just as he did. In this connection, Wright quotes but avoids addressing the balance of Joseph's letter, in which Joseph wrote that he spent the time "recounting occasionally the history of the Book of Mormon, roving over the mounds of that once beloved people of the Lord, picking up their skulls & their bones, as proof of its divine authenticity." In Wright's view, Joseph was recounting the history of Mesoamerica, picking up skulls and bones in Ohio as proof of the divine authenticity of a Mesoamerican record.

Despite these problems applying the hinterlands approach to North America, the hinterlands approach has many promising implications and suggests new avenues for additional research—especially if it is applied in the opposite direction. This article proposes that the text of the Book of Mormon, considered in light of the historical, geographical, archaeological, and geological evidence, points to *Mesoamerica* as the hinterlands to the Book of Mormon narrative. Under this approach, the bulk of the narrative, from the land of Nephi to Zarahemla to Cumorah, took place in North America.

In *Mormon's Codex*,[265] John Sorenson proposed using filters to assess any proposed setting. This article applies the filters Sorenson formulated, along with three additional filters based on the text of the Book of Mormon itself. It thus sets aside the *Times and Seasons* articles and other extra-textual statements to focus on the merits of Mesoamerican theories based on the text of the Book of Mormon and other scriptures.

Zarahemla as *axis mundi*

Efforts to locate the setting of the Book of Mormon commonly focus on Zarahemla because that is the most important city in the book. The text contains 139 references to Zarahemla (including the city, the land, the people, and the leader), by far the most of any city, and it is the only Book of Mormon city mentioned in the Doctrine and Covenants. The importance of the city is reflected in a passage explaining that at one point in their history, the Lamanites "had come into the center of the land, and had taken the capital city which was the city of Zarahemla." (Helaman 1:27). Zarahemla is located on the western bank of the River Sidon, a prominent feature of Book of Mormon geography. Finding Zarahemla is key. As Dr. John Lund put it, "Once Zarahemla or the 'small neck' of land has been identified, one has found the *axis mundi* of the lands of the Jaredites, Mulekites, and the children of Lehi."[266]

Of the dozens of proposed Book of Mormon geographies, only two rely on modern statements about the location of ancient Zarahemla: the 1842

Times and Seasons articles for the Mesoamerican theory[267] and D&C Section 125 for the American theory.[268] (As used in this article, the American theory places the Book of Mormon events within The United States circa 1842, including states and territories, as well as portions of Canada.) Mesoamerica and America, therefore, are the two candidates for "main setting" and "hinterlands." Although neither of the Zarahemla statements will be considered determinative, or even influential, in assessing the viability of the two alternative models discussed in this article, it is important at the outset to briefly acknowledge some of the issues associated with each setting for Zarahemla.

Winchester used the *Times and Seasons* to focus Book of Mormon studies on Central America. His motivation was likely a combination of three discrete interests. First, his sincere belief in the inference he made from the text (p. 49 in the 1830 edition, 1 Nephi 18:23 now) that Lehi landed in or near Panama. Second, his desire to link the Book of Mormon to a national bestseller, John Lloyd Stephens' *Incidents of Travel in Central America, Chiapas, and Yucatan*. Third, his desire to repudiate critics who claimed Joseph Smith had copied the Book of Mormon from Solomon Spaulding or Ethan Smith. (Winchester wrote the first pamphlet against the Spaulding theory.) Recognizing that Zarahemla was the center of the Nephite world, Winchester placed it in Guatemala (Quirigua) knowing that all other geographical references would flow from there. Although they have rejected Quirigua per se, Sorenson, Lund and other Mesoamerican advocates have placed Zarahemla in various locations within Mesoamerica, rationalizing that the *Times and Seasons* articles focused on Guatemala but left room for a variety of settings within that general area.[269]

For the American setting, Section 125:3 is a key to locating Zarahemla. "Let them build up a city unto my name upon the land opposite the city of Nauvoo, and let the name of Zarahemla be named upon it." Section 125 was the first mention of the name Zarahemla in connection with the Iowa development. Some commentators have argued that this area of Iowa had been called Zarahemla prior to March 1841, the date Joseph received the revelation, but all such references were added retroactively (and after Joseph died) by historians and compilers by way of explanation.[270] With the Iowa Zarahemla as the *axis mundi*, the American setting has Lehi landing in the Florida panhandle, the Land of Nephi in the mountains of Tennessee,

Bountiful in Indiana and Ohio, Zarahemla in Iowa, the Sidon River comprising the river system that includes the Missouri and Ohio Rivers plus the Upper Mississippi, with the West Sea South being the lower Mississippi, the West Sea North being Lake Michigan, the narrow neck being the Niagara Peninsula, and Cumorah in New York, outside of Palmyra—where Joseph Smith found the plates. Essentially, this is the United States from 1838 to 1842, including states and territories.

Filters and Terms of Reference

Sorenson lists terms of references, or "filters," that he believes must be applied to any real-world candidate for The Book of Mormon setting. This article examines his three "major filters,"[271] applies them to the text and evidence, and then performs the same assessment using three additional filters. The six filters are:

1. Scope of territory (Sorenson)
2. Destruction in 3 Nephi (Sorenson)
3. Sophisticated society (Sorenson)
4. Law of Moses
5. Promised land
6. Infrastructure (Ores, Towers, Fortresses, Buildings, Roads)

Filter 1—Scope of Territory. "A hemispheric or continental scope is contrary to the text. Mormon's map cannot possibly be matched by such a large territory as North or South America, let alone by the entire hemisphere. The total extent of lands that Mormon know about, based on his own words, did not exceed about 600 miles (965 km) in length and half that in width."[272]

This filter makes an important point. One of Sorenson's most important contributions has been calling attention to the practical, real-world implications of the text. "Important to his legacy is the shrinking of the potential Book of Mormon lands from the entire Western hemisphere to a region roughly comparable to the geographic scope of the history of the Hebrews in the Old World."[273]

That said, the premise of this filter is flawed: Mormon's "own words" say nothing about miles or kilometers. The distances Sorenson cites here are purely the product of *Sorenson's* assumptions about how far someone could travel in a given manner over a given terrain in a given time frame. For example, he claims the distance between the city of Zarahemla and the city of Nephi was "on the order of 180 miles (290 km)" based on this reasoning:

> Accounts of travel by groups between the two cities report (or imply) that a party of ancient travelers (at least one time including women, children, and flocks) required about 22 days to make the trip, much of it evidently *through mountainous terrain.*[274] (emphasis added)

However, there is no indication in the text that Alma crossed a mountain, let alone mountainous terrain. Mosiah 24:25 speaks of Alma's group departing a valley and traveling through "wilderness," not "mountainous terrain." A valley is a "hollow or low area of land between *hills* or mountains." A valley can also be a "low extended plain, usually alluvial, penetrated or washed by a river."[275]

In fact, the Book of Mormon text contains only 13 references to mountains in the new world, none in connection with Alma's route. Several references involve the Gadianton robbers who "dwelt upon the mountains" and in the wilderness (Helaman and 3 Nephi), but there is no description of the mountains themselves. (As an aside, dwelling "upon" and sending an army "upon the mountains" suggests a more flat and livable "mountain" than the steep mountains one finds in Mesoamerica. One would dwell "upon" something more like a large hill than "upon" a volcano.[276]) Samuel the Lamanite made a specific prediction: "And behold, there shall be great tempests, and there shall be many mountains laid low, like unto a valley, and there shall be many places which are now called valleys which shall become mountains, whose height is great" (Helaman 14:23). It's anyone's guess how high terrain would have to be to qualify as "great," especially compared with the land's former valley elevation. However, 3 Nephi only mentions a single "great mountain" with no reference to height (8:10).

The term "mountain" is relative; it refers to a "natural elevation of the earth's surface having considerable mass, generally steep sides, and a height greater than that of a hill."[277] There is another scriptural reference to mountains that may offer additional insight. On July 8, 1838, Joseph Smith received a revelation at Far West, Missouri, canonized as Section 117. Verse 8 reads, "Is there not room enough on the mountains of Adam-ondi-Ahman, and on the plains of Olaha Shinehah, or the land where Adam dwelt, that you should covet that which is but the drop, and neglect the more weighty matters?" Adam-ondi-Ahman is located in Davies County, Missouri, about 70 miles north of Kansas City. Section 117 refers to "mountains" in this area, suggesting a possible example of how the Book of Mormon uses the term. The Book of Mormon distinguishes between hills and mountains without clearly delineating between the two, raising the inference that the difference is a continuum, a matter of degree or perspective. (E.g., 3 Nephi 4:1). The highest elevation at Adam-ondi-Ahman currently is 124 feet above the river—a site named Spring Hill in Section 116, which suggests ambiguity about the terms "hill" and "mountain" as used in these scriptures.

Nevertheless, Sorenson makes an important point in this filter by asking how far one can travel in the real world under specified conditions. Groups can travel by foot 15 to 20 miles a day; even the Mormon handcart companies traveled this much. The participants on Zion's Camp walked 20 to 40 miles per day[278]—including through and across valleys. (There are over 500 named valleys or hollows in Indiana and Illinois. Joseph and the others crossed the Illinois River at Valley City, just north of Zelph's Mound.) At that pace, Alma's group could have traveled as much as 880 miles—far more than the limits Sorenson imposes on the entire length of territory Mormon was familiar with. Of course, few groups would travel 40 miles a day on foot over any kind of terrain for twenty-two days straight, but the likelihood of a particular distance is a judgment call, not an explicit statement in the text.

It is one thing to recognize the text does not support a 9,000-mile-long hemispheric geography—typified by Orson Pratt's concept that South America was Lamanite territory, North America was Nephite territory, and Panama was the narrow neck of land between them[279]—and something altogether different to presume that the text supports only a territory 600 miles by 300 miles. Recognizing that such a limitation is set by Sorenson's assumptions, not the text, the filter is still useful for providing a feasible range of distances in the real world. The limited geography Mesoamerican models such as Sorenson's easily pass through this filter.

By comparison, the American model contemplates a distance of about 750 miles between Zarahemla and Cumorah. The land of Nephi, including the city Lehi-Nephi, would be about 500 miles southeast from Zarahemla and 700 miles south of Cumorah. These distances are reasonably close to

Sorenson's estimates (although in entirely different configurations), and well short of the continental distances that the filter rejects.

Conclusion: Both models pass filter #1.

Filter 2—Destruction in 3 Nephi. "The configuration of the lands cannot have been modified by catastrophic geological events in the historic past. Ancient geographical features were for practical purposes the same as we see today; for example, references to the narrow neck and narrow pass were the same in Moroni's day as in the day of General Moroni, several centuries earlier."[280]

This part of filter #2 is important for making the point that the Moroni who completed the record and hid the plates recognized the same geological features that General Moroni had described centuries earlier. Regarding that point, both the Mesoamerica and American theories pass the filter.

Actually, Filter #2 is illusory; i.e., there is no known place in the Western Hemisphere that has experienced a "major change in the shape or extent of the lands" in the last 2,500 years, so *any* proposed geography in the Western Hemisphere would pass through this filter. Perhaps the purpose of this filter is to reject any proposed theory that claims Book of Mormon geography is unrecognizable today. If so, then both the Mesoamerican and the American models pass this filter.

To make this filter meaningful, it should be compared with the requirements of the text. The first column below is the entire filter. The second column is the text from 3 Nephi.

Filter #2	3 Nephi 8:11-13
The configuration of the lands cannot have been modified by catastrophic geological events in the historic past.	11 And there was a great and terrible destruction in the land southward.
Ancient geographical features were for practical purposes the same as we see today; for example, references to the narrow neck and narrow pass were the same in	12 But behold, there was a more great and terrible destruction in the land northward; for behold, the whole face of the land was changed, because of the tempest and the whirlwinds and the thunderings and

Moroni's day as in the day of General Moroni, several centuries earlier." No credible evidence exists from real-world research that justifies believing that major physical events have drastically changed the present boundaries of the seas or other major physiographic features in the Western Hemisphere within the period of human habitation. In fact, evidence from archaeology contradicts the idea of any major change in the shape or extent of the lands, since archaeological studies in all Western Hemisphere land areas show uninterrupted human occupation over thousands of years.	the lightnings and the exceedingly great quaking of the whole earth; 13 And the highways were broken up, and the level roads were spoiled, and many smooth places became rough. 16 And there were some who were carried away in the whirlwind; and whither they went no man knoweth, save they know that they were carried away. 17 And thus the face of the whole earth became deformed, because of the tempests, and the thunderings, and the lightnings, and the quaking of the earth. 18 And behold, the rocks were rent in twain; they were broken up upon the face of the whole earth, insomuch that they were found in broken fragments, and in seams and in cracks, upon all the face of the land.

The side-by-side comparison shows that here are two key elements integral to the purpose of this filter which are not expressly stated in the filter itself.

First, while there was there was "a great and terrible destruction in the land southward," "there was a *more great and terrible destruction* in the land northward" (emphasis added). No Mesoamerican proponents have explained why there would be a difference between the two areas. Sorenson[281] and others[282] assert the destruction was caused by earthquakes and volcanic activity throughout the area, with no geological basis for distinguishing between north and south. Setting aside the text's lack of any mention of

volcanoes in 1,000 years of history in Mesoamerica—itself a stunning
omission given the dominance of volcanoes in that area—there is no
geological or historical basis for a difference in destruction between the north
and the south in the Mesoamerican model. The terrain and geological
formations are continuous. At best, one could argue the text is describing an
epicenter—or volcanic eruption—in the north, but if that's the case, how
could there be "great and terrible destruction" in the south? The impact of
earthquakes and volcanoes drops quickly with distance, but shaking from
earthquakes is stronger in areas that have softer surface layers, such as
accumulated sediment. When an earthquake strikes, "as the thickness of
sediment increases, so too does the amount of shaking."[283] Mountain areas
experience less shaking than sediment areas; shaking is amplified where
sediments are thicker. When the text differentiates between the impact in the
northern and southern lands, it implies a difference in the type of terrain and
geology between north and south.

In contrast to Mesoamerica, the American setting offers a sharp
distinction between the land southward and the land northward. The land
southward is dominated by the Appalachian Mountains in present-day
Tennessee, Alabama and Georgia. The risk of earthquake there is far less
than along the Mississippi and Ohio River valleys, areas that extend into the
land northward and are characterized by thick sediment. Actual historical
accounts of the New Madrid earthquakes in 1811-1812—the biggest
earthquakes in American history—describe conditions much like those
described in 3 Nephi. The damage was far worse along the Mississippi River
than in the mountains of Tennessee, just as expected from the respective
geology. This is also consistent with the distinction made in 3 Nephi 8. In
the earthquake of 1895, damage was documented along the Ohio and Upper
Mississippi Rivers (part of the River Sidon), while shaking was felt but no
damage experienced in eastern Tennessee and Alabama and Georgia.

The evidence indicates that the American model passes through this
implied element of filter #2, but Mesoamerica does not.

The second implied element involves the scriptural requirement that "the
face of the whole earth became deformed." Recall that the original filter
states, "The configuration of the lands cannot have been modified by
catastrophic geological events in the historic past." This requirement is

imposed by the geological record in Mesoamerica, not by the text of the Book of Mormon.

What does the scripture mean? What kind of terrain could be "deformed" while retaining major landmarks and configuration, yet without leaving obvious geological evidence?

As Sorenson notes, there is no evidence of a deformation of "the face of the whole earth" in Mesoamerica. In fact, because of the mountainous and relatively rigid terrain, such a deformation could not have occurred without obvious geological evidence. Mesoamerica simply can't pass through this implied element of filter #2.

By contrast, land that is relatively flat, or at least not featuring tall mountains, could satisfy the description in the text. A major earthquake can shake a flat area and cause tremendous destruction without leaving the massive landslides and sheared rock face that occurs in mountainous areas and leaves behind telltale signs.

As noted in Wright's paper, the Book of Mormon refers to plains in several places, including the "plains of Nephihah" (Alma 62:18), the plains between Mulek and Bountiful (Alma 52:20), the "plains of Heshlon" (Ether 13:28) and the "plains of Agosh" (Ether 14:15). Such flat areas would qualify for events—earthquakes, tornadoes, and floods—that deform the face of the whole earth without leaving the type of "major change in the shape or extent of the lands" that Sorenson's filter guards against. Flat terrain also is far more susceptible to "whirlwinds" and "tempests" as described in 3 Nephi 8; tornadoes are relatively rare in mountainous terrain, but common in open, flat lands. Consequently, this filter both excludes Mesoamerica, and points toward any area characterized by flat open spaces; i.e., plains.

Zarahemla in the American model is located between the plains of Iowa on the west and Illinois on the east, roughly in the center of FEMA's Wind Zone IV (the strongest rating).[284] It is also on the banks of the Mississippi, a river notorious for changing course and deforming the face of the land. Even in the absence of a cataclysmic earthquake, the changing course of the Mississippi River has been well documented. For example, the first capitol of Illinois, Kaskaskia, located about 250 miles downstream from Zarahemla, was a major French colonial town of 7,000 residents in the 1700s. For a hundred years, it was a commercial and cultural center. In the 1840s, the Mississippi River shifted course and by 1881, the city was cut off from

Illinois and destroyed by flooding. Kaskaskia ended up on the west of the river—in Missouri. The city was flooded again in 1993 and the current population is only 14 people.

The Missouri River has also changed the face of the land. In the 1800s, hundreds of steamboats sank along these rivers, most of them buried and long lost. One, the steamship Arabia, sank in 1856. Salvagers finally located it in 1987—underneath a farm, half a mile away from the river and buried beneath *45 feet* of topsoil that had accumulated in 130 years.[285]

The specific language of the text—the "face of the whole earth became deformed"—describes changes to the surface. Somehow earth was "carried up upon the city of Moronihah" to become a "great mountain" (not a "tall mountain"). What besides strong winds could "carry up" earth in this manner? The text describes not volcanoes but fire, earthquakes, tempest, and whirlwinds (tornadoes[286]). Cities sank into the earth and were buried. Such surface changes could include earth and sand being blown in huge quantities from one area to another, rivers changing course, old riverbeds being filled in, etc. According to the U.S. Geological Survey, the New Madrid earthquakes "caused the ground to rise and fall… opening deep cracks in the ground. Deep-seated landslides occurred along the steeper bluffs and hillsides; large areas of land were uplifted permanently; and still larger areas sank and were covered with water that erupted through fissures or craterlets."[287]

Given Sorenson's point that there has been no "major change in the shape or extent of the lands," and recognizing the topology and geology of Mesoamerica precludes any undetectable change to "the whole face of the land," Mesoamerica simply cannot pass through this element of filter #2.

By contrast, not only the topology and geology of the American setting, but actual historical experience, closely matches the description of destruction—the deformation of the face of the whole earth—contained in the text.

Conclusion: Both models pass Sorenson's original illusory filter #2 (as would every other potential location in the Americas), but as to the implied elements of filter #2—the ones required by the text—the American model passes filter #2 and Mesoamerica does not.

Filter 3—Sophisticated society. "Cultural criteria described in the text must be accounted for in any acceptable theory. Most of the lands about which Mormon wrote were described as having characteristics of advanced civilization, such as 'cities.' Furthermore, many of the people involved were literate; the existence of 'many books' (Helaman 3:15) was a cultural feature of note. Only one area in ancient America had cities and books: Mesoamerica."[288]

These cultural criteria do not directly lead to the conclusion Sorenson reaches in his last sentence. First, what constitutes a "city" anciently? The Book of Mormon text distinguishes between *villages* and *cities* (and, beginning around AD 363, *towns*), but never mentions what defines a "city." Is it a function of population, civic infrastructure, architecture, specialization of occupation, or something else?

The 1828 Webster's dictionary defines "city" as: "In a general sense, a large town; a large number of houses and inhabitants, established in one place. In a more appropriate sense, a corporate town."[289] The same dictionary defines a "village" as "A small assemblage of houses, less than a town or city, and inhabited chiefly by farmers and other laboring people."[290] The definition goes on to explain that in England, the lack of a market distinguishes a village from a town. This suggests a plausible meaning of the term "city" as used in The Book of Mormon; i.e., a village is where farmers live, while a city is where not only farmers, but tradespeople, merchants, and government officials live and markets exist. In fact, the only mention of a "market" in The Book of Mormon is in connection with a city: "the highway which led to the chief market, which was in the city of Zarahemla." (Helaman 7:10)

Perhaps a Book of Mormon city was defined by architecture, such as a city wall or barrier. Or it could be a formal administrative designation—a "corporate town." This could be analogous to modern usage, whereby a city is technically defined by its formal incorporated area. The largest city in California in terms of territory—California City—encompasses over 200 square miles but actually has a small population (14,000 people).

A city need not have a large population. "Many ancient cities had only modest populations, however (often under 5,000 persons)."[291] When Lehi left Jerusalem, the city had a population of only about 25,000 people.[292]

At any rate, the term "city" does connote an advanced civilization. Other indicia should also be considered, such as evidence of advanced mathematics,

Jonathan Neville

knowledge of astronomy, including solar and lunar cycles, and public works large enough to require organization and coordinated effort.

The Book of Mormon describes "banks of earth" that fits this meaning of the term (Alma 48:8 and 49:22). Moroni cased that his armies "should commence in digging up heaps of earth round about all the cities" (Alma 50:1). As Kennedy indicates, not only towns but graves were built up. According to the Book of Mormon text, bones "have been heaped up on the earth" (Alma 2:38) similar to the mounds that Kennedy—and Joseph Smith—described. "Nevertheless, after many days their dead bodies were heaped up upon the face of the earth, and they were covered with a shallow covering" (Alma 16:11). "The bodies of many thousands are moldering in heaps upon the face of the earth," explains Alma 28:11. Mormon "saw thousands of them hewn down in open rebellion against their God, and heaped up as dung upon the face of the land." Mormon 2:15. The Jaredites, too, noted mounds: "their bones should become as heaps of earth upon the face of the land." Ether 11:6.

Applying these criteria, Mesoamerica is hardly the only civilization in ancient America that qualifies as "advanced." Any inference that the inhabitants of North America were not "advanced" ignores the actual evidence. Kennedy wrote: "In the Ohio and Mississippi valleys, tens of thousands of structures were built between six and sixty-six centuries ago... The antiquities of Mexico or of Egypt are far better known than those of Indiana, Illinois, or Ohio, and not because they are larger or more ambitious intellectually."[293] The archaeological evidence demonstrates that ancient people living in North America enjoyed advanced and well-organized civilizations with agriculture, commerce, cities, and roads.

Both the Mesoamerican and American settings satisfy the first prong of Filter #3.

The "books" prong of filter #3 is problematic. Sorenson cites Helaman 3:15 for the existence of "many books" which he claims are characteristic of both Mesoamerican and Book of Mormon culture, but the entire verse leads to the opposite conclusion:

15 But behold, there are many books and many records of every kind, and they have been kept chiefly by the Nephites.

Moroni's America

If, as Sorenson claims, Mesoamerica was the only civilization in America that had "books," and the books were kept chiefly by the Nephites, how is it that there is not a scintilla of evidence of Nephite books in Mesoamerica? One must invert the meaning of Helaman 3:15 to consider the decidedly *non-Nephite* books found in Mesoamerica as evidence of *Nephite* culture and civilization.

For Mesoamerican books to be evidence of Book of Mormon people, verse 15 would have to read that the books and records were kept chiefly by the *Lamanites* (or another non-Nephite groups).

Worse, to the extent the Nephites had books, they were all destroyed, as explained in Helaman 3:16 (the Nephites were "plundered, and hunted, and driven forth, and slain…even becoming Lamanites"). It was the destruction of the Nephites' "many books and many records of every kind" that made the "sacred records" so precious. (4 Nephi 1:48-9; Mormon 1:1) The title page of The Book of Mormon emphasizes that the plates Joseph translated were "written and sealed up, and hid up unto the Lord, that they might not be destroyed."

This fear about Lamanite treatment of the records was not unique to Moroni's day. Many centuries earlier, Enos had written about this characteristic of Lamanite culture. "For at the present our strugglings were vain in restoring them to the true faith. And they swore in their wrath that, if it were possible, they would destroy our records and us, and also all the traditions of our fathers." (Enos 1:14).

Ultimately, it was the *Lamanites* who destroyed the Nephites and their culture, and it was the *Lamanites* who *did not* keep books and records. If we accept The Book of Mormon account, we should be looking for an ancient American civilization that did *not* value books and records.

The Book of Mormon itself gives us an example of the type of ancient civilization we should be looking for. After the Mulekites settled in the promised land:

their language had become corrupted; and they had brought no records with them; and they denied the being of their Creator . . . after they were taught in the language of Mosiah, Zarahemla gave a genealogy of his fathers, according to his memory.[294]

339

Jonathan Neville

Like the Lamanites, the Mulekites did not value records. Their history was transmitted orally, by memory. The only reason the text mentions an engraved stone—a ubiquitous feature of Mayan culture—was because the people couldn't read it. (Omni 1:20) An engraved stone was so exceptional that the people of Zarahemla brought it to Mosiah to translate.

Such a culture is directly opposite of the engraved stone lintels, tablets, stairs, statues and stelas archaeologists find throughout Mesoamerica.

Conclusion: Both models pass through the first prong of filter #3. Mesoamerica satisfies the second prong (books) and the American model does not—but that prong contradicts the text. A filter that reflects the text would require a society without books, in which an engraved stone is unusual and not comprehensible. The American model passes through such a filter and Mesoamerica does not.

Filter 4—Law of Moses. Criteria related to the law of Moses as described in the text must be accounted for in any acceptable theory. "Lehi and his people diligently kept the law of Moses. Nephi affirmed… that they did 'keep the law of Moses, and look forward with steadfastness unto Christ, until the law shall be fulfilled' (2 Nephi 25:24).... The Nephites were to continue to keep the law of Moses until it was fulfilled."[295]

The Book of Mormon people did not casually observe the Law of Moses. They "were strict in observing the ordinances of God, according to the law of Moses." Alma 30:3. It was obedience to the law of Moses that Korihor criticized:

"Korihor said unto him: Because I do not teach the foolish traditions of your fathers, and because I do not teach this people to bind themselves down under the foolish ordinances and performances which are laid down by ancient priests, to usurp power and authority over them, to keep them in ignorance, that they may not lift up their heads, but be brought down according to thy words." (Alma 30:23)

When groups failed to observe the law of Moses, they "had fallen into great errors." Alma 31:9.

The law of Moses and its implications for Book of Mormon geography deserve an entire article, but this filter can serve its purpose with just a few of the key points.

Architecture

One major difference between the Mesoamerican and American settings is visible in architecture. Mayan architecture is typified by large stone temples, made of cut stones and featuring steps by which one ascends to altars or the tops of the temples. By contrast, Hopewell architecture relies on uncut stone and ramps to ascend. Altars and ramps of earth are also common.

According to the law of Moses, observers of the law must use ramps and uncut stones. "An altar of earth thou shalt make unto me, and shalt sacrifice thereon thy burnt offerings, . . . And if thou wilt make me an altar of stone, thou shalt not build it of hewn stone, for if thou lift up thy tool upon it, thou hast polluted it. Neither shalt thou go up by steps unto mine altar, that thy nakedness be not discovered thereon" (Exodus 20:24-26). Ramps were also important for leading animals to be sacrificed.

This distinction is apparent in Israel, where archaeologists can use the distinction between ramps and stairs to determine whether an ancient site was built according to the law of Moses. One archaeologist describing the discovery of Joshua's Altar on Mt. Ebal, Israel, explains it this way:

Hebrew altars can be distinguished from pagan altars in 5 respects: 1. They are made of uncut natural stone. 2. Ramps, never stairs. 3. Hebrew altars are square. 4. Hebrew altars have their sides oriented to the 4 points of the compass (NSEW), as we see in the orientation of the tabernacle.[296]

In Mesoamerican sites, there are no ramps; in the American setting, sites have no steps. In Mesoamerica, stones are carved; in the American setting, they are unhewn. Whoever created the Hopewell structures complied with this aspect of the Law of Moses, intentionally or not. Whoever created the Mesoamerican structures did not comply with the Law of Moses, even in the Nephite time period.

Calendar

Another aspect of the Law of Moses was determining the time for various religious events. The ancient Hebrews used a lunar calendar. Psalm 81:3-6 notes that the moon determined the time for feasts: "Blow up the trumpet in the new moon, in the time appointed, on our solemn feast day. For this was a statute for Israel, and a law of the God of Jacob."

Sorenson notes that "A lunar-based calendar was apparently basic to Nephite/Mulekite calendrical calculations (Omni 1:21). That being the case, a systematic record of moon phenomena would have been an element in their astronomy/calendar knowledge system... The moon-based calendar of the Jews of Jerusalem surely was carried forward by the Lehites and Mulekites when they emigrated from the near East to the New World."[297] He notes that some scholars believe the Mayans used lunar months at one time, but their primary calendar was solar. In fact, the Mayan lunar series was not incorporated until the 3rd Century AD.[298] The best-known calendar, used by the lowland Maya, used 13 numbered days in connection with 20 named days, producing a 260-day cycle. Another version of Mayan calendars was based on the Haab', a roughly solar calendar consisting of eighteen 20-day months plus five days at the end of the year. This resembled the Egyptial solar calendar.

Like the Hebrews (and presumably the Nephites), the Hopewell culture also used a lunar calendar to schedule feasts.[299] The largest geometric earthworks complex in the world is near Newark, Ohio, and is around 2,000 years old. The site's "lunar alignments precisely encode the orb's very complex cycle, with moonrises and moonsets rotating north and south over an 18.61-year cycle."[300]

To summarize, Mesoamerican culture was based primarily on a solar calendar, while the ancient American (Hopewell) culture, like the culture of ancient Israel, was based primarily on a lunar calendar.

Plants and Animals

Proof of the existence of species at the time and place mentioned in the Book of Mormon requires first, determining what species were mentioned, and second, where the species were encountered. Consideration of the Law of Moses is important because it filters out species that would not, and could not, be used as part of strict observance of the law. Specific species of plants and animals are essential for observing the law of Moses. Strict obedience to the law of Moses does not allow substitutions; for example, for a peace offering, the law specifies "a bullock, a sheep, or a goat," (Leviticus 22:27). When he arrived in the land of promise, Nephi indicated that he found the animals they needed to observe the law of Moses. He wrote "we did find upon the land of promise... that there were beasts in the forests of every kind, both the cow and the ox, and the ass and the horse, and the goat and the wild goat." 1 Nephi 18:25.

One unnamed animal pertains directly to the law of Moses. The Book of Mormon has sixty-six references to "flocks." Mosiah 2:3 explains the significance: "And they also took of the firstlings of their flocks, that they might offer sacrifice and burnt offerings according to the law of Moses." The flocks were so important that when Limhi prepared his people to escape from the Lamanites, he "caused that his people should gather their flocks together…the people of king Limhi did depart by night into the wilderness with their flocks and their herds." Mosiah 22:10-11. When Alma led his people out of bondage, he "and his people in the night-time gathered their flocks together." Mosiah 24:18. Presumably the reason they took their flocks when they escaped, despite the evident complications and the pursuit by the Lamanites, was because they needed them for their offerings and sacrifices.

The Hebrew term translated as "flock" ordinarily applies to sheep, but when used as the plural "flocks" it can include other kinds of domesticated animals. "Book of Mormon terminology fails to clarify what species composed Nephite 'flocks' and 'herds,'" according to John Sorenson.[301] However, Alma defines the term flock as meaning sheep. "For what shepherd is there among you having many sheep doth not watch over them, that the wolves enter not and devour his flock?" (Alma 5:59) Other uses of the term, such as "flocks of sheep" in 3 Nephi 20:16, could be interpreted as purely metaphorical, but if the people did not have sheep, what sense would the metaphor make? Christ is referred to as the Lamb of God throughout the text, from 1 Nephi through Ether.

Sheep, of course, are one of the animals required under the law of Moses, along with goats, bulls, and oxen. Enos reiterated that the people of Nephi did raise "flocks of herds, and flocks of all manner of cattle of every kind, and goats, and wild goats, and also many horses." Enos 1:21. Mosiah emphasized that the people grew wheat and barley, both needed for the law of Moses. Mosiah 9:9. None of these species are found in Mesoamerica, which is why Mesoamerican advocates suggest the small Mexican brocket deer might be a goat and the tapir an ass.[302] By contrast, there is evidence of each of these species in the American setting.

Pre-Columbian wheat and barley have both been documented in North America (but not in Mesoamerica). Wade E. Miller and Matthew Roper have noted, "beginning in the 1980s, discoveries of pre-Columbian barley started to be made, substantiating the Book of Mormon claim."[303] The Fort

Jonathan Neville

Ancient State Memorial Museum in Oregonia, Ohio, has this ancient barley on display. Miller and Roper also note that the Vikings claimed to find wheat in North America when they arrived in the year 1000 A.D. Despite this evidence in North America, because they are defending the Mesoamerican setting, Miller and Roper write, "while the Book of Mormon makes reference to wheat (e.g., Mosiah 9:9), it might have been another grain translated as 'wheat.'"[304] Sorenson explains: "Exactly what species Nephite 'wheat' referred to is unclear, but it apparently was not the wheat familiar to us, which was unknown in Mesoamerica; presumably the name was applied to one of the aforementioned grains."[305] But if the Nephites were using a different grain, how did they comply strictly with the Law of Moses?

Animals that match the terms used in the Book of Mormon apparently existed in North America before Columbus. Nephi claimed he found "the goat and the wild goat." (1 Nephi 18:25). These species were permitted as food under the Law of Moses (Deuteronomy 14:4-5). It's interesting that Deuteronomy also specifies "the hart, and the roebuck, and the fallow deer… and the pygarg, and the wild ox, and the chamois," but Nephi listed none of these. Early French explorers noted the presence of "wild goats" along the Mississippi River, in Indiana and Illinois, and in Florida.[306] Miller and Roper suggest the "goat" may have been a species of domesticated deer that resembled a goat. They note that men accompanying De Soto observed "herds of tame deer"[307] in Ocale, a town in northern Florida. Another Spanish historian recorded a similar observation in Apalachicola[308]—right in the area where Lehi landed, according to the American model.

As evidence that ancient people in Ohio had goats, the Mound City Group Visitors Center, a Hopewell Culture National Historic Park near Chillicothe, Ohio, features a copper goat horn that dates to Book of Mormon times.

Sheep and lambs are mentioned 77 times in the Book of Mormon. Many references are figurative, but as Alma 5:59 indicates, the people were familiar with sheep and did tend to them. William Richie, an archaeologist, reported that he found remains of domestic sheep in western New York dating to 100 A.D., about 30 miles east of the Hill Cumorah.[309] At least one Hopewell sculpture of an animal that looks like a sheep has been found.

Enos referred to "all manner of cattle of every kind," a description similar to that of French explorers who described seeing "wild bulls, wild cows, wild cattle, and vaches sauvages" that are now considered to be terms used "as the designation of both the moose and the elk."[310] Buffalo, or bison, were often described as cattle. There are several accounts from the 1500s of buffalo-like creatures in Florida, but it is not known what species the explorers were describing.[311]

Evidence of the specific animals required by the Book of Mormon is far more abundant in the American setting than it is in the Mesoamerican setting. Sorenson notes that there is evidence of other Book of Mormon animals from the right time period that fit the American model, such as the horse, mammoth and mastodon remains at St. Petersburg, Florida, that date around 100 B.C.[312]

Regarding Mesoamerica, Sorenson concludes that "there are plausible creatures to match each scriptural term."[313] He suggests that the deer or tapir may qualify as horse, ox, ass and goat, while the paca or agouti may qualify as sheep, his theory being that Joseph Smith didn't know a more accurate term to translate the original word on the plates. But "deer" and "pygarg" (the term for antelope) were both terms used in Deuteronomy that presumably could have been used in the translation of the Book of Mormon and would have been better fits to the species in Mesoamerica. It is inconceivable that a paca or agouti, both of which are rodents and therefore unclean under the law of Moses, would have been considered "sheep" by the Nephites and used for their sacrifices.

At any rate, calendars, architecture, plants, and animals all tend to show that this important aspect of Nephite culture was feasible in America, but not in Mesoamerica.

Conclusion: The American model passes filter #4 and Mesoamerica does not (unless one assumes the Book of Mormon was not translated accurately when it came to naming animal and plant species).

Filter 5—Promised Land. The lands and societies must satisfy the attributes given in the text for the land of promise or promised land. Some of the descriptions are subjective, but enough are objective and straightforward enough that we should be able to determine whether a proposed setting meets the requirements set out on the text. Presumably the text includes these attributes so readers would identify the place.

In the abstract, any place where someone lives may be considered a "promised land" to that person. The gospel covenants apply wherever one lives. However, there are many verses in the Book of Mormon that refer to a specific land of promise. These descriptions or attributes of the promised land were recorded by the prophets so future readers could identify it. Only a few can be mentioned here.

2 Nephi 10:10 – But behold, this land, said God, shall be a land of thine inheritance, and the Gentiles shall be blessed upon the land.

2 Nephi 10:11 – And this land shall be a land of liberty unto the Gentiles, and there shall be no kings upon the land, who shall raise up unto the Gentiles.

2 Nephi 10:12 – And I will fortify this land against all other nations.

3 Nephi 10:22 – this people will I establish in this land, unto the fulfilling of the covenant which I made with your father Jacob; and it shall be a New Jerusalem.

Ether 13:2-3 – it became a choice land above all other lands… it was the place of the New Jerusalem.

D&C 45:66 – it shall be called the New Jerusalem.

D&C 57:2 – [Jackson County, Missouri] is the land of promise, and the place for the city of Zion.

D&C 84:2-3 – the gathering of his saints to stand upon Mount Zion, which shall be the city of New Jerusalem. Which city shall be built, beginning at the temple lot, which is appointed by the finger of the Lord, in the western boundaries of the State of Missouri.

The Book of Mormon text refers to the promised land as the place where the Nephites lived and claims that the land will be the site of the New Jerusalem. The D&C cites that language and places it specifically in Missouri. Which model passes through this filter best, the Mesoamerican or the American?

The American model puts Zarahemla less than 200 miles from Independence, Missouri, in Jackson County. Jackson County borders the Missouri River, part of the River Sidon system in the American model. The Kansas City Hopewell culture was the farthest west group of the Hopewell tradition, dating to about the time of Christ. There are around 40 known sites in and around Kansas City where people migrated from the Lower Illinois Valley areas and left pottery, tools and weapons characteristic of the Hopewell.[314]

The Mesoamerican model puts Zarahemla 1,500 air miles from Independence, (about 2,000 miles by land). There are no known connections between the Mayans and the Native Americans in the Kansas City area. While there are some similarities between artifacts found in Ohio and Mesoamerican artifacts, the relationships between the two cultures, if any, are unclear.

Sorenson does not address this filter, apart from general references such as "Nephi's/Lehi's Mesoamerican land of promise."[315] However, some Mesoamerican advocates have proposed that the phrase "this land" as used in the Book of Mormon and Doctrine and Covenants means anywhere on the American continent, encompassing the totality of North and South America, including Central America.[316] They claim there are only two continents—the "eastern" and "western," or the "old" and the "new," essentially equating the phrase "this land" with an entire hemisphere.

Substituting "North and South America" for "this land" in the verses listed above renders them incoherent. For example, "North and South America became a choice land above all other lands." If there are only two continents, what "other lands" (plural) could this verse refer to? "North and South America was the place of the New Jerusalem." How useful is it to designate an entire hemisphere as the site of a city?

Furthermore, blurring the distinction between countries—pretending there is no border between Guatemala and Mexico, or between Mexico and the United States—makes the text even more meaningless. How could such a promised land be fortified if there is no border?

Paradoxically, on one hand, Mesoamerican advocates assert that the lands of the Book of Mormon are confined to a "limited geography" of about 600 miles in length and about 300 miles in width. On the other hand, they claim references to "this land" extend from the tip of South America to the Arctic. Simple consistency would confine the scope of "this land" to an area the Nephite prophets would have been familiar with.

In some cases, the phrase unambiguously refers to a specific site, such as D&C 58:57, a revelation given in Zion, Jackson County, Missouri. "And let my servant Sidney Rigdon consecrate and dedicate *this land*, and the spot for the temple, unto the Lord." Surely Rigdon was not dedicating the entire hemisphere as the site for the temple. In D&C 59:1, also given in Zion, Jackson County, Missouri, a similar narrow meaning applies: "Behold, blessed, saith the Lord, are they who have come up unto *this land* with an eye single to my glory, according to my commandments." Section 101:80 refers to the United States: "And for this purpose have I established the Constitution of *this land*, by the hands of wise men whom I raised up unto this very purpose, and redeemed the land by the shedding of blood." D&C 57:1 specifically identifies Missouri as "this land" in these words: "Hearken, O ye elders of my church, saith the Lord your God, who have assembled yourselves together, according to my commandments, in *this land*, which is the land of Missouri, which is the land which I have appointed and consecrated for the gathering of the saints."

With those verses in mind, Section 10:49-51 relates the phrase directly to the Book of Mormon: "Now, this is not all—their faith in their prayers was that this gospel should be made known also, if it were possible that other nations should possess *this land*; And thus they did leave a blessing upon *this land* in their prayers, that whosoever should believe in this gospel in *this land* might have eternal life; Yeah, that it might be free unto all of whatsoever nation, kindred, tongue or people they may be." The preposition "it" in the last clause refers back to "this land," making a close connection between D&C 101:80 and 2 Nephi 10:11-12. "This land" would be "free" unto whoever came to it. And, of course, the gospel was restored—made known—in the American setting, not in Mesoamerica.

At the risk of deviating from the original premise of this article (avoiding extraneous statements about the text of the Book of Mormon), in this case it is impossible to discuss the meaning of "this land" without examining the literature on the topic. For example, for the proposition that Joseph Smith meant the totality of North and South America when he wrote the Wentworth letter, one author cites a long list of examples from Benjamin Winchester, John E. Page, and William Smith, as well as Parley and Orson Pratt.[317] Aside from the problems inherent with these authors,[318] one example from the Wentworth letter shows that Joseph Smith was quite specific about the topic.

Joseph wrote "The remnant are the Indians that now inhabit this country." Taken by itself, in the context of a letter in which he also referred to the Savior's appearance "upon this continent," the phrase "this country" might be ambiguous. But this sentence was not written in a vacuum.

Much of the Wentworth letter, including most of the passage containing this sentence, Joseph copied word for word from Orson Pratt's 1840 pamphlet, cited above, that was published in the *Millennial Star*. However, Joseph made specific edits that have great significance. Here is the sentence Pratt wrote:

Orson Pratt 1840: The remaining remnant, having dwindled into an uncivilized state, still continue to inhabit the land, although divided into a "multitude of nations," and are called by Europeans the "American Indians."

Pratt's version describes the hemispheric model, which Sorenson and others have collapsed into the Mesoamerican model. The key phrases are:
1) "inhabit the land" which (unlike "this land") can mean anywhere in the hemisphere;
2) "multitude of nations" which can mean the many nations established by the Europeans (including Chile, Peru, Panama, Guatemala, Mexico, etc.); and
3) "called by the Europeans the 'American Indians'" which was the term commonly used for all indigenous inhabitants of the Americas, North and South.
Here is how this sentence looked *after* Joseph Smith's edit:

Wentworth Letter 1842 (Joseph Smith): The remnant are the Indians that now inhabit this country.

Joseph corrected Pratt's language and narrowed it considerably. According to Joseph, the remnant don't inhabit "the land" but "this country." The remnant are not the "American Indians" generically, and they are not divided into a multitude of nations. Instead, the remnant are, simply—and exclusively—the "Indians that now inhabit this country."

It is difficult to imagine how Joseph Smith could have been more clear and specific about this point. He was well known for allowing others to think as they pleased, rarely correcting them (which made his public rebukes of Benjamin Winchester all the more exceptional). Whether he corrected Orson Pratt in private we'll never know—Pratt had other problems in Nauvoo in 1842—but it is clear that, in the Wentworth letter, Joseph corrected Pratt's mistaken identification of the remnant of the Book of Mormon people. Joseph left no room for speculation that the Lamanites were any people other than the Indians who inhabited the United States in 1842.

Jonathan Neville

Returning to the scriptural excerpts listed at the start of this filter, concepts of blessedness, liberty and fortification are inherently subjective. Fortunately, we are considering only two alternatives: the Mesoamerican setting (consisting of southern Mexico and Guatemala) on one hand, and the American setting on the other. Blessedness may be intangible, but surely it connotes a measure of education, economic prosperity and societal peace (all of which unquestionably point toward the American setting). Streams of refugees, including parentless children on top of trains, offer a more objective measure of blessedness and liberty. All one has to do is see which way they are traveling. Are U.S. citizens seeking refuge in southern Mexico and Guatemala, or are Mexicans and Guatemalans seeking opportunities in the United States?

The disparity between the Mesoamerican and American settings is not a recent phenomenon or aberration. Poverty in Mexico dates to the earliest colonial period, and was not significantly alleviated even when the government ceded land to the general population after the Mexican Revolution. Poverty in Guatemala is even worse and always has been.

Which geographical model places Book of Mormon events in a land that has been fortified against all other nations? The United States has invaded both Mexico and Guatemala, not the other way around. The U.S. border, however porous in practical terms, remains fortified. Beyond that, though, what other nation is, and has been, more fortified against "all other nations" than the United States? The United States spends more on defense—fortification—than the rest of the world combined.

There are many more attributes of the promised land, including the history described by Nephi, that could be added to this filter. They all point to the American setting.

Conclusion: The American model passes filter #5 and Mesoamerica does not.

Filter 6— Infrastructure (Ores, Towers, Fortresses, Buildings, Roads). Available resources and infrastructure in a proposed setting must match the requirements in the text. The manner of war, implements of war fortifications, buildings, and roads must be consistent with descriptions in the Book of Mormon.

Shortly after the Nephites separated themselves from the Lamanites (establishing the land of Nephi), Nephi states that he "did take the sword of Laban, and after the manner of it did make many swords, lest by any means the people who were now called Lamanites should come upon us and destroy us." 2 Nephi 5:14. He also writes, "I did teach my people to build buildings, and to work in all manner of wood, and of iron, and of copper, and of brass, and of steel, and of gold, and of silver, and of precious ores, which were in great abundance." 2 Nephi 5:15. These ores are all found in Tennessee in the area near Ducktown. The mine there has extracted over 15 million tons of copper ore in modern times. The French Huguenots enjoyed friendly relations with the Mountain Apalachee Indians, who were mining gold, copper and silver near their villages. The gold came from what is now Georgia; the silver from western North Carolina; and the copper from southeast Tennessee. To honor his friendship with these Native Americans, De Laudonniére named the region, "Les Montes Apalachiens."[319]

The Hopewell towers and fortresses consisted of earth walls "heaped up" and topped with timbers, precisely as described in the Book of Mormon. They were typically circular, again as described in the text. In at least one case, archaeologists in Ohio have shown that an existing settlement was later surrounded with a defensive wall, exactly as General Moroni explained.

Along the Ohio River there are ruins of towers on both sides of the river that date to Book of Mormon times. Hilltop fortresses (places of resort) are common throughout the Midwest, dating to Book of Mormon times. Farmers and archaeologists have found metal breastplates, head plates, and other armor, along with abundant arrow heads and atlatl heads. Every aspect of warfare described in the Book of Mormon matches what is known from the archaeology and topography of the American model.

By contrast, earth berms or walls are relatively unusual in Mesoamerica, which is dominated by massive stone structures. The examples cited by Sorenson consist of moats outside the city wall, a technique never mentioned in the Book of Mormon text.

A related requirement from 3 Nephi 8:13 is this: "And the highways were broken up, and the level roads were spoiled." This distinction between highways and roads also occurs when the manner of construction is alluded to: "there were many highways cast up, and many roads made, which led from city to city, and from land to land, and from place to place." 3 Nephi 6:8.

The term "cast up" is used in three places to describe piling earth. In Ether 10:23, "they did cast up mighty heaps of earth to get ore." In Alma 49:2, "they had cast up dirt round about to shield them." In Alma 52:6, "he was preparing to defend himself against them, by casting up walls round about and preparing places of resort." This usage suggests the term is synonymous with "piling" up. The only other mention of "cast up" is in connection with the highways. Presumably this means the highways, too, were constructed by "casting up" or piling dirt. In the American setting, ancient highways were, in fact, constructed by piling up dirt along both sides of the passageway. European observers called them walls. The most famous is the Great Hopewell Road that connected Newark and Chillicothe, a distance of sixty miles through Ohio. This fits well with the Book of Mormon description. There were also lesser roads. One of De Soto's chroniclers described "streets" built by the Indians that "are fifteen or twenty feet in width and are bordered with walls constructed of thick pieces of wood."

By contrast, in Mesoamerica the common highway is the "sacbe," a Mayan term for "white road." The sacbe had "edges made of great limestone blocks. Between the limestone edges, coarse fill was leveled with fine gravel and then paved with plaster."[320] These highways are elevated but do not feature dirt or earth "cast up" as the Book of Mormon describes.

Conclusion: The American model passes filter #6 and Mesoamerica does not.

This analysis has demonstrated that while there are a few textual filters through which the Mesoamerican model can pass, most of them disqualify Mesoamerica as a candidate for the real-world setting of the Book of Mormon narrative. By contrast, the American model passes easily through all six filters.

Back to Wright's "hinterlands" approach, the ninety-nine percent of Nephite (and Jaredite) history not accounted for in the text could encompass Mesoamerica. One plausible theory is that the Jaredites who were not killed off in "this north country" (Ether 1:1), meaning the New York area in the American model, expanded into the rest of the hemisphere, including Mesoamerica. The text also mentions Nephites escaping "into the south countries" (Mormon 6:15). Any similarities between the text and various cultural, linguistic, mythological, anthropological and other attributes of Mesoamerica can be accounted for through this application of the hinterlands approach. This explains why Mesoamerican advocates can point to correspondences, but not direct ties, between ancient Mesoamerica and the Book of Mormon. This is a promising area of study that will surely produce results in the future.

But for Book of Mormon studies per se—the study of the times, places, and people actually described in the text—the best available evidence places the core narrative of the Book of Mormon squarely in America.

Jonathan Neville

NOTES

[259] Matthew Roper, Paul J. Fields, Atul Nepal, "Joseph Smith, the *Times and Seasons*, and Central American Ruins," *Journal of the Book of Mormon and Other Restoration Scripture* 22/2 (2013): 84-97. In that article, the authors present the results of a stylometric analysis that show none of the three candidates tested could have written the articles. The authors nevertheless conclude that "Joseph Smith is the most likely author of the composite text" because they erroneously assume that no one else was "said to be working in the printing office." In fact, there were several employees, but most importantly, William Smith was publishing the Wasp from the same office and much—often most—of the content of the Times and Seasons consisted of articles mailed to Nauvoo or excerpted from other publications.

[260] Jonathan Neville, *The Lost City of Zarahemla* (Legends Library, Rochester NY 2015).

[261] For example, Joseph Fielding Smith included one of them in *Teachings of the Prophet Joseph Smith*, and they have been widely cited and quoted in books and articles about Book of Mormon geography, including *Mormon's Codex*, cited below, and numerous articles published by FARMS and the Neal A. Maxwell Institute for Religious Studies, both affiliated with BYU.

[262] John L. Sorenson, The Geography of Book of Mormon Events: A Source Book (FARMS 1990, 1992) p. 210.

[263] Mark Alan Wright, "Heartland as Hinterland: The Mesoamerican Core and North American Periphery of Book of Mormon Geography," *Interpreter: A Journal of Mormon Scripture* 13 (2015): 111-129, available online here: http://www.mormoninterpreter.com/heartland-as-hinterland-the-mesoamerican-core-and-north-american-periphery-of-book-of-mormon-geography/

[264] Ibid, p. 118. Wright erroneously claims Joseph's letter "was actually penned by James Mulholland and then signed by Joseph." His citation to the Joseph Smith Papers explains that the version of the letter is in Mulholland's handwriting, but it is found in JS Letterbook 2, which is a book containing copies of Joseph's correspondence—not the actual correspondence. Mulholland was one of seven scribes who copied material into Letterbook 2. Mulholland was not a participant on Zion's Camp and could not have written the original letter.

[265] John L. Sorenson, *Mormon's Codex* (Deseret Book, Salt Lake City, UT 2013), pp. 20-21.

[266] John L. Lund, *Joseph Smith and the Geography of the Book of Mormon* (The Communications Company, SLC, UT, 2012), p. 10.

²⁶⁷ There are many variations of the Mesoamerican theory, but the most prominent is Sorenson's. Most Mesoamerican settings share the characteristics addressed herein.

²⁶⁸ The American model consists of the states and territories of the United States as of March, 1842. It includes what Wright calls the "Heartland," plus the south, eastern seaboard, and northeastern areas of the United States and contiguous areas of Canada. See Jonathan Neville, *Moroni's America* (Legends Library, Rochester NY 2015).

²⁶⁹ E.g., Dr. John L. Lund, "Joseph Smith Identified Zarahemla as Being in Guatemala," *FunForLessTours Newsletter*, Oct. 8, 2012, http://www.funforlesstours.com/newsletter/17/2012-10-08/

²⁷⁰ See *Lost City*, p. 332

²⁷¹ Numbers 1-3 are copied verbatim from *Mormon's Codex*, pp. 20-21.

²⁷² Mormon's Codex, p. 20.

²⁷³ Brant A. Gardner and Mark Alan Wright, "John L. Sorenson's Complete Legacy: Reviewing Mormon's Codex," *Interpreter: A Journal of Mormon Scripture* 14 (2015): 209-221, p. 210.

²⁷⁴ Mormon's Codex, p. 18.

²⁷⁵ "Valley," Webster's 1828 dictionary, http://webstersdictionary1828.com/Dictionary/valley

²⁷⁶ Webster's 1828 dictionary defines the term this way: "A large mass of earth and rock, rising above the common level of the earth or adjacent land, but of no definite altitude. We apply mountain to the largest eminences on the globe; but sometimes the word is used for a large hill...The word is applied to a single elevation, or to an extended range." See "Mountain," http://webstersdictionary1828.com/Dictionary/mountain

²⁷⁷ American Heritage dictionary, https://www.ahdictionary.com/word/search.html?q=mountain

²⁷⁸ Zion's camp included 200 men, 12 women and 9 children who walked 900 miles from Kirtland, Ohio, to Missouri. See http://prophetjosephsmith.org/index/life_joseph_smith/joseph_smith_timeline/1834-1844/joseph_smith_zions-camp.

²⁷⁹ Orson Pratt, *A[n] Interesting Account of Several Remarkable Visions*, 1840, http://josephsmithpapers.org/paperSummary/appendix-orson-pratt-an-interesting-account-of-several-remarkable-visions-1840

²⁸⁰ Mormon's Codex, 20-21.

²⁸¹ Mormon's Codex, pp. 638-653.

²⁸² E.g., Alvin K. Benson, "Geological Upheaval and Darkness in 3 Nephi 8-10," *The Book of Mormon: 3 Nephi 9-30, This is My Gospel*, Monte S. Nyman and

Charles D. Tate, Jr., eds, (Religious Studies Center, Brigham Young University, Bookcraft, Inc., Salt Lake City, Utah 1993): 59-72.

283 "Earthquake Shaking-Accounting for 'Site Effects,'" Southern California Earthquake Center, http://www.scec.org/phase3/overview.html

284 Wind Zones in the United States, Federal Emergency Management Agency, available at http://www.fema.gov/media-library-data/20130726-1619-20490-0806/ra1_tornado_risks_in_midwest_us_final_9_14_07.pdf

285 The story of the Steamboat Arabia is explained on the web page associated with the museum that contains the artifacts recovered from the ship. http://1856.com/arabias-story/the-arabia-rediscovered/

286 "TORNADO, n. [from the root of turn; that is, a whirling wind]: A violent gust of wind, or a tempest, distinguished by a whirly motion. Tornadoes of this kind happen after extreme heat, and sometimes in the United States, rend up fences and trees, and in a few instances have overthrown houses and torn them to pieces. Tornadoes are usually accompanied with severe thunder, lightning and torrents of rain; but they are of short duration, and narrow in breadth." "tornado." Noah Webster's 1828 American Dictionary of the English Language. 2015. http://1828.mshaffer.com/d/word/tornado (8 February 2015). The same dictionary defines a "tempest" as "An extensive current of wind, rushing with great velocity and violence; a storm of extreme violence."

287 Historic Earthquakes, USGS, http://earthquake.usgs.gov/earthquakes/states/events/1811-1812.php

288 Mormon's Codex, p. 21.

289 "city." Noah Webster's 1828 American Dictionary of the English Language. http://1828.mshaffer.com/d/search/word,city (8 February 2015).

290 Ibid, "village."

291 Michael E. Smith, "Ancient Cities," The Encyclopedia of Urban Studies (R. Hutchison, ed., Sage, 2009): 24. Available at http://www.public.asu.edu/~mesmith9/1-CompleteSet/MES-09-AncCities-SageEncy.pdf.

292 John W. Welch and Robert D. Hunt, "Culturegram: Jerusalem 600 B.C.," Glimpses of Lehi's Jerusalem (Foundation for Ancient Research and Mormon Studies (FARMS), Provo, Utah 2004): 5.

293 Hidden Cities, p. 2.

294 Omni 1:17-18.

295 John W. Welch and Stephen D. Ricks, editors, King Benjamin's Speech, (Foundation for Ancient Research and Mormon Studies, Provo, Utah 1998), pp. 150-151.

296 Adam Zertal, Ph.D , Joshua's Altar on Mt. Ebal, Israel, http://www.bible.ca/archeology/bible-archeology-altar-of-joshua.htm (accessed 29 April

2015). See another description of the altar at Mt. Ebal here: http://www.ucg.org/the-good-news/the-bible-and-archaeology-archaeology-and-the-book-of-joshua-the-conquest

[297] Mormon's Codex, p. 432-435.

[298] See, e.g., http://mayan-calendar.com/ancient_supplementary.html

[299] E.g., see Brad Lepper, Hopewell Astronomy, Ohio History Connection Archaeology Blog http://apps.ohiohistory.org/ohioarchaeology/hopewell-astronomy/

[300] Stephanie Woodard, "Ohio's Magnificent Earthworks, an Ancient Astronomical Wonder," Indian Country Today, June 16, 2012, accessed April 29, 2015 at http://indiancountrytodaymedianetwork.com/2012/06/16/ohios-magnificent-earthworks-ancient-astronomical-wonder-118726

[301] Mormon's Codex, p. 313.

[302] Ibid.

[303] Wade E.Miller and Matthew Roper, "Animals in the Book of Mormon: Challenges and Perspectives," *Interpreter: A Journal of Mormon Scripture*, (herein *Animals*), http://www.mormoninterpreter.com/animals-in-the-book-of-mormon-challenges-and-perspectives/, note 69, citing Daniel B. Adams, Last ditch archaeology. *Science 83/4 (1983), 28-37;* N. B. Asch and D. L. Asch, "Archaeobotany." *In* C. R. McGimsey and M. D. Conner (eds.) Deer Track: A late Woodland Village in the Mississippi Valley (Kampsville, Illinoise, *Center for American Archaeology, 1985): 79-82.* Note that this discovery was made in the Mississippi Valley.

[304] Ibid.

[305] Mormon's Codex, p. 306.

[306] *Memoirs of the Museum of Comparative Zoology at Harvard College, Volume 4* (Harvard University, Museum of Comparative Zoology 1874) pp. 81, 88 and 133, available online on google books. (herein, *Memoirs*).

[307] *Animals*, footnote 97, citing Hernando De Soto, *Narratives of the Career of Hernando De Soto* (New York: Allerton Book, 1922), 162.

[308] Ibid.

[309] William Richie, *The Archaeology of New York* (The Natural History Press, Garden City, NY 1965), p. 242.

[310] Memoirs, p. 87.

[311] Memoirs, pp. 99-100.

[312] John L. Sorenson, *An Ancient American Setting for the Book of Mormon* (Deseret Book Company, Salt Lake City, Utah, 1996), p. 298.

[313] Ibid, p. 299.

[314] "Kansas City Hopewell," University of Kansas Museum of Anthropology, http://www2.ku.edu/~arc/cgi-bin/hopewell/kchopewell.php (accessed 29 April 2015).

[315] Mormon's Codex, 226.

---

[316] E.g., Matthew Roper, "Joseph Smith, Revelation, and Book of Mormon Geography," *FARMS Review 22/2* (2010): 15-85, available from the Neal W. Maxwell Institute for Religious Scholarship at
http://publications.maxwellinstitute.byu.edu/publications/review/22/2/S00003-5176a03b6d5fc3Roper.pdf

[317] Ibid, pp. 37-45.

[318] See *The Lost City of Zarahemla.*

[319] http://www.examiner.com/article/georgia-s-mountains-conceal-ruins-of-ancient-gold-miners

[320] *Mormon's Codex*, p. 357-8.

Chapter 29 – Latin America and The Book of Mormon

IN *THE LOST CITY OF ZARAHEMLA*, I DISCUSSED THE IMPACT of the North American setting on people who live outside the United States. I suggested three ways in which native peoples in Central and South America can be Book of Mormon people

First, they could be among the "other sheep" Christ visited. The numerous legends of a "white God" and other elements of a Biblical nature could be attributable to such visits, even though there are no records extant.

Second, the "Hinterlands" theory suggests that descendants of Lamanites migrated southward.

Third, the Jaredite civilization, which came from Asia, expanded throughout the continent. As I wrote there, "In some respect, the Book of Ether is largely forgotten as a history of the inhabitants of the American continent, probably because of a widely held perception in the Church that the Jaredites were completely killed off, leaving only a sole survivor to meet the Mulekites. I propose that this notion is incorrect and that the Jaredites are at least one of the sources of the Asian DNA found in indigenous Latin Americans."

From a theological perspective, there is another way to address the question of Lamanites and Latin America.

In 3 Nephi 16, the Lord gave an extended sermon about the "lost sheep of Israel," the Gentiles, and the house of Israel. There are several key points.

1. The Lord said he had "other sheep which are not of this land." If, as I propose, "this land" refers to North America, then Christ could have been referring to people in Mesoamerica and South America, as well as anywhere

else in the world. The heading to the chapter refers to the "lost sheep of Israel," but the text itself does not use that phrase. In fact, according to Mosiah 26:21, "he that will hear my voice shall be my sheep and him shall ye receive into the church and him will I also receive." This suggests that the "sheep" in 3 Nephi 16 were not necessarily of the house of Israel, but anyone who hears the Lord's voice. The Lord's sheep could be Mesoamericans, Asians, Africans—anyone.

2. The Lord's sayings were to be kept and manifested unto the Gentiles, "that through the fullness of the Gentiles" the remnant of their seed—meaning the Lord's people at Jerusalem, or the Jews—may be brought to a knowledge of their Redeemer, and thereby be gathered.

3. The truth was to come unto the Gentiles, who were to scatter the Lord's people who are of the house of Israel. The Europeans did scatter the tribes from Eastern North America (through the Removal Act of 1830 and the many treaties that placed them on reservations), but the indigenous people in Latin America still live where they always have.

4. At a future date, the Gentiles would rebel. "At that day when the Gentiles shall sin against my gospel, and shall reject the fullness of my gospel," the Lord will bring the fullness of the gospel from among them. And *then* he will remember his covenant with the house of Israel. So it seems consistent with the scriptures for the gospel to be taken to the Gentiles—including the people in Latin America—before it is taken to the descendants of the people to whom the Lord was speaking; i.e., the Lamanites. At this point—still future—the Lord says:

> 12 And I will show unto thee, O house of Israel, that the Gentiles shall not have power over you; but I will remember my covenant unto you, O house of Israel, and ye shall come unto the knowledge of the fullness of my gospel.
> 13 But if the Gentiles will repent and return unto me, saith the Father, behold they shall be numbered among my people, O house of Israel.
> 14 And I will not suffer my people, who are of the house of Israel, to go through among them, and tread them down, saith the Father.
> 15 But if they will not turn unto me, and hearken unto my voice, I will suffer them, yea, I will suffer my people, O house of Israel, that they shall go through among them, and shall tread them down, and they shall be as salt that hath lost its savor, which is thenceforth good for nothing but to be cast out, and to be trodden under foot of my people, O house of Israel.

16 Verily, verily, I say unto you, thus hath the Father commanded me—that I should give unto this people this land for their inheritance.

At the end of this sermon, the Lord told the people, "I perceive that ye are weak, that ye cannot understand all my words which I am commanded of the Father to speak unto you at this time. Therefore, go ye unto your homes and ponder upon the things which I have said, and ask of the Father in my name that ye may understand." (3 Nephi 17: 1-2) That advice applies to us today as well. (My novel, *The Rule of Equity*, proposes one possible way the promises in chapters 16 and 20 of 3 Nephi could be fulfilled.)

The Lord did resume this sermon, starting with 3 Nephi 20:10. In verse 22, he explains, "this people will I establish in this land . . . and it shall be a New Jerusalem."

The New Jerusalem, of course, will be in Jackson County, Missouri.

Chapter 30 – A Whole New World of Book of Mormon Studies

→≫ ≪←

[NOTE: The following comments are adapted from *The Lost City of Zarahemla*.]

FOR OVER 170 YEARS, CHURCH MEMBERS, LEADERS, and scholars have been influenced by the anonymous articles in the *Times and Seasons*. This has led to an unfortunate focus on Mesoamerica in the search for Book of Mormon lands. Joseph Smith never described sites in Mesoamerica as places where Book of Mormon events occurred. By contrast, he did name specific places in North America.

Concluding as I have that the Mesoamerican theory originated out of misplaced missionary zeal, and has been perpetuated by an inordinate focus on the Hinterlands, I was curious about what a "correct" geography would look like. The work of Brother Sorenson and others has been invaluable in this pursuit—but it led me to a much different conclusion because I think their work *excludes* Mesoamerica as a viable setting for the Book of Mormon.

Hopefully we can redirect our efforts, energy, and resources to North America. People respond to the truth. The more we learn about the Book of Mormon, the more the truth becomes apparent. A correct understanding of Book of Mormon geography and anthropology will facilitate acceptance of the book on a broader scale than ever before. Replacing Mesoamerica with North America will strengthen the faith of members, encourage missionaries, and remove an unnecessary stumbling block for investigators.

We can all look forward to a whole new world of Book of Mormon studies.

→≫ ≪←

Moroni's America

Made in the USA
Las Vegas, NV
05 December 2024

13435304R00213